GANGS

STORIES OF LIFE AND DEATH FROM THE STREETS

GANGS
STORIES OF LIFE AND
DEATH FROM THE STREETS

EDITED BY SEAN DONAHUE
SERIES EDITOR CLINT WILLIS

Thunder's Mouth Press
New York

GANGS: STORIES OF LIFE AND DEATH FROM THE STREETS

An Adrenaline Book®

Published by
Thunder's Mouth Press
An Imprint of Avalon Publishing Group Incorporated
161 William Street, 16th floor
New York, NY 10038

Book design: Sue Canavan

frontispiece photo: Crips gang members in L.A., © Daniel Lainé/Corbis

Library of Congress Cataloging-in-Publication Data

Gangs: stories of life and death from the streets / edited by Sean Donahue.
    p.cm.
  "An Adrenaline book"--Copyright p.
  ISBN 1-56025-425-4
    Gangs--United States. I. Donahue, Sean.

HV6446.G36 2002
364.1'06'60973--dc21   2002141674

Printed in the United States of America

Distributed by Publishers Group West

for Carol

c o n t e n t s

p h o t o g r a p h s

introduction

A friend of mine living in Oakland, California found himself trapped one evening by a group of about eight street kids. The oldest might have been fourteen. They blocked the sidewalk in front of him, demanding money, while other kids arrived as reinforcements. My friend turned over a few bucks, all he had, but the kids weren't satisfied. Maybe they wanted an excuse to hurt him. They gave my friend an impressive beating.

How did these kids take down a big, strong college student? It's not just that their numbers trumped his individual size and strength. They gained a further edge by surprising him. My friend didn't anticipate their willingness—eagerness—to abrogate basic principles of the social contract that comfortably governed his life. He was thinking, "This is a typical shakedown for money, and these are kids. Really, how far can it go?" Somewhere in the gap between his expectations and their intentions, these kids found the advantage they needed to overwhelm him.

Gangs don't live by our rules. Instead, they create shadow worlds, cults of outsiderness complete with elaborate codes, symbols, visual clues, social rituals, and standards of behavior. The violence those kids were so quick to unleash is just one of the realities of a gang's world.

Modern society is supposed to protect us from the constant struggle for survival, reducing violence to an anomaly. That's why gangs—though bred mainly in city streets and inescapably linked to modern social problems— seem like ancient artifacts. They are like ghosts from a time when life, as the famous phrase puts it, was nasty, brutish and short. In fact, the phrase perfectly describes the lives of many gang members.

Because they live in a world so apart from ours, it's easy to dismiss gang members as sociopaths. Very Bad People. The detritus of modern society. But it turns out that gang members (with a few notable exceptions) are in many ways ordinary. The bored California teenagers in William Finnegan's *Cold New World* seem unremarkable apart from their attraction to neo-Nazi gangs and sectarian skinhead violence. The dangerous crack-dealing Chambers brothers in William Adler's book *Land of Opportunity* are businessmen—good ones. It's easy to imagine any of these characters living without gangs, given easier circumstances.

Many of the writers in this collection attempt to make sense of gangs' intrusions into our ordered world. British author Anthony Burgess wrote *A Clockwork Orange*, his famous novel about a savage young criminal, after thugs assaulted and nearly killed his wife. Journalist Bill Buford's encounter with a trainload of rampaging football hooligans on an otherwise unremarkable night inspired him to investigate and write about violent soccer fans. He didn't emerge unscathed from the experience, which he describes in his book *Among the Thugs*.

Some of the stories in this book are told by gang members themselves, who want to describe gang life. "Monster" Kody Scott considered murder a duty. Scott and others also make it clear that gang membership is a privilege. Piri Thomas describes the aftermath of a fight with a gang member in his new neighborhood:

> "You deal good," I said.
> "You too," he muttered, pressuring out. And just like

that, the fight was over. No more words. We just separated, hands half up, half down. My heart pumped out, *You've established your rep. Move over, 104th Street. Lift your wings, I'm one of your baby chicks now.*

Five seconds later my spurs were given to me in the form of introductions to streetdom's elite.

As we get closer to gang members, their tough postures dissipate. What's left is fear, sadness, tragedy and the damage that gangs inflict on themselves. Reporter Scott Wallace in his investigation of U.S.-bred street gangs in El Salvador introduces us to Murra, a gangster now in his mid-20s who wishes he could escape his gang past. While describing the first murder he committed—at age thirteen—for his gang, Murra sums up the trap of gang life:

> "I felt joy and sadness," Murra told me. "I had killed my first. But then I knew I was no longer safe walking on the street. You live with the fear they're going to do the same thing to you . . . if someone had been there when I was younger to offer advice, I wouldn't have gotten involved."

Such moments reach across the divide between gang members' world and ours. Wallace's unadorned portrait of Murra—or Fredric Dannen's detailed account of the lives destroyed by the murderous rise and fall of Chinatown's Green Dragons—requires a reader's engagement. We must drop the filter we usually apply to news reports about gangs or pop culture references to them. The best gang stories are about people we recognize—maybe people we know.

—Sean Donahue

from Among the Thugs
by Bill Buford

Bill Buford—former editor of the literary journal Granta *and current literary editor of* The New Yorker*—is an unlikely street fighter. But he found himself in the thick of the action while reporting his book on England's football hooligans. Buford's adventures included a trip to Turin, Italy, with a group of Manchester United supporters. The Turin soccer match was a prelude to mayhem.*

When the buses of United supporters pulled up into the cool evening shadow cast by the Stadio Comunale, a large crowd was already there. The fact of the crowd— that it would be waiting for the English—was hard to take in at first.

It was especially hard for Harry. Harry was the supporter I found myself sitting next to. But then, Harry was having difficulty taking in much—of anything. Like so many others, Harry had enjoyed the long hot afternoon, and all about him there was that gamey smell that comes from perspiring without interruption for a very long, though interdeterminate, period of time. Harry had been drinking since five that morning and had, by his own estimate, five imperial gallons of lager in his stomach, which, every time he turned, rolled of their own accord. Harry had been busy. He had been one of those who had abused the bus driver on the ride into the city, and he had abused the bus driver on the ride to the ground. He had urinated on a café table that had, in his inimitable phrasing, a number of "Eyetie cows" sitting around it, and he had then proceeded to abuse the waiters. In fact he had spent most of the day abusing waiters—many, many waiters. Who could know how many? They all looked so much alike that they blurred into one indiscriminate shape (round and short). He had abused the Acting British Consul, the police, hotel managers, food vendors of every description, and any onlooker who didn't speak English—*especially* anybody who didn't speak English. All in all, Harry had had a good day out, and then, in the full, bloated arrogance of the moment, he saw the following: thousands of Italian supporters converging on Harry's bus. They had surrounded it and were pounding on its sides—jeering, ugly, and angry. What right had they to be angry?

Do you see what they're doing? Harry said to the bloke behind me, full of indignation. And then if there's trouble, Harry said, they'll blame the English, won't they?

The fellow behind him agreed, but before he could say, "Fuckin' Eyeties," the bus started to rock from side to side. The Italians were trying to push the bus, our bus—the bus that had me inside it—on to its side.

I had not appreciated the importance of the match that evening, the semifinals for the Cup-Winners Cup. It had sold out the day the tickets—seventy thousand of them—had gone on sale, and at that moment all seventy thousand ticket holders seemed to be in view. In my ignorance, I had also not expected to see the English supporters, who were meant to be the hooligans, confronted by Italians who, to my untutored eye, looked like hooligans: their conduct—rushing towards the buses, brandishing flags—was so exaggerated that it was like a caricature of a nineteenth-century mob. Was this how they normally greeted the supporters of visiting teams?

We remained sitting inside the buses. The drivers weren't opening their doors until more police arrived, and you could see the members of the *carabinieri* just beyond the mob, pushing the Italian supporters out of the way until all four buses were encircled. They formed a cordon leading to the gate; and only then were we let out, escorted, and then frisked by four different, very young and very nervous policemen. All around us Italians were fighting to break through the cordon, shouting and gesticulating, their fingers forming the familiar upturned V. This was turning into a very peculiar experience.

It took a long time for the buses to empty and fill the area set aside for us, enclosed by a chain-link fence. All along the fence were more Italians, their jeering insistent. One tried to go over the top, and the police ran up to him, pulling him down by his trousers. As the last English supporter made his way into the enclosure, we were told something that I found hard to believe: that, inside, there were no seats.

I realized that I had never been given my match ticket and now I understood why: it didn't exist. Was it possible that a package tour had been arranged without tickets in the confidence that the authorities, afraid of English supporters on the streets, would somehow find a way of getting them into the ground? Bobby Boss, true to character, was not to be found.

And so we remained: standing, surrounded by a police guard and angry Italians, while somebody looked for a place to put the visiting English. At least I hoped somebody was doing that. At some point, during this long wait, the Italian supporters at the very top of the stadium—the top row that could overlook the grounds outside—realized that there was a gaggle of English below them. It must have been an exciting discovery: unlike their compatriots, they were not circumvented by a police cordon; they could—within the laws of gravity—do whatever they wanted. And they did. I remember the moment, looking up into the evening's pink sky, and watching the long, long slow arc of an object hurled from far above as it came closer and closer, gaining speed as it approached, until finally, in those milliseconds before it disclosed its target, I could actually make out what it was—a beer bottle—and then, *crash*: it shattered within three feet of one of the supporters.

Distant muted laughter from up high.

I feared what would follow. An English supporter went down, his forehead cut open. A policeman looked on. He was at a loss about what to do, even though his choices seemed fairly obvious: he could help the injured supporter (an ethical impossibility, since the supporter was a violent criminal); he could send police into the ground to stop the miscreants above us (an ethical contradiction, since *they* were the ones needing protection); he could move the English supporters into a more sheltered position, which must not have occurred to the policeman because what he did was this: nothing. He continued staring blankly as more things rained down upon us. Eventually he became a target as well. Eventually we all became targets, helpless underneath a barrage that consisted principally of beer bottles and oranges. There were so many bottles and so many oranges that the pavement, covered with juice and pulp and skins, was sticky to look at and sparkled from the shattered glass.

Mr. Wicks appeared, having arrived in an embassy car. He looked frantic and pale. As he hurried past, I heard him mutter, perhaps as a muted greeting, "Fucking Boss."

Alas, Mr. Wicks. He may have lost his friendliness, but he retained his democratic principles to the end. He must have known that this was his last chance to prevent what he now knew was certain to happen. Was there any possible doubt? He had the police at his disposal; he had the perfect excuse—no seats! Wasn't this the time to gather everyone together and bundle them back to England? But, no, Mr. Wicks, the democrat, did this: alternating between English and Italian, he shouted first for the beleaguered Jackie, whom he found hiding behind a policeman—the missiles, despite Mr. Wicks's intervention, continued to fall from above—and demanded to know why there were no seats. He then shouted at the police officer in charge, dramatically pointing (the gestures, I thought, were impressively Mediterranean) to the ground around them with its array of objects recently shattered or smashed or squashed from impact. And then he shouted at one of the stadium stewards, who began shouting instructions to the other stadium officials, with the result that in very little time we were told that a space inside had been cleared to accommodate the English supporters.

When finally we were ushered through a tunnel that led to the ground, police in front and police behind, it became apparent that, while the English supporters may have been accommodated, their accommodation wasn't in the most salubrious part of the stadium. We were heading for the bottom steps of the terraces, directly beneath the very people who had been hurling missiles at us while we waited outside.

I did not like the look of this.

I kept thinking of the journalist from the *Daily Star*, the one who ran off when things got violent. He emerged in my mind now as an unequivocally sympathetic figure. He had, the supporters said, shit himself, and it was worth noting that this phrase had now entered my vocabulary.

I was not, I found myself muttering, going to shit myself.

One by one, we walked from out of the darkness of the tunnel into the blinding light of the ground—the sun, though setting, was at an angle and still shining bright—and it was hard to make out the figures around us. There were not many police—I could see that—and it appeared that Italians had spilled on to the pitch in front of the terraces where we were meant to stand, separated only by a chain-link perimeter fence. Once again things were coming at us from the air: not just bottles and pieces of fruit but also long sticks—the staffs of Juventus flags—firecrackers, and smoke bombs. The first one out of the tunnel, drunk and arrogant and singing about his English pride, was hit on the back of the head by an eight-foot flag pole and he dropped to the concrete terrace. Out of the corner of my eye I saw a Union Jack had been set alight, its flames fanned as it was swirled in the air. I saw this only out of the corner of my eye because I was determined not to look up at the Italians above me, who were hurling things down, or down to the Italians below, who were hurling things up. I had the suspicion that if I happened to make eye contact with anybody I would be rewarded with a knock on the head. Also I didn't want to lose my concentration. Looking straight ahead, I was concentrating very hard on chanting my new refrain.

I will not shit myself, I will not shit myself.

As we arrived at the patch of concrete allocated to us, television cameramen appeared along the edges of the pitch. They looked Italian (thin, not beer drinking) and were squatting between the missile-throwing Juventus fans. There was also a number of newspaper photographers. They looked English (fat, clearly beer drinking). The curious thing about both the television and newspaper men was this: they were only a couple of feet away from the masked, missile-throwing Juventus fans. They could see that the English supporters were being felled—several people were on their knees holding their heads. I couldn't help thinking: it wouldn't take much effort to grab someone's arm, just as it was pulled back to hurl another pole or flare or smoke bomb or beer bottle; it would take even less effort to give one of them a little nudge; it would take virtually no effort at all to say a word or two urging these masked terrorists of the terraces to stop behaving in this way. Nobody did a thing. And while there is the old argument that to have done so would have been considered interventionist—participating in the event that they were meant to be reporting—for me, as one of the targets, such an argument was not very persuasive. They were not worried about getting in the way of the event. They were trying to create it. Not only were they not stopping the masked, missile-throwing Juventus fans, but they were also not photographing them. It was images of the English they wanted.

They wanted the English tattoos; their sweaty torsos, stripped to the waist; their two fingers jabbing the air; the vicious expressions on their faces as they hurled back the objects that had been thrown at them. Italians behaving like hooligans? Unheard of. English behaving like English? *That* was interesting! I remember thinking: if the day becomes more violent, who do you blame? The English, whose behavior on the square could be said to have been so provocative that they deserved whatever they got? The Italians, whose welcome consisted in inflicting injuries upon their visitors? Or can you place some of the blame on these men with their television equipment and their cameras, whose misrepresentative images served only to reinforce what everyone had come to expect?

• • •

Somehow the match started, was played, ended. And, while it could be said that there was no single serious incident, it could also be said that there was no moment without one. Several people were hurt, and one supporter was taken away to the hospital. During half time, when yet another Manchester lad was felled by a beer bottle, the English supporters, with a sudden roar, rushed to the top of the terraces, trying to climb the wall that separated them from the Italians. The wall was too high to scale, and the supporters ended up jumping up and down, trying to grab the Italians by their shoes until the police arrived to pull them away.

Police kept pouring through the tunnel, now wearing riot gear— moon helmets and blue uniforms instead of green—with obvious instructions to place themselves between each English supporter and everybody else. It was evident that the police continued to regard the English supporters as the problem, and they probably were the problem simply because they were there. But they were not the only problem, which the police discovered after surrounding every English supporter and ignoring the Italians above them, who, in that uninhibited way that has come to characterize the Mediterranean temperament, continued to express their strong feelings. By the end it appeared to me that the police were being struck down more frequently than the English.

It was a peculiar setting for watching a sporting event, although, oddly, it didn't seem so at the time. The day had consisted of such a strange succession of events that, by this point in the evening, it was the most natural thing in the world to be watching a football game surrounded by policemen: there was one on my left, another on my right, two directly behind me, and five in front. It didn't bother me; it certainly didn't bother the supporters, who, despite the distractions, were watching the match with complete attentiveness. And when Manchester United tied, the goal was witnessed, as it unfolded, by everyone there (except me; I was looking over my shoulder for missiles), and jubilation shot through them, their cheers and songs suddenly tinny and small in that great cavity of the Juventus football ground, its seventy thousand Italians now comprehensively silent. The United supporters jumped up and down, fell over each other, embraced.

But the euphoria was brief. In the final two minutes Juventus scored again. The exhilaration felt but minutes before by that small band of United supporters was now felt—magnified many times—by the seventy thousand Italian fans who, previously humiliated, directed their powerful glee into our corner. The roar was deafening, invading the senses like a bomb.

And with that explosive roar, the mood changed.

What happened next is confusing to recall. Everything started moving at great speed. Everything would continue to move at great speed for many hours. I remember that riot police started kicking one of the supporters who had fallen down. I remember hearing that Sammy had arrived and then coming upon him. He was big, well-dressed, with heavy horn-rimmed glasses that made him look like a physics student, standing underneath the bleachers, his back to the match, an expensive leather bag and camera hanging over his shoulder, having (like Robert) just come from France by taxi. I remember watching Ricky and Micky, the improbable pair I had met on my early morning minibus in London, scooting underneath the stands, exploiting the moment in which the Italians were embracing, crushed together in their celebrations, to come away with a handful of wallets, three purses, and a watch, got by reaching up from below the seats. And I remember some screaming: there had been a stabbing (I didn't see it) and, with the screaming, everyone bolted—animal speed, instinct speed—and pushed past the police and rushed for the exit. But the gate into the tunnel was locked, and the United supporters slammed into it.

It was impossible to get out.

Throughout this last period of the match, I had been hearing a new phrase: "It's going to go off."

It's going to go off, someone said, and his eyes were glassy, as though he had taken a drug.

If this keeps up, I heard another say, then it's going to go off. And the phrase recurred—it's going to go off, it's going to go off—spoken softly, but each time it was repeated it gained authority.

Everyone was pressed against the locked gate, and the police arrived moments later. The police pulled and pushed in one direction, and the supporters pushed in another, wanting to get out. It was shove and counter shove. It was crushing, uncomfortable. The supporters were humorless and determined.

It's going to go off.

People were whispering.

I heard: "Watch out for knives. Zip up your coat."

I heard: "Fill up your pockets."

I heard: "It's going to go off. Stay together. It's going to go off."

I was growing nervous and slipped my notebook into my shirt, up against my chest, and buttoned up my jacket. A chant had started: "United. United. United." The chant was clipped and sure. "United. United. United." The word was repeated, *United*, and, through the repetition, its meaning started changing, pertaining less to a sporting event or a football club and sounding instead like a chant of unity—something political. It had become the chant of a mob.

"United. United. United. United. United. United . . ."

And then it stopped.

There was a terrible screaming, a loud screaming, loud enough to have risen above the chant. The sound was out of place; it was a woman's screaming.

Someone said that it was the mother of the stabbed boy.

Someone said that it was no such thing, just a "fucking Eyetie."

The screaming went on. It appeared that a woman had been caught by the rush to get away and swept along by it. I spotted her: she was hemmed in and thrashing about, trying to find some space, some air. She couldn't move towards the exit and couldn't move away from it, and she wasn't going to be able to: the crush was too great, and it wouldn't stay still, surging back and forth by its own volition, beyond the control of anyone in it. She was very frightened. Her scream, piercing and high-pitched, wouldn't stop. She started hyperventilating, taking in giant gulps of air, and her screams undulated with the relent-less rhythm of her over-breathing. It was as if she were drowning in her own high-pitched oxygen, swinging her head from side to side, her eyes wild. I thought: Why hasn't she passed out? I was waiting for her to lose consciousness, for her muscles to give up, but she didn't pass out. The scream went on. Nobody around me was saying a word. I could tell that they were thinking what I was thinking, that she was going to have a fit, that she was going to die, there, now, pressed up against them. It went on, desperate and unintelligible and urgent.

And then someone had the sense to lift her up and raise her above his shoulders—it was so obvious—and he passed her to the person in front of him. And he passed her to the person in front of him. And in this way, she was passed, hand to hand, above everyone's heads, still screaming, still flailing, slowly making her way to the exit, and then, once there, the gate was opened to let her out.

And it was all that was needed. Once the gate had been opened, the English supporters surged forwards, pushing her heavily to one side.

I was familiar with the practice of keeping visiting supporters locked inside at the end of a match until everyone had left and of using long lines of police, with horses and dogs, to direct the visitors to their buses. The plan in Turin had been the same, and the police were there, outside the gate, in full riot regalia, waiting for the United supporters. But they weren't ready for what came charging out of the tunnel.

For a start, owing to the trapped woman, the supporters came out earlier than expected—the streets were filled with Juventus supporters—and when they emerged, they came out very fast, with police trailing behind, trying to keep up. They came as a mob, with everyone pressed together, hands on the shoulders of the person in front, moving quickly, almost at a sprint, racing down the line of police, helmets and shields and truncheons a peripheral blur. The line of police led to the buses, but just before the bus door someone in the front veered sharply and the mob followed. The police had anticipated this and were waiting. The group turned again, veering in another direction, and rushed out into the space between two of the buses. It came to a sudden stop, and I slammed into the person in front of me, and people slammed into me from behind: the police had been there as well. Everyone turned around. I don't know who was in front—I was trying only to keep up—and nothing was being said. There were about two hundred people crushed together, but they seemed able to move in unison, like some giant, strangely coordinated insect. A third direction was tried. The police were not there. I looked behind: the police were not there. I looked to the left and the right: there were no police anywhere.

What was the duration of what followed? It might have been twenty minutes; it seemed longer. It was windy and dark, and the trees, blowing back and forth in front of the street lamps, cast long, moving shadows. I was never able to see clearly.

I knew to follow Sammy. The moment the group broke free, he had handed his bag and camera to someone, telling him to give them back later at the hotel. Sammy then turned and started running backwards. He appeared to be measuring the group, taking in its size.

The energy, he said, still running backwards, speaking to no one in particular, the energy is very high. He was alert, vital, moving constantly, looking in all directions. He was holding out his hands, with his fingers outstretched.

Feel the energy, he said.

There were six or seven younger supporters jogging beside him, and it would be some time before I realized that there were always six or seven younger supporters jogging beside him. When he turned in one direction, they turned with him. When he ran backwards, they ran backwards. No doubt if Sammy had suddenly become airborne there would have been the sight of six or seven younger supporters desperately flapping their arms trying to do the same. The younger supporters were in fact very young. At first I put their age at around sixteen, but they might have been younger. They might have been fourteen. They might have been nine: I take pleasure, even now, in thinking of them as nothing more than overgrown nine-year-olds. They were nasty little nine-year-olds who, in some kind of prepubescent confusion, regarded Sammy as their dad. The one nearest me had a raw, skinny face with a greasy texture that suggested an order of fish'n'chips. He was the one who turned on me.

Who the fuck are you?

I said nothing, and Fish'n'chips repeated his question—Who the fuck are you?—and then Sammy said something, and Fish'n'chips forgot about me. But it was a warning: the nine-year-old didn't like me.

Sammy had stopped running backwards and had developed a kind of walk-run, which involved moving as quickly as possible without breaking into an outright sprint. Everybody else did the same. The idea, it seemed, was to be inconspicuous—not to be seen to be actually running, thus attracting the attention of the police—but nevertheless to jet along as fast as you could. The effect was ridiculous: two hundred English supporters, tattooed torsos tilted slightly forwards, arms straight, hurtling stiffly down the sidewalk, believing that nobody was noticing them.

Everyone crossed the street, decisively, without a word spoken. A chant broke out—"United, United, United"—and Sammy waved his hands up and down, as if trying to bat down the flames of a fire, urging people to be quiet. A little later there was another one-word chant. This time it was "England." They couldn't help themselves. They wanted so badly to act like normal football supporters—they wanted to sing and behave drunkenly and carry on doing the same rude things that they had been doing all day long—and they had to be reminded that they couldn't. Why this pretense of being invisible? There was Sammy again, whispering, insistent: no singing, no singing, waving his hands up and down. The nine-year-olds made a shushing sound to enforce the message.

Sammy said to cross the street again—he had seen something—and his greasy little companions went off in different directions, fanning out, as if to hold the group in place, and then returned to their positions beside him. It was only then that I appreciated fully what I was witnessing: Sammy had taken charge of the group—moment by moment giving it specific instructions—and was using his obsequious little lads to ensure that his commands were being carried out.

I remembered, on my first night with Mick, hearing that leaders had their little lieutenants and sergeants. I had heard this and I had noted it, but I hadn't thought much of it. It sounded too much like toyland, like a war game played by schoolboys. But here, now, I could see that everything Sammy said was being enforced by his entourage of little supporters. Fish'n'chips and the other nine-year-olds made sure that no one ran, that no one sang, that no one strayed far from the group, that everyone stayed together. At one moment, a cluster of police came rushing towards us, and Sammy, having spotted them, whispered a new command, hissing that we were to disperse, and the members of the group split up—some crossing the street, some carrying on down the center of it, some falling behind—until they had got past the policemen, whereupon Sammy turned around, running backwards again, and ordered everyone to regroup: and the little ones, like trained dogs, herded the members of the group back together.

I trotted along. Everyone was moving at such a speed that, to ensure I didn't miss anything, I concentrated on keeping up with Sammy. I could see that this was starting to irritate him. He kept having to notice me.

What are you doing here? he asked me, after he had turned around again, running backwards, doing a quick head count after everyone had regrouped.

He knew precisely what I was doing there, and he had made a point of asking his question loudly enough that the others had to hear it as well.

Just the thing, I thought.

Fuck off, one of his runts said suddenly, peering into my face. He had a knife.

Didja hear what he said, mate? Fish'n'chips had joined the interrogation. He said fuck off. What the fuck are you doing here anyway, eh? Fuck off.

It was not the time or the occasion to explain to Fish'n'chips why I was there, and, having got this far, I wasn't about to turn around now.

I dropped back a bit, just outside of striking range. I looked about me. I didn't recognize anyone. I was surrounded by people I hadn't met; worse, I was surrounded by people I hadn't met who kept telling me to fuck off. I felt I had understood the drunkenness I had seen earlier in the day. But this was different. If anyone here was drunk, he was not acting as if he was. Everyone was purposeful and precise, and there was a strong quality of aggression about them, like some kind of animal scent. Nobody was saying a word. There was a muted grunting and the sound of their feet on the pavement; every now and then, Sammy would whisper one of his commands. In fact the loudest sound had been Sammy's asking me what I was doing there, and the words of the exchange rang round in my head.

What the fuck are you doing here anyway, eh? Fuck off.

What the fuck are you doing here anyway, eh? Fuck off.

I remember thinking in the clearest possible terms: I don't want to get beaten up.

I had no idea where we were, but, thinking about it now, I see that Sammy must have been leading his group around the stadium, hoping to find Italian supporters along the way. When he turned to run backwards, he must have been watching the effect his group of two hundred walk-running Frankensteins was having on the Italian lads, who spotted the English rushing by and started following them, curious, attracted by the prospect of a fight or simply by the charisma of the group itself, unable to resist tagging along to see what might happen.

And then Sammy, having judged the moment to be right, suddenly stopped, and, abandoning all pretence of invisibility, shouted: "Stop."

Everyone stopped.

"Turn."

Everyone turned. They knew what to expect. I didn't. It was only then that I saw the Italians who had been following us. In the half-light, streetlight darkness I couldn't tell how many there were, but there were enough for me to realize—holy shit!—that I was now unexpectedly in the middle of a very big fight: having dropped back to get out of the reach of Sammy and his lieutenants I was in the rear, which, as the group turned, had suddenly become the front.

Adrenaline is one of the body's more powerful chemicals. Seeing the English on one side of me and the Italians on the other, I remember seeming quickly to take on the properties of a small helicopter, rising several feet in the air and moving out of everybody's way. There was a roar, everybody roaring, and the English supporters charged into the Italians.

In the next second I went down. A dark blur and then smack: I got hit on the side of the head by a beer can—a full one—thrown powerfully enough to knock me over. As I got up, two policemen, the only two I saw, came rushing past, and one of them clubbed me on the back of the head. Back down I went. I got up again, and most of the Italians had already run off, scattering in all directions. But many had been tripped up before they got away.

Directly in front of me—so close I could almost reach out to touch his face—a young Italian, a boy really, had been knocked down. As he was getting up, an English supporter pushed the boy down again, ramming his flat hand against the boy's face. He fell back and his head hit the pavement, the back of it bouncing slightly.

Two other Manchester United supporters appeared. One kicked the boy in the ribs. It was a soft sound, which surprised me. You could hear the impact of the shoe on the fabric of the boy's clothing. He was kicked again—this time very hard—and the sound was still soft, muted. The boy reached down to protect himself, to guard his ribs, and the other English supporter then kicked him in the face. This was a soft sound as well, but it was different: you could tell that it was his face that had been kicked and not his body and not something protected by clothing. It sounded gritty. The boy tried to get up and he was pushed back down—sloppily, without much force. Another Manchester United supporter appeared and another and then a third. There were now six, and they all started kicking the boy on the ground. The boy covered his face. I was surprised that I could tell, from the sound, when someone's shoe missed or when it struck the fingers and not the forehead or the nose.

I was transfixed. I suppose, thinking about this incident now, I was close enough to have stopped the kicking. Everyone there was off-balance—with one leg swinging back and forth—and it wouldn't have taken much to have saved the boy. But I didn't. I don't think the thought occurred to me. It was as if time had dramatically slowed down, and each second had a distinct beginning and end, like a sequence of images on a roll of film, and I was mesmerized by each image I saw. Two more Manchester United supporters appeared—there must have been eight by now. It was getting crowded and difficult to get at the boy: they were bumping into each other, tussling slightly. It was hard for me to get a clear view or to say where exactly the boy was now being kicked, but it looked like there were three people kicking him in the head, and the others were kicking him in the body—mainly the ribs but I couldn't be sure. I am astonished by the detail I can recall. For instance, there was no speech, only that soft, yielding sound—although sometimes it was a gravelly, scraping one—of the blows, one after another. The moments between the kicks seemed to increase in duration, to stretch elastically, as each person's leg was retracted and then released for another blow.

The thought of it: eight people kicking the boy at once. At what point is the job completed?

It went on.

The boy continued to try to cushion the blows, moving his hands around to cover the spot were he had just been struck, but he was being hit in too many places to be able to protect himself. His face was now covered with blood, which came from his nose and his mouth, and his hair was matted and wet. Blood was all over his clothing. The kicking went on. On and on and on, that terrible soft sound, with the boy saying nothing, only wriggling on the ground.

A policeman appeared, but only one. Where were the other police? There had been so many before. The policeman came running hard and knocked over two of the supporters, and the others fled, and then time accelerated, no longer slow motion time, but time moving very fast.

We ran off. I don't know what happened to the boy. I then noticed that all around me there were others like him, others who had been tripped up and had their faces kicked; I had to side step a body on the ground to avoid running on top of it.

In the vernacular of the supporters, it had now "gone off." With that first violent exchange, some kind of threshold had been crossed, some notional boundary: on one side of that boundary had been a sense of limits, an ordinary understanding—even among this lot—of what you didn't do; we were now someplace where there would be few limits, where the sense that there were things you didn't do had ceased to exist. It became very violent.

A boy came rushing towards me, holding his head, bleeding badly from somewhere on his face, watching the ground, not knowing where he was going, and looked up just before he would have run into me. The fact of me frightened him. He thought I was English. He thought I was going to hit him. He screamed, pleading, and spun round backwards to get away and ran off in another direction.

I caught up with Sammy. Sammy was transported. He was snapping his fingers and jogging in place, his legs pumping up and down, and he was repeating the phrase, It's going off, it's going off. Everyone around him was excited. It was an excitement that verged on being something greater, an emotion more transcendent—joy at the very least, but more like ecstasy. There was an intense energy about it; it was impossible not to feel some of the thrill. Somebody near me said that he was happy. He said that he was very, very happy, that he could not remember ever being so happy, and I looked hard at him, wanting to memorize his face so that I might find him later and ask him what it was that made for this happiness, what it was like. It was a strange thought: here was someone who believed that, at this precise moment, following a street scuffle, he had succeeded in capturing one of life's most elusive qualities. But then he, dazed, babbling away about his happiness, disappeared into the crowd and the darkness.

There was more going on than I could assimilate: there were violent noises constantly—something breaking or crashing—and I could never tell where they were coming from. In every direction something was happening. I have no sense of sequence.

I remember the man with his family. Everyone had regrouped, brought together by the little lieutenants, and was jogging along in that peculiar walk-run, and I noticed that in front of us was a man with his family, a wife and two sons. He was shooing them along, trying to make them hurry, while looking repeatedly over his shoulder at us. He was anxious, but no one seemed to notice him: everyone just carried on, trotting at the same speed, following him not because they wanted to follow him but only because he happened to be running in front of us. When the man reached his car, a little off to the side of the path we were following, he threw open the door and shoved the members of his family inside, panicking slightly and badly bumping the head of one of his sons. And then, just as he was about to get inside himself, he looked back over his shoulder—just as the group was catching up to him—and he was struck flatly across the face with a heavy metal bar. He was struck with such force that he was lifted into the air and carried over his car door on to the ground on the other side. Why him? I thought. What had he done except make himself conspicuous by trying to get his family out of the way? I turned, as we jogged past him, and the supporters behind me had rammed into the open car door, bending it backwards on its hinges. The others followed, running on top of the man on the ground, sometimes slowing down to kick him— the head, the spine, the ass, the ribs, anywhere. I couldn't see his wife and children, but knew they were inside, watching from the back seat.

There was an Italian boy, eleven or twelve years old, alone, who had got confused and ran straight into the middle of the group and past me. I looked behind me and saw that the boy was already on the ground. I couldn't tell who had knocked him down, because by the time I looked back six or seven English supporters had already set upon him, swarming over his body, frenzied.

There was a row of tables where programs were sold, along with flags, T-shirts, souvenirs, and as the group went by each table was lifted up and overturned. There were scuffles. Two English supporters grabbed an Italian and smashed his face into one of the tables. They grabbed him by the hair on the back of his head and slammed his face into the table again. They lifted his head up a third time, pulling it higher, holding it there—his face was messy and crushed—and slammed it into the table again. Once again the terrible slow motion of it all, the time, not clock time, that elapsed between one moment of violence and the next one, as they lifted his head up—were they really going to do it again?—and smashed it into the table. The English supporters were methodical and serious; no one spoke.

An ambulance drove past. Its siren made me realize that there were still no police.

The group crossed a street, a major intersection. It had long abandoned the pretense of invisibility and had reverted to the arrogant identity of the violent crowd, walking, without hesitation, straight into the congested traffic, across the hoods of the cars, knowing that they would stop. At the head of the traffic was a bus, and one of the supporters stepped up to the front of it, and from about six feet, hurled something with great force—it wasn't a stone; it was big and made of a metal, like the manifold of a car engine—straight into the driver's windshield. I was just behind the one who threw this thing. I don't know where he got it from, because it was too heavy to have been carried for any distance, but no one had helped him with it; he had stepped out of the flow of the group, and in those moments between throwing his heavy object and turning back to his mates, he had a peculiar look on his face. He knew he had done something that no one else had done yet, that it had escalated the violence, that the act had crossed another boundary of what was permissible. He had thrown a missile that was certain to cause serious physical injury. He had done something bad—extremely bad—and his face, while acknowledging the badness of it, was actually saying something more complex. It was saying that what he had done wasn't all that bad, really; in the context of the day, it wasn't that extreme, was it? What his face expressed, I realized—his eyes seemed to twinkle—was no more than this: I have just been naughty.

He had been naughty and he knew it and was pleased about it. He was happy. Another happy one. He was a runt, I thought. He was a little shit, I thought. I wanted to hurt him.

The sound of the shattering windshield—I realize now—was a powerful stimulant, physical and intrusive, and it had been the range of sounds, of things breaking and crashing, coming from somewhere in the darkness, unidentifiable, that was increasing steadily the strength of feeling of everyone around me. It was also what was making me so uneasy. The evening had been a series of stimulants, assaults on the senses, that succeeded, each time, in raising the pitch of excitement. And now, crossing this intersection, traffic coming from four directions, supporters trotting on top of cars, the sound of this thing going through the windshield, the crash following its impact, had the effect of increasing the heat of the feeling: I can't describe it any other way; it was almost literally a matter of temperature. There was another moment of disorientation—the milliseconds between the sensation of the sound and knowing what accounted for it, an adrenaline moment, a chemical moment—and then there was the roar again, and someone came rushing at the bus with a pole (taken from one of the souvenir tables?) and smashed a passenger's window. A second crashing sound. Others came running over and started throwing stones and bottles with great ferocity. They were, again, in a frenzy. The stones bounced off the glass with a shuddering thud, but then a window shattered, and another shattered, and there was screaming from inside. The bus was full, and the passengers were not lads like the ones attacking them but ordinary family supporters, dads and sons and wives heading home after the match, on their way to the suburbs or a village outside the city. Everyone inside must have been covered with glass. They were shielding their faces, ducking in their seats. There were glass splinters everywhere: they would cut across your vision suddenly. All around me people were throwing stones and bottles, and I felt afraid for my own eyes.

We moved on.

I felt weightless. I felt nothing would happen to me. I felt that anything might happen to me. I was looking straight ahead, running, trying to keep up, and things were occurring along the dark peripheries of my vision: there would be a bright light and then darkness again and the sound, constantly, of something else breaking, and of movement, of objects being thrown and of people falling.

A group of Italians appeared, suddenly stepping forward into the glare of a street lamp. They were different from the others, clearly intending to fight, full of pride and affronted dignity. They wanted confrontation and stood there waiting for it. Someone came towards us swinging a pool cue or a flag-pole, and then, confounding all sense, it was actually grabbed from out his hands—it was Roy; Roy had appeared out of nowhere and had taken the pole out of the Italian's hands—and broken it over his head. It was flamboyantly timed, and the next moment the other English supporters followed, that roar again, quickly overcoming the Italians, who ran off in different directions. Several, again, were tripped up. There was the sight, again, of Italians on the ground, wriggling helplessly while English supporters rushed up to them, clustering around their heads, kicking them over and over again.

Is it possible that there were simply no police?

Again we moved on. A bin was thrown through a car showroom window, and there was another loud crashing sound. A shop: its door was smashed. A clothing shop: its window was smashed, and one or two English supporters lingered to loot from the display.

I looked behind me and I saw that a large vehicle had been overturned, and that further down the street flames were issuing from a building. I hadn't seen any of that happen: I realized that there had been more than I had been able to take in. There was now the sound of sirens, many sirens, different kinds, coming from several directions.

The city is ours, Sammy said, and he repeated the possessive, each time with greater intensity: It is *ours, ours, ours.*

A police car appeared, its siren on—the first police car I had seen—and it stopped in front of the group, trying to cut it off. There was only one car. The officer threw open his door, but by the time he had got out the group had crossed the street. The officer shouted after us, helpless and angry, and then dropped back inside his car and chased us down, again cutting us off. Once again, the group, in the most civilized manner possible, crossed the street: well-behaved football supporters on their way back to their hotel, flames receding behind us. The officer returned to his car and drove after us, this time accelerating dangerously, once again cutting off the group, trying, it seemed to me, to knock down one of the supporters, who had to jump out of the way and who was then grabbed by the police officer and hurled against the hood, held there by his throat. The officer was very frustrated. He knew that this group was responsible for the damage he had seen; he knew, beyond all reasonable doubt, that the very lad whose throat was now in his grip had been personally responsible for mayhem of some categorically illegal kind, but the officer had not personally seen him do anything. He hadn't personally seen the group do anything. He had not seen anyone commit a crime. He saw only the results. He kept the supporter pinned there, holding him by the throat, and then in disgust he let him go.

A fire engine passed, an ambulance, and finally the police—many police. They came from two directions. And once they started arriving, it seemed that they would never stop. There were vans and cars and motorcycles and paddy wagons. And still they came. The buildings were illuminated by their flashing blue lights. But the group of supporters from Manchester, governed by Sammy's whispered commands, simply kept moving, slipping past the cars, dispersing when needing to disperse and then regrouping, turning this way, that way, crossing the street again, regrouping, reversing, with Sammy's greasy little lieutenants bringing up the rear, keeping everyone together. They were well-behaved fans of the sport of football. They were once again the law-abiding supporters they had always insisted to me that they were. And, thus, they snaked through the streets of the ancient city of Turin, making their orderly way back to their hotels, the police following behind, trying to keep up.

"We did it," Sammy declared, as the group reached the railway station. "We took the city."

from Cold New World: Growing Up
in a Harder Country
by William Finnegan

New Yorker staff writer William Finnegan (born 1952) immersed himself in the worlds of four young Americans growing up in difficult environments. His subjects included Mindy, a teenager caught in a war between rival skinhead gangs—the Nazi Low Riders and the antiracist Sharps—in the crumbling suburbs of California's Antelope Valley.

M indy Turner's favorite escape from the valley was going to raves in the city. I asked her about a small poster on the wall in her bedroom, advertising something called THE INSOMNIAC RAVE.

"Oh," she said. "*Oh.* That was so great. It was the first real rave I went to. *Dang.* It was in Hollywood. Raves are like big parties, with all different races dancing. They're not really known to the cops. And there's never any fights. The people like rent a warehouse and they have deejays and everything. You have to phone for directions just before it happens. The Insomniac Rave had an *Alice in Wonderland* theme. A lot of people were in costume. There were big rabbits walking around, queens, guys in tall hats. I took Ecstasy, and I just danced all night. Usually I'm self-conscious when I dance, but not that night. A guy started squirting me with cold water from a squirt gun and"— Mindy threw her head back, giving a convincing demonstration of rapture—"*it felt so good.*"

She sighed. "Jaxon can't stand it that I go to raves," she said. "He says I don't act white. But what is acting white? Me and him have been getting drunk almost every night lately, and I ask him, 'What do you think black people do that's so different from whites? They just sit around getting drunk and listening to music. Drive around in cars. Just like us.' "

I looked forward to hearing Jaxon's counterargument. In the meantime, he and Mindy seemed to fight nonstop. "I don't see why we can't be together and just have different beliefs," she said.

"Beliefs" made up a strikingly large part of Mindy's world. The word sometimes referred to racial attitudes, but it just as often encompassed questions of religion, sex, politics, music, history, or personal heroes. Kicking around teenage Lancaster, I sometimes felt like I had fallen in with a thousand little cultural commissars, young suburban ideologues whose darkest pronouncement on another kid—a kid deviating from, say, the hardcore punk anarchist line on some band or arcane point of dress—was, inevitably, "He's *confused.*"

Mindy's own beliefs were nothing if not eclectic. Her brave and principled rejection of racism, even her devotion to Alicia Silverstone, did not mean she had embraced enlightened liberalism in all matters. She still had a soft spot, for instance, for Adolf Hitler—she claimed she was the only NLR who had actually read *Mein Kampf*—and her all-time favorite "leader" was still Charles Manson. "My mom thinks I'm sick, but I think he's cute," she told me. "In a weird, gross way, I think he's attractive. He has the real fuck-you blood. He's been in jail for so long but he doesn't let it bother him. He acts as his own lawyer. He talks for himself. I've read some of *Helter Skelter.* I wouldn't, like, buy a poster of him and put it up. My mom wouldn't let me do it if I tried. But I don't think it would fit my room, anyway, with all my nice John Lennon and Beatles stuff."

We were talking in Mindy's room, where the walls were indeed adorned with Beatles posters. Her father, she said, had been a big John Lennon fan. Her own favorite musician at that moment was Tori Amos—a frail-voiced, folk-rock poetess whose music was popular with sensitive, alienated teenage girls. But Mindy also loved Trent Reznor, of

Nine Inch Nails, whose best-known lyric was "I wanna fuck you like an animal!" I asked about a framed photograph, set next to her bed, of a shirtless, tattooed young man. The picture had obviously been taken in prison.

"That's Tory," she said. "He's my brother." She meant close friend, not blood relative. "He's twenty-three. He says he's in love with me, but he knows I can't get over Jaxon. He's in for armed robbery. I didn't know him too well before he went to jail, but then we started writing letters. We're going to Florida together after he gets out. He's SFV Peckerwood."

The Peckerwoods were a white gang, known mainly for mindless violence and methamphetamine dealing. (They should also be known for having the worst gang name in America.) They were big in the Antelope Valley but bigger, reportedly, in the San Fernando Valley, or SFV. They were biggest of all in prison. "Tory has his beliefs," Mindy said. "He believes whites are better than blacks, and he'll never eat or smoke after a black person, whatever that means. But he knows I don't think like that, so we don't talk about it. He's got WHITE PRIDE tattooed on the backs of his arms in Olde English."

Now she pointed at another rave poster and said, "This one is happening this Sunday. Probably in Hollywood. You should come. Me and my friend Stephanie and her boyfriend Mike are going." I said I would be glad to go along, my heart sinking at the thought of an entire night in a warehouse with a bunch of kids on Ecstasy. This rave was to be called, inscrutably, the Return of Fuck—No Screw on Monday.

"Maybe Darius can come," Mindy said.

I must have given her a strange look, because she added, hastily, "I just want to see him dance."

Darius was Darius Houston, one of the Sharps to whom Mindy had turned for protection. Darius was half black, half white, and was probably the NLRs' least favorite skinhead. "I don't think Darius really likes me," Mindy said. "Because when I hung out with the boneheads"—this was the generic term for racist skinheads—"I used to call him a nigger. All the Sharps have good reason to hate me. I was stupid."

I knew Darius pretty well by then, so I agreed to ask him to come along to the rave on Sunday. I asked Mindy if she might be hoping to become a Sharp herself.

She said no. "Most people here say, 'Mindy Turner? Oh, you mean Nazi Mindy.' So I don't want to start being Sharp Mindy. I want to be just *Mindy*. If somebody asks me what I am now, I just tell them I'm Free Unity. That's not a gang. It's just what I believe."

"Sharp" stands for Skinheads Against Racial Prejudice. It is not, as I first thought, a local Antelope Valley sect. Skinheads claim Sharp throughout the United States, in Europe, even, reportedly, in Japan. There is no formal organization—just an antiracist ideology, a street-fighting tradition, and a few widely recognized logos, usually worn on jacket patches. Sharp's raison d'être is its evil twin, the better-known white-supremacist and neo-Nazi skinhead movement. Many, if not most, skinheads in this country are actually nonpolitical (and non-racist) and simply resent the disastrous public image that the bone-heads give them. Sharps do more than resent it.

"It's all about working-class"—this was the surprising reply I kept getting from the Antelope Valley Sharps when I first asked why they were skinheads. All of them, I found, were amateur social historians, determined to rescue the skinhead movement—or simply skinhead, as they call it—from the international disrepute into which it had fallen. In their version, which seems broadly accurate, the original skinheads emerged in England in the mid-sixties out of other youth cultures, notably the "hard mods" and the Rude Boys, stylish Jamaicans who wore porkpie hats and listened to reggae and ska. Skinheads were clean-cut, working class, nonracist ("two-tone"), and tough. They loathed hippies for reasons of both class and hygiene, loved soccer and beer, fighting and ska, scooters and Fred Perry tennis shirts. They wore extra-shiny boots, extra-wide Levis, and narrow braces. The meticu-lous, distinctive look they developed has been described as a "carica-ture of the model worker." For a detailed history of skinhead, the Antelope Valley Sharps all urged on me a book, published in Scotland, called *Spirit of '69: A Skinhead Bible*.

By the seventies, the movement had been hijacked, according to the Sharps, by the anti-immigrant National Front in England. Skinheads had already become notorious for "Paki-bashing," but that was at first less racial, the Sharps insisted, than territorial. In any case, it was the second wave of British skinhead that crossed over to the United States, in the late seventies, as part of the great punk-rock cultural exchange, and by then neo-Nazism and white supremacism were definitely in the mix. Traditional American racist and neo-Nazi groups began to see the political potential in skinhead in the mid-eighties, and a host of unholy alliances were formed between racist skinheads and old-line extremist organizations such as the Aryan Nations, White Aryan Resistance, the Church of the Creator, and the Ku Klux Klan. The Anti-Defamation League, which monitors neo-Nazi skinheads in more than thirty countries, estimated in 1995 that there were only thirty-five hundred active neo-Nazi skinheads in the United States—a figure apparently derived from a narrow definition of its subjects, since there were, from everything I could tell, more white-supremacist gang members than that in California alone. But after a decade of hate crimes and racist violence, white-power skinheads were becoming increasingly familiar figures in the American social landscape, particularly among teenagers, who tended to know much more about them and their rabid views than adults did.

"The boneheads are looking *forward* to a race war."

"They like Bic their heads, and grow out a little goatee so they look like the devil, just to scare other kids."

"They're all on some harsh drug."

"*Somebody's* got to stand up to these guys," Darius Houston said.

Six or seven Sharps were sitting around Jacob Kroeger's mother's house in Lancaster. They were a picturesque lot in their boots and braces, their extra-short ("flooded") jeans, their Andy Capp–type "snap caps." Some sported "suedeheads," others had skulls that gleamed. Most were white kids and, though girls came and went, it was clear that all the main players were boys. They were voluble with me, and easy with each other, even though the mood that evening was rather grim and besieged. This was late 1995, and Darius's girlfriend, Christina Fava, had just been involved in a nasty incident with the Nazi Low Riders. It seemed that a girl from the NLRs had called her a "nigger lover" in a hallway at Antelope Valley High School, where Christina was a junior. A black student named Todd Jordan, who knew and cared nothing about skinheads, had become involved on Christina's side, and the next day half a dozen NLRs had jumped Todd on a deserted athletic field, stabbing him five times with a screwdriver. Todd was now in the hospital. The doctors were saying he would not play basketball—he was on the school team—again. Christina, for her part, was transferring to a new school.

And this wasn't the only violent attack of the preceding weeks. Less than a month before, some two dozen NLRs and their allies had stormed Jacob's house during a party, knocking down the front door, chasing everyone out, breaking windows, smashing holes in the walls. The house was still being repaired, as I could see, and there was some question about whether or not it had been insured against Bonehead Attack.

Somehow, I said, being a Sharp seemed to mean, more than anything else, a lot of fighting with white-power skinheads.

I was wrong, I was assured.

"It's the music, the fashions, the friendships, the whole lifestyle."

"It's like a big fuckin' family."

"Everybody's got everybody else's back."

"It's all about working-class."

This curious, almost un-American class consciousness among the Antelope Valley Sharps turned out, upon examination, to be a very American miscellany. The kids themselves came from a wide range of backgrounds, everything from two-parent middle-class families to drug-addled welfare mothers who dumped them on the streets as adolescents. For some, "working-class" meant, I learned, simply having a job, any job, as opposed to being a "bum." For others, it was synonymous with "blue-collar," and it distinguished them from richer kids who might decide to be skinheads and buy all the gear but who weren't really streetwise and so might just have to be relieved of their new twelve-hole Doc Martens.

Sharp membership was itself in constant flux. Earlier that year, there had been scores of kids in the valley claiming Sharp, but the antics of some of the "fresh cuts" had started causing problems for the inner circle, who were tougher and more deeply committed to skinhead and had to tell the new guys to cool it. There were still dozens of kids "backing it up" when I started visiting—young antiracists who said they were punk rockers or traditional skinheads or unity skins—but only a handful actually claiming Sharp. Hanging out with the Sharps and their allies, I came to see that there was, in fact, much more to their little brotherhood than rumbling with the boneheads. They were a haven, a structure, a style, a sensibility, set against the bleakness, uncertainty, and suffocating racial tension of teenage life in the valley.

For Darius, in particular, Sharp was a godsend. An orphan since his mother died when he was thirteen, he had been a skater and a punk rocker before discovering skinhead. As a half-black kid in a largely white town, being raised by various white relatives—it was his white mother's family that had settled in the Antelope Valley—he had always been something of an outsider. Skinhead, as he understood it, was a complete, ready-made aesthetic and way of life. It was exotic yet comfortable, it fit. He identified with its "blue-collar pride," its underground energy, and its music, and he was soon playing bass in a multiracial ska band called the Leisures. Darius was a stickler for the dress code. Indeed, one of his main complaints about the boneheads seemed to be that they were always doing "cheesy" things like writing slogans in felt pen on their jeans and T-shirts and bomber jackets, instead of getting proper patches. He was planning, he told me, to get a huge tattoo on his back of a crucified skinhead with the caption THE LAST RESORT, which was, among other things, the name of a legendary skinhead music shop in London. Unfortunately, the mere idea of a black skinhead drove neo-Nazi skinheads into a fury, so Darius had been fighting on a regular basis for years. He was a skilled fighter—

he once showed me a kick-boxing trophy he had won—but the backup that the other Sharps provided was still, for Darius, a life-saver. Going to school had become too dangerous, so he was on independent study. After graduating, he said, he planned to join the Navy and become a medical technician. He was eighteen, beefy, soft-spoken, watchful, with skin the color of light mahogany. When we met, he was homeless and had been sleeping on a couch in Jacob's mother's house.

Billy Anderson, another Sharp, was sleeping on the other couch. He was seventeen, pink-skinned, big-boned, round-faced. He came from a chaotic family, plagued by alcoholism and drug abuse. According to both Billy and his older sister, a punk rocker who lived down below, their mother, who had been on public assistance most of her life, was a methamphetamine addict, given to tearing up carpets and tearing out phone wires in search of secret microphones; her current husband was an alcoholic; her previous husband was a tweaker; their favorite aunt died of a heroin overdose; and their father, who lived in a trailer park in Compton, was a pothead. "It's so wack to see your parents all tweaked on drugs," Billy said. "That's why I've never tried any drugs." Drinking and fighting were all right, though, he thought, particularly if you were fighting boneheads, whose crudity and racism gave the name of his beloved skinhead a white-trash taint. Like Darius, Billy was on independent study when we met and was planning to join the Navy. He had been into skinhead since he was fifteen, and he always seemed to be "dressed down"—in immaculate, classic skinhead gear—which was a feat, since he was usually homeless and broke.

Jacob Kroeger still had his hair when we first met, though he was getting ready to become a full-fledged Sharp. Eighteen, sardonic, fair-haired, he was a rare, second-generation Lancaster native. Jacob struck me as a street-fighting liberal (an even rarer breed), so affronted by the boneheads' racism that he was ready to defend his town's good name with his fists. After a clash with the NLRs that left one of them with a gash in his scalp, Jacob told me, "I just hope it knocks some *sense* into his head." His mother was often away with a boyfriend, leaving her house—a modest ranch-style bungalow in a seedy older tract—to become, at least for a while, the Sharps' main hangout.

Christina Fava claimed to be horrified by what Jacob and his younger brother had been allowed to do to the room they shared—they had totally covered the walls with graffiti, much of it obscene, including some vivid pornographic tableaux—but she didn't let it stop her from coming around daily in her parents' late-model, black-and-silver, 4 x 4 sport-utility vehicle. Her romance with Darius was unpopular at home, she said, so much of her hanging out was semi-clandestine. Christina was slim but not fragile, and when I met her she had just trimmed her blond hair into a "fringe," which is the standard skin girl haircut and made her look reasonably tough. She was the only non-racist in her family, she said. In fact, she had an uncle who had been in prison and joined the Aryan Brotherhood, a widely feared white prison gang. Christina doubted that Darius would really join the Navy. "He just says it so that all his friends will say, 'No, don't go!' " she said, not unkindly. "He always does that. 'I'm ugly.' 'No!' 'I'm moving.' 'No!' He can't leave his friends."

Justin Molnar was another regular at Jacob's. He played keyboards for the Leisures, and claimed traditional skinhead, though he had gone through many phases, including grunge, punk, glam, and Gothic rock, before finding what he called "my niche." Justin, who was twenty, lived with his parents in a swank tract west of Lancaster, and was close to his family—he even bowled in a league with his parents and sister. Short and almost comically intense, he was studying engineering at Antelope Valley College. Though he told me he backed up Sharp, he was clearly less enthusiastic about fighting than some of the others, causing them to question privately just how down for the cause he was.

Johnny Suttle was also taking classes at the college, but nobody questioned how down he was. He was twenty, half Mexican, half Anglo, diminutive but super-aggressive. He worked graveyard shifts at a Taco Bell, and had a great deal to say about skinhead. On the patriotism question, for instance, he was one of those who said the Paki-bashing by the founding skinheads had been justified, because the victims were buying neighborhood pubs and kicking out the local boys. Skinhead was about loyalty—to your class, hometown, soccer team, *and* nationality, according to Johnny. Thus, if a Japanese or a Chinese skinhead decided to beat up a foreigner, it was okay, "because they're just defending their country, and that's good," he said. "The thing is, America is not a white man's country, never mind what the boneheads say. It's a melting pot. And we're about defending that."

Johnny always seemed ready to weigh the moral dimensions of violence. His girlfriend, Karen, had immigrated from Khomeini's Iran with her parents, and she had told him about the revolutionary regime's practice of hanging thieves from the lampposts. Johnny couldn't argue with it. "I'm sure people started thinking twice before they boosted anybody else's shit!" (Karen's parents were cool, he said. "They're racist about blacks, but that's just because they can't understand why some of them are kind of loud and obnoxious. And they totally hate Armenians, but that's just an Iran thing.") I once heard him deliberate one of the timeless questions: Was it ethically permissible to drop bonehead chicks before taking on the boneheads? The answer, ultimately, was yes. While it was not right to hit females, bonehead chicks were simply too dangerous to leave standing while you fought their boyfriends. They would probably stick a knife in your back. Ergo, they had to be dropped at the outset. Q.E.D.

Jacob's mother, Sheryl, an attractive, weary-looking woman in her thirties, was dubious about the Sharps. At one time, she had admired them for standing up to the racist bullies in the community, she said. "But then I got my house smashed up. I've got three kids, including a ten-year-old daughter, and I don't want anything worse to happen. I just wish the whole stupid thing would go away."

"We believe in Hitler's ways," Tim Malone, of the Nazi Low Riders, explained. "But that don't mean we worship him. He was smart, but he was a homosexual. I think what he did with the Jews was right, mainly. They was coming into Germany, buying up the businesses, treating the Germans like slaves. I think he killed *more* than six million. That was just all they could find."

Chris Runge, another NLR, told me that Hitler had actually been working for the Vatican. "That's why the Jews were put in the concentration camps. The Pope went to Hitler and said, 'These people aren't giving in. We'll give you weapons, we'll give you ammunition.' "

It took me some time to get past the NLRs' mistrust of strangers bearing notebooks, but once I did I found them garrulous, even fascinating, expounders of misinformation and sulfurous opinion. Chris Runge seemed to be the theorist of the Lancaster clique. He was nineteen, hairless, blue-eyed, pale-skinned, with an athlete's physique and an odd manner that, at least with me, alternated between an exaggerated serenity and a worried seriousness—an alternation occasionally interrupted by big, goofy smiles. "I'm basically what you call a political Nazi," he said. "A lot of these Nazis out here are unorganized. They're mostly street skins, like Storm Troopers, doing the dirty work. I want to start getting them organized. I'm not down for the government, but I'm interested in military service, because that's really getting inside the political system. I want to know how to use weapons, and get inside the government, so I can help bring it down and start my own. You saw what happened in North Carolina? We're already in there."

Chris was referring to the discovery, in late 1995, of a group of violent white-supremacist paratroopers at Fort Bragg.

"People don't really understand what Nazism is about," he went on. "They think it's all just Adolf Hitler. But Nazism is about a society with no upper class, no lower class. We'd have equality. We wouldn't have homelessness—because we keep the factories going and everybody has a place. It's like a machine, a robot. Democracy doesn't work. As you can see right now, it's falling apart. With a Nazi government, we'd just take out all the unwanted and start over again—even whites, if they're doing the same thing as the niggers are. . . . I'm here for the future. I'm for a lot of restrictions. You can't let too much freedom in." Chris gave me one of his big, blue-eyed smiles.

He grew serious again. "White supremacism just comes from growing up and seeing what's happening in society," he said. "We're going down. I mean, what's up with all this United Negro College Fund? Why is there no United White College Fund? We're just all sitting out here on the corner while they're getting all the scholarships." He frowned. "I haven't seen any of them yet show me they really deserve to be in this society. They deserve to be taken out—any way possible."

Chris was trying to change his own ways, he said. "Before, I was just like a street thug. 'Fuck you, nigger!' I see 'em in an alley, say, 'Hey, you're in the wrong neighborhood,' and beat 'em down. But our superiority is a superiority of the *mind*. You can't kill 'em all. You gotta be smarter. Whites are more civilized, so you should act more civilized—present yourself in a good manner, so people respect you."

Chris credited a recent eight-month stint in jail for his new insight. He had been convicted for participating in the same drive-by shooting that sent Jaxon Stines, who was his best friend, to jail. And he had "found the Lord" in his cell, he said, an experience that seemed to be the source of his beatific grins. It may have also softened some of his judgments. Of Mindy, for instance, Chris merely said, "She's confused. She's young." This was notably gentler than the pronouncements of other NLRs on the subject. Chris even showed some self-awareness when he talked about his life. He told me that his mother's ex-husband used to beat her so badly when he was drunk that she would come lie in bed with Chris in the hope that it would make him stop. It didn't. "And that's a lot of the hate I got inside me now," Chris said quietly.

Chris's mother was, by all accounts, a serious tweaker. (His grandfather was an executive with the Xerox Corporation, Chris said—a point of reference, perhaps, for his bitter assessment, "We're going down.") She and he had moved to the Antelope Valley when he was thirteen. He had dropped out of school in the ninth grade, and had largely been on his own since. For a while, he was a Deadhead, following the band around California, and he had lived for a patch in

Oakland. When we met, he was working at a Burger King and living with the Malones.

The Malones' house was still the NLR hangout. Though I stopped by many times, day and night, I never saw Mrs. Malone there. She worked in a plastics factory in Pasadena, more than an hour's drive away, and, according to Tim, she left the house at dawn and got home only late in the evening. When I first met Tim, who was seventeen, he had just spent two months in jail; he had been locked up as a suspect in the Todd Jordan stabbing, but had been released for lack of evidence. He was wiry and well built, with close-cropped dark hair and, tattooed on the back of his neck, an Iron Cross. He described himself as "more of the Gestapo Storm Trooper type than a political Nazi—the type that's ready to go to war over things. There's gonna be a race war around the year 2000."

I asked Tim how he had become a Nazi. He said that his father had been a Hell's Angel, "so it was kind of inherited." His dad drank, did speed, and abused his mother—that was why his parents broke up. The family had lived in a black neighborhood in Montclair, east of Los Angeles, where Tim, at the age of ten, joined a local Crips set for self-protection. He was the middle brother of three, and his joining a black gang did not please his brothers. "Both my brothers was punk rockers, into speed metal, and they used to beat me up, trying to teach me a lesson," he said. "I thank them for it now. I was on the wrong road. You gotta stick with your own race. Now ain't nothing I hate more than a wigger." (This charming term means "white nigger.") The news that Tim was an ex-Crip helped explain why he often sounded like a white thug doing a flawless imitation of a black thug. He even had a set of elaborate hand and arm gestures that I had never before seen a white kid use—the same moves gangsta rappers use in performance.

Tim and his brothers, Jeff and Steve, became skinheads after moving to the Antelope Valley, in 1992, and meeting the local neo-Nazis. They were, however, no longer calling themselves Nazi Low Riders, he said. I was surprised; that was what everyone, including the police and the press, called them. But it seemed that Willie Fisher, the leader of the

Lancaster NLRs, had been beaten up when he arrived in prison claiming NLR. "It's a prison gang," Tim explained to me. This had obviously been news to the Lancaster set. "You gotta be in prison to be a member. That's why they jumped Willie, because he never been in prison before. See, NLRs are a clique off of Aryan Brotherhood, and Aryan Brotherhood ain't recruiting no more. Now it's just everybody white in prison. But Willie's been talking to the older homeboys, so now it's cool. But we're under his wing, so if we mess up, the older homeboys will take it out on him. So we gotta jump up and take the blame for any brothers in trouble, jump up if anybody disses NLR, back it up a hundred percent. See, you can be down for NLR but not claim it yet, because you're not eligible."

Stints in juvenile detention—Tim had twice done time for methamphetamine possession—evidently didn't count toward NLR eligibility. "But the real NLRs can always just call on us if they need something taken care of," Tim said. "They just say, 'Hey, brother,' and we take care of it." The once and future NLRs of Lancaster were, in any case, eagerly awaiting, as Mindy said, the release of their leader, Willie. "When he gets out, he might take us all to Idaho," Tim said wistfully. "That's a white-power state."

In the meantime, they were a warm little nest of vipers. "We're all family," Tim said. "Even the little kids. Trouble's son, who's only, like, nine months old, already knows how to Sieg Heil." Tim imitated an infant giving a Nazi salute, and laughed. (Trouble was the street name of Robert Jones, one of the three NLRs, as I shall continue to call them, charged with firing into a parked car full of black people, including a baby, in Lancaster in 1995. Jones was convicted and sentenced to twelve years. One of his companions, Chris Parker, fondly known around the Malones' house as Evil, was the shooter; he got twenty-two years.)

There were certain limits that even Tim acknowledged, though. "Like my little sister, we don't want to get her into it too bad yet," he said. His sister, who was always parked in front of a TV playing video games when I came by the house, was, Tim estimated, approximately ten. (He really had no idea.) "She knows how to salute, and throw up a W"—that's a white-power gang sign, done with crossed fingers—"but one day she got down to it with some black kid at school, called him a nigger, and the school called my mom, and she got mad at us, because she knew where my sister picked it up."

The ranks of the boneheads were swelling, Tim said. Everywhere he went in the Antelope Valley, guys were throwing Nazi salutes at him. "Some of them I don't even know," he said. "We get hooked up that way." Standing in the Malones' front yard, talking with Tim and his friends, I did notice a startling number of passing cars honking in greeting, with white arms often jutting out the windows. The NLRs would respond with quick, stiff-armed salutes and the occasional deep shout, "White power!" Then they would grin. This, I thought, was why the local Sharps called their hometown Klancaster.

"When we first come up here, there was hardly any blacks," Tim told me. "So there wasn't much trouble. But then they started hearing about this place, wanting to come up here, starting stuff, thinking they're hard. So we're just trying to push 'em back."

The NLRs' main enemies, however, were the Sharps. "Most all Sharps are straight pussies," Tim said vehemently. "They're just a bunch of preppy white boys who want to run with the blacks because they're afraid to fight them."

The one Sharp who most infuriated Tim and his friends was, of course, Darius Houston. "There's no such thing as a black skinhead," Tim fumed. "Skinheads are *white*. Everybody knows that. Darius is bullshit."

I asked Tim if he knew where skinhead originated.

"Germany," he said. He wasn't sure when.

I asked if he had ever read anything about skinheads.

"There really ain't no book about skinheads," he said. (There are many.) He had heard about a magazine, though, a neo-Nazi "skinzine" called *Blood and Honor*, published in Long Beach, California. He asked if I could help him find some copies. "They'll hold some concerts out here for us, we heard."

On the whole, the neo-Nazi skinheads I met in the Antelope Valley seemed to have only vague, subpolitical connections to the white-supremacist world beyond their turf—through the methamphetamine trade, through prison gangs and outlaw motorcycle gangs, through racist music (white-power punk bands like Skrewdriver and Rahowa—for "Racial Holy War"—and country-and-western lynch-mob nostalgists like the Coon Hunters). They knew and admired groups like the Ku Klux Klan and White Aryan Resistance but, as far as I could tell, had little or no contact with such organizations.

I did meet one young man at the Malones' who was clearly not from the valley. He said his name was Scott Larson (I doubted that), that he was nineteen (he seemed older), and that he came from Ventura, a town on the coast north of Los Angeles, where he belonged to a gang called the Ventura Avenue Skinhead Dogs. Scott was wound extremely tight; he could not sit still while we talked. He was barechested and prison-yard fit, with a swastika tattooed on his chest and SWP (for Supreme White Power) on one shoulder. He told me that all his older male relatives were Klansmen, and that he had just served eight months in jail, "for stabbing a nigger." Before that, he said, "My girlfriend got killed by four niggers. They knew my truck—it had a big Swazi on the back—and we were coming home from a movie, just sitting at a light, and they just started capping. They were aiming at me, but they got her, twice. Now all them niggers is six feet under. But I'll be with her soon!"

Scott didn't think too much of the Antelope Valley. "This is all petty here," he said. "But I'm trying to get these guys organized. That's why I'm here."

Scott reckoned the American race war would be with us "in about ten years. And after that it'll be all segregated. Each city will be, like—Lancaster will be white, L.A. will be Mexican, New York and San Francisco will be niggers." In the meantime, he said, "We're against everything about blacks. We're against black gangs, black kids, everything. Fuck niggers!"

There were always kids at the Malones' house, and I noticed a number of them gathered around now, listening to Scott. "We're just like the Nazis," he went on, grinning intently. "We're the Storm Troopers, trying to get everybody *out.*"

Trying to get who out of where? I asked.

"Trying to get all the niggers and Mexicans out of *existence.*"

Among the kids who were usually around the Malones' were some who could not have been more than ten. I wondered if their parents had any notion what kinds of things their children were seeing and hearing there. Not all the older kids were skinheads—one regular, Tom Forney, who was perhaps seventeen, and who always seemed to be fiddling with an electric guitar, had a long red ponytail—and not all the NLR skinheads were willing to talk to me. Tim's older half-brother, Jeff, whose gang name was Demon, was polite to me but kept his distance. Angela Jackson, one of Mindy's tormentors, was often around but elusive. I sometimes heard her mention Mindy—loudly refusing to use a stick of lip balm, say, that she thought Mindy might have touched. She once sat in the kitchen and told me a few things about herself—that she lived with her grandmother, that her father had died of a heroin overdose, that the Antelope Valley had used to be all white people but was now full of "toads"—but mostly she stayed in front of the TV with the Malones' little sister.

Angela, who was seventeen, struck me as intelligent but eerily immature. She was chunky, wore boys' clothes, and, whenever I was around, seemed to be wearing a strange, sweet, dissociated smile. The NLRs called her La La, and Tim Malone told me that even he had to defer to her passion for taking revenge on the defector Mindy. "I'd really just like to work with Mindy, and get her back this way," he said. "But my brothers and sisters think she should be punished, so I keep quiet."

The attractions of the Malones' house as a hangout were not mysterious. The illicit atmosphere was exciting—all the in-your-face racism, the edge of violence, the skinhead outrageousness, the sex-and-drugs-and-rock-and-roll. The house was like a child's idea of a pirate's den: scruffy and run by tattooed brigands. I even got the feeling sometimes that a rough, retrograde, neo-communal sort of social experiment was being conducted. A boy would be opening a can of beans to heat up on the stove. Someone would bellow, "Only bitches cook in this house!" The boy would drop the can, while onlookers guffawed. Angela would tear herself away from the TV and finish opening the can, declaring herself "a skin bitch, a Featherwood." Someone at the window would shout, "Check out this Fender!" And the others would rush to the window to study two young Latinos walking past the house carrying a guitar. The questions in the air were charged and clear: Can they be robbed? Right here and now? In front of this reporter guy from New York? What can we *not* get away with?

There are many versions of what happened in the little brown tract house on East Avenue J-4 in Lancaster on the night of March 9, 1996. I heard at least two dozen. A few facts are undisputed. The Sharps were having a party. There were roughly fifty kids there, most of them white, not all of them antiracists. A keg of beer was flowing. Darius, who was drunk, got into a dispute in the kitchen with Ronda Hardin, who was wearing a bomber jacket with a Confederate flag patch on one sleeve. The dispute may have been over the patch. Darius may have choked Ronda. In any case, Ronda fled. Tom Forney, the ponytailed guitarist who hung out at the Malones', remonstrated with Darius for attacking Ronda. A number of Sharps beat up Tom. Not seriously hurt, he also fled. A boy named Sebastian McCrohan drove Ronda to the Malones' house. When the NLRs heard what had happened, three of them—Tim Malone, Jeff Malone, and somebody named Javier—went back to the party with Sebastian and Ronda in Sebastian's car.

The boys went inside. Ronda remained in the car. A confrontation took place almost immediately, not far from the front door. Jeff Malone, the quiet nineteen-year-old whose gang name was Demon, waved a knife at a girl who approached him. He was wearing sneakers and wraparound sunglasses. She later said she had been trying to warn him to leave. Darius, standing in a knot of his friends, threw a cup of beer at Tim Malone. One of the Malones challenged Darius. The NLRs were standing in close formation, their backs against a living-room wall. Darius ran toward them, a knife in his right hand. With his first thrust, he stabbed Jeff Malone through the heart. Jeff fell. His friends dragged him out the door.

Ronda ran to a neighbor's to phone the police. Sebastian drove Jeff to the hospital. On the way Jeff's friends tried to stop the bleeding. Tim was slapping his brother hard in the face, shouting, "Breathe! Breathe!" To Sebastian, he yelled, "Run this light! Go! Go!" It was only a few minutes' drive to Antelope Valley Hospital. By the time they got there, Sebastian said, Jeff's body was cold. They carried him inside. He was pronounced dead an hour later.

"Homeboy deserved it," Johnny Suttle said. "He shouldn't have come to that party. He wasn't invited."

Johnny himself wasn't at the party. He was at Taco Bell, working. But he heard about the stabbing soon after it happened, and he helped direct the Sharps' flurry of subsequent moves. The party had broken up immediately, and Juan, Fred, Billy, and Jacob had bundled Darius away. They drove first to a cemetery behind Antelope Valley High, and there, at Juan's suggestion, they all spat on the bloody knife and buried it under a bush. Next, they went to a park and cleaned up Darius, whose clothes and arms were covered with blood. Then, unaware that Jeff was dead, they dispersed for the night.

But the news was soon flying around town. Jacob was lying in bed a couple of hours later when he got a phone call. He jumped up and woke his mother, brother, and sister. Within minutes, they had packed their bags and moved to his grandmother's house. Some of Darius's relatives were also on the move before daybreak. NLR death threats were already in the air.

Johnny called the police in the morning, and he liked what he heard. The police had interviewed a number of witnesses, and to them the killing sounded like self-defense. Johnny, who knew where Darius was hiding, agreed to bring him in for questioning. He did so, and Darius was questioned but not arrested. Darius then went deeper into hiding, with some relatives in Orange County.

The police wanted the knife used in the killing. They also wanted to know why, if the stabbing *had* been self-defense, the knife had been thrown away. The Sharps, frightened by police mutterings about possible charges, asked me to accompany them to the cemetery to look for the knife. This was now three days after the killing. I declined to go with them. They eventually retrieved the weapon and turned it in.

The killing became a crossroads of sorts for the Sharps. Johnny, who was nothing if not down, took a hard line. "We gotta get *more* aggressive now," he told me. "You always gotta show the boneheads you're crazier than they are. That's the only way they won't fuck with you. If you punk it and run, you're finished."

Jacob, on the other hand, decided to let his hair grow out—"to hang up my boots and braces," as he put it. When I asked him why, he looked nonplussed. "Why? Death, that's why," he said. "This is just not a win-win situation." His friends understood, he said. He would still back them up. He just wouldn't claim skinhead. Like many Sharps (and ex-Sharps), Jacob was angry at Darius. "Why did he do it? He had no right to play God, to take another man's life. And now we all have to lie low. We can't go out and get drunk like we used to. We just have to stay in our houses and watch for boneheads."

Jacob's house was actually empty. As the Sharps' old hangout, it was now too dangerous to live in. In fact, less than a week after the killing, Jacob's entire family moved to Utah, where his mother's boyfriend had relatives. Jacob refused to go with them. He'd spent his whole life in Lancaster and he didn't want to leave. But a few weeks later he, too, moved to Utah.

Billy Anderson wanted to leave the valley, but he had no plans to grow any hair. "I'm a skinhead for life," he said. "I just hate this place. I totally despise it. The boneheads are multiplying like cockroaches, and we're just getting smaller and smaller. Everywhere else, the skinheads outnumber the boneheads, but we're stuck in this dead-end desert town where people are raised on hate. I just want to go up north, where it's more secluded and nobody knows me and I can just start over. Go to college, live with my friends."

The Sharps as a group seemed intent on putting Jeff Malone's death behind them as fast as possible. They joked about "that killer party" and soon began referring glibly to "the time Darius shanked that fool." But they each had their own odd angle on the tragedy.

Justin Molnar said his first thought after seeing Darius stab Jeff Malone was for the Leisures, their ska band. "Right away I knew we were going to need another bass player," he said. "And probably a new name, too, because without Darius it's really not the same band." Justin was also angry at Darius. "Because it affects all of us. We all have to change our routines. I can't take my girl to the movies dressed like a skin." He was now less inclined than ever, he said, to claim Sharp. "I'm not that political. I hate boneheads because they make people think that our pure little movement, just kids listening to ska, that we're all like them: racists. That's it." He shrugged. "I'm not a violent person. I don't mind a boxing match, but to throw your life away, your whole career, just in twenty seconds, just by pulling a trigger or shanking somebody, that's such a waste. There's too much I want to accomplish."

Natalie Blacker thought that the death of Jeff Malone would be the end of the local Sharps. Darius, she said, would be unable to return to the valley soon, if ever. "And without Darius I just think the Sharps here will dwindle," she said. "It's so terrible. Darius has so much potential. And just before he got into that fight in the kitchen he was so happy. I was talking to him and he was saying, 'This is such a mellow party. It's going to be so much fun.'"

Natalie had mixed feelings about her friend Christina Fava's reaction to the tragedy. Christina, who as Darius's girlfriend was now in real peril, had chosen not to lie low. She still went to school, still worked in a shop on Lancaster's main drag. She talked to Darius on the phone regularly, and drove down to see him every chance she got. "I mean, it's great that she's so loyal," Natalie said. "But girls around here can be too loyal. Sometimes it's like Christina doesn't realize that he *killed* someone."

Mindy realized, and she was devastated. We were sitting in the Hang 'n Java coffeehouse, in Lancaster, a week after the killing, and she could not seem to take her eyes off the floor. "I keep thinking about this one time with Jeff," she said. Her voice was low and dull. "It wasn't that long ago. We were at a party, and he was on a trampoline, just jumping up and down, and he was *so happy*. We went back to my house, and he was hungry, and all I could find was a can of pork and beans. He wouldn't even let me heat it up for him. He just ate it cold. I can't get that out of my mind."

The Malones were about to bury Jeff, and Mindy was not invited to the funeral. "They should think about what Jeff would want," she said. "Jeff would want me there. But I'm not a Nazi, so I'm not welcome." Her breath was ragged. "I think I'll go buy this Danzig CD Jeff liked and listen to it while they're having the funeral. One of his favorite songs is on there. He sang it to me one time when we were lying on his bed. I had such a crush on him. He always had a crush on me, too. I remember one night lying on the roof of his house, just rubbing Jeff's head until we both passed out."

Tears were trickling down Mindy's cheeks. We sat and sipped coffee in silence for a couple of minutes.

"The NLRs will never forgive me for saying Darius was fine," Mindy said suddenly. "It was true, though, he really was good-looking. But I've lost all respect for him now. If I saw him, I wouldn't even talk to him. I would just give him a dirty look."

Mindy seemed unaware that Darius had left town to avoid mishaps worse than her dirty look.

"I don't want to go back to being a bonehead," she said. "But the way things are happening out here . . . I don't want to have a label on me, but Tim says I already have one. He says I'm a 'gang hopper.' "

It was news to me that Mindy was talking to Tim Malone. As it happened, Tim had just told me that the NLRs were on strict orders from Willie Fisher, who was still in prison, to do nothing. The police were watching them, he said, expecting them to retaliate against the Sharps. This ceasefire might mean that Mindy herself was safe, at least temporarily, I thought—a hopeful possibility that I mentioned to her. She thought about it but seemed uncomforted.

"Willie is an evil person," she said quietly. "Evil, and wicked, and sweet, all at the same time."

Two burly young men had come into the coffeehouse and were standing behind Mindy. Both wore baseball caps, and both had goatees. I wondered if they were boneheads. As they began to walk past us, one of them turned and gave me a startling, sparkly-eyed look right in the face. It was a practiced, frightening, prison-yard challenge. I had never seen the guy before, but I now had no doubt whatsoever that he was a neo-Nazi. He kept walking. The skin on the back of my neck was crawling. Mindy hadn't noticed a thing.

"Once, I was drinking beer at Jacob's," she said. "And I asked Darius what he wanted to be when he grew up. And he said, 'An elephant.' Is that the sweetest thing you ever heard? An *elephant*." Mindy shook her head. "People keep asking me, 'What's wrong?' And I say, 'Oh, my friend killed my friend.' That's the way it's been coming out. It doesn't matter if they disagreed in their beliefs."

The spooky guys in the baseball caps were now chalking pool cues. I didn't know what to make of them, except that with one glance I had felt jolted out of my journalist's protective pocket for the first time, really, in months of visiting the Antelope Valley. I was so distracted that I suggested we leave, and we did. We drove to Stephanie's. Mindy told Stephanie that she couldn't hang out that night, though. She wanted to go home and finish a poem she had been working on for Mrs. Malone.

When I asked Tim Malone how his mother was taking Jeff's death, he said, "Like she should. Hard and dry."

That wasn't true, I found, when I talked to her. Mrs. Malone was tearful and despondent, and was wishing aloud that she had never moved her family to the Antelope Valley. "I wanted to get Tim away from the gangs in Montclair," she said. "But there are bad influences here, too, and my boys have gotten under their wing, and I'm hardly ever home to protect them." She knew almost no one in the valley, she said, and added, "But I've met more people in the last few days, people just calling up to offer condolences, than I'd met in the three years before this happened."

Even Heather Michaels, the NLRs' fierce "Aryan Mother," wasn't "hard and dry" when we spoke. "They didn't want no trouble," she said, meaning, improbably, the NLRs who had rushed to the party that night. "If they wanted trouble, they would've taken guns. They thought there was just five or ten Sharps there. Then they get there, turns out it's like fifty or a hundred Sharps." Heather's eyes welled at the thought. "If one of us had killed this nigger, or even stabbed him, we'd all be locked up," she snapped.

Tim Malone said the same thing, calling the police treatment of Darius "reverse discrimination." He and Chris Runge and I were standing in the Malones' front yard, watching traffic pass and talking desultorily. It was a sunny afternoon. Both of them were barechested and wore boots and jeans. Tim had on a pair of red suspenders, which he occasionally pulled up over his shoulders but mostly left to dangle. Chris, I noticed, was not flashing his goofy smile.

"Vengeance is mine, saith the Lord, and tenfold," Chris intoned. "Darius will get a lot worse than what Jeff got."

Tim nodded, his face both somber and livid. "That's right, brother," he said. To me, he said, "You know, we didn't expect Darius to be there. Because he usually runs if he thinks we might be coming."

I asked what had happened.

"We saw him in there, standing with his friends, and when he saw us he started bouncing up and down." Tim demonstrated. I had seen Darius do that fighter's bounce during the mélée at the oi show in San Bernardino. "We saw him pull something out and hide it behind his leg. We figured it was Mace. Then somebody offered me a beer, and when I went to take it Darius threw a cup of beer at me. I caught it, threw it down, and called him on." Tim demonstrated his quick reactions, his forceful challenge. " 'Come on, nigger, let's go! Right now! Mace me!' Then I spit in his face."

Nobody else had remembered the scene quite this way.

"Then four guys rushed me, and Darius came in behind them, low, and reached around me and stuck Jeff. I saw it go in. It was a pocket knife, with a black handle. Jeff didn't even know he'd been stuck. Then he looked down at his shirt and saw it. He went, 'Fuck you, nigger!' " Tim imitated Jeff crouching, both middle fingers raised before him like guns. Again, nobody else remembered anything like this. "Then we all started backing up toward the door. Jeff didn't go down till we got outside. We dragged him to the car, and we beat the shit out of him on the way to the hospital. 'Wake the fuck up!' But he died before we got there."

We stood and watched the traffic pass. I asked if Jeff had said anything in the car. "No," Tim said. "But I know what he would have said: 'Get that nigger!' "

Tim and Chris looked at each other, their shaved heads slowly nodding.

I found Darius somewhere in the suburban wilderness of Orange County. We met at a Taco Bell. Juan and Christina were also there. Darius looked much the same—a little warier, less abashed, slightly exhilarated. We had talked on the phone a few days before, and I had asked how he felt. "I'm going to be more mellow," he had said. "I was sick the first couple of days. I haven't felt that feeling since my parents died. Some people probably get off on it, and some people don't like it. I don't like it. It's weird. You've taken somebody's life, and they're never coming back on this earth. At the same time, you feel happy because he was, like, your enemy."

To my amazement, Darius didn't know the name of the person he had killed. At first I thought he was just confused by the fact that the newspapers were calling Jeff by his real father's last name, Crowther. But Darius said he hadn't seen any newspapers. He just didn't know the guy's name. If he hadn't seen the papers, I thought, then he also probably didn't know that the *Antelope Valley Press* was describing him as a "mulatto."

I ran Tim Malone's version of the killing past Darius and Juan. When I got to the part about Jeff's noticing he had been stabbed, throwing up his middle fingers in defiance, and bellowing, "Fuck you, nigger!" Juan and Darius gaped.

"He did what?" Juan said.

I told them again.

Juan and Darius looked at each other. Darius laughed. Juan shrugged. "Okay," Juan said. "They want to go out in a blaze of glory. That's cool. They can have their story."

In Darius's version, the boneheads had arrived with two knives. Darius had kicked one of them loose—he wasn't sure who was holding it—and then picked it up. That was the knife he had used to stab Jeff. None of the other witnesses I interviewed had seen this kick, or anything like it. Darius, I thought, didn't look abashed enough as he told this story.

I watched Christina from the corner of my eye. She fidgeted, checked her watch, said nothing. I noticed her studying Darius, her expression both cool and oddly contented. This fugitive skinhead was her main project now, even the center of her life. Other kids in the Antelope Valley were starting to talk about her with awe. Her black boyfriend— *Mandingo*—killed a bonehead. He was in hiding. She stuck by him, defying her parents. It was a romantic role, far larger than ordinary valley teenage life. I wondered if Christina still had the shrewd perspective on Darius she had shown when she told me that he didn't really want to join the Navy, that he just wanted to hear his friends say, "No!"

Christina and Juan set off on the long drive back to the valley.

Darius took me to meet some new friends he had made. "It's a good thing I cliqued up with some other heads," he said. "Because Huntington Beach is just a few miles from here, and that's where the O.C. Skins are from. Remember those guys from the oi show? I heard they're looking for me. So I need people to watch my back."

Darius's friends lived in a vast low-rise apartment complex. We passed through an empty white-brick foyer and were buzzed into a courtyard that seemed to ramble on for blocks—through plots of grass and stands of tattered bamboo, past a lighted swimming pool, around a thousand plastic tricycles and abandoned toys. All the ground-floor apartments had sliding glass doors without curtains. Behind them, virtually in public, people watched TV, ate sushi, and scratched their bellies, oblivious of path traffic like us. There were Asians, Latinos, blacks, whites, bikers, yuppies, buppies, old Samoans, young Cambodians. It was a Free Unity world, I thought. It felt like a vision of the next American century: ramshackle, multiracial, cut-rate. White supremacists, it struck me, fear the future for a reason: It's going to be strange and very complicated.

We came finally to the apartment of Darius's friends. But they were not there. Some other guys were, and they let us in. They looked like skaters. Two were white, one was Asian. They were smoking a bong, listening to music. Darius and I sat on a couch to one side and talked. He was staying with one of his many half-brothers, he said, not far away. He was thinking about moving to Germany. He had a lot of relatives in Germany. First, though, he was going to enroll in the local community college to learn German. Then he thought he might join the Navy. In the meantime, he thought Christina should move down here. It was too dangerous for her in the Antelope Valley now.

I wasn't sure why Darius wanted me to meet his new friends. But I figured I had seen enough of his new world. It was just a more historically mature Antelope Valley, I thought. I wished him luck. We shook hands, finishing off with a clean, only slightly self-conscious solidarity knuckle punch. And then I made my way back out through the long, complex, low-rise courtyard of the future.

The first time I talked to the Lancaster prosecutor in charge of investigating Jeff Malone's death, he shared with me his feeling about gang killings in general. "I say lock 'em all up in a room and prosecute the survivor," he said. I took this to mean that Darius did not have to fear prosecution.

Later, when a decision was officially made not to prosecute, the same assistant district attorney explained his reasoning to me. The victim and his friends had gone to a house where a hostile or opposing gang was having a party. The victim had a knife. He attacked Mr. Houston. Mr. Houston's claim that the knife he used belonged to the victim or to the victim's friends was not credible. But it was not illegal for him to possess that knife inside that house. There were conflicting eyewitness versions of the attack. It was certainly not a particularly vicious attack. The fact that a single knife thrust had killed the victim was simply bad luck. The crucial question for the prosecution was whether a jury could be persuaded that the killing had *not* been self-defense. That seemed unlikely; the victim was a Nazi skinhead, who would not be viewed sympathetically. Mr. Houston was on his own turf, minding his own business. "I'm not saying Mr. Houston is a great guy," the prosecutor concluded. "He's not. He's a jerk. You need to call me in about six months to see if he is still alive. I do not believe he will be."

To the Malone family's bitter contention that it was really because Jeff was a skinhead from a poor family that no one would be prosecuted for his death, I could think of no rejoinder. It was true.

from The Gangs of New York
by Herbert Asbury

Newspaperman and author Herbert Asbury
(1889–1963) was a self-appointed chronicler
of America's underworld. His 1928 cult classic
The Gangs of New York presents a startling
phantasmagoria of violence and lawlessness.

The original Five Points gangs had their genesis in the tenements, saloons, and dance halls of the Paradise Square district, but their actual organization into working units, and the consequent transformation of the area into an Alsatia of vice and crime, closely followed the opening of the cheap green-grocery speakeasies which soon sprang up around the Square and along the streets which debouched into it. The first of these speakeasies was established about 1825 by Rosanna Peers in Center street just south of Anthony, now Worth street. Piles of decaying vegetables were displayed on racks outside the store, but Rosanna provided a back room in which she sold the fiery liquor of the period at lower prices than it could be obtained in the recognized saloons. This room soon became the haunt of thugs, pickpockets, murderers, and thieves. The gang known as the Forty Thieves, which appears to have been the first in New York with a definite, acknowledged leadership, is said to have been formed in Rosanna Peers' grocery store, and her back room was used as its meeting-place, and as headquarters by Edward Coleman and other eminent chieftains. There they received the reports of their henchmen, and from its dimly lit corners dispatched the gangsters on their warlike missions. The Kerryonians, composed of natives of County Kerry, Ireland, was also a product of Rosanna's enterprise. This was a small gang which seldom roamed beyond Center street and did little fighting; its members devoted themselves almost exclusively to hating the English.

The Chichesters, Roach Guards, Plug Uglies, Shirt Tails, and Dead Rabbits were organized and had their rendezvous in other grocery stores, and in time these emporiums came to be regarded as the worst dens of the Five Points, and the centers of its infamy and crime. The Shirt Tails were so called because they wore their shirts on the outside of their trousers, like Chinamen, and the expressive appellation of the Plug Uglies came from their enormous plug hats, which they stuffed with wool and leather and drew down over their ears to serve as helmets when they went into battle. The Plug Uglies were for the most part gigantic Irishmen, and included in their membership some of the toughest characters of the Five Points. Even the most ferocious of the Paradise Square eye-gougers and mayhem artists cringed when a giant Plug Ugly walked abroad looking for trouble, with a huge bludgeon in one hand, a brickbat in the other, a pistol peeping from his pocket and his tall hat jammed down over his ears and all but obscuring his fierce eyes. He was an adept at rough and tumble fighting, and wore heavy boots studded with great hobnails with which he stamped his prostrate and helpless victim.

The Dead Rabbits were originally part of the Roach Guards, organized to honor the name of a Five Points liquor seller. But internal dissension developed, and at one of the gang's stormy meetings someone threw a dead rabbit into the center of the room. One of the squabbling factions accepted it as an omen and its members withdrew, forming an independent gang and calling themselves the Dead Rabbits.[*]

---

[*] In the slang of the period a rabbit was a rowdy, and a dead rabbit was a very rowdy, athletic fellow.

Sometimes they were also known as the Black Birds, and achieved great renown for their prowess as thieves and thugs. The battle uniform of the Roach Guards was a blue stripe on their pantaloons, while the Dead Rabbits adopted a red stripe, and at the head of their sluggers carried a dead rabbit impaled on a pike. The Rabbits and the Guards swore undying enmity and constantly fought each other at the Points, but in the rows with the water-front and Bowery gangs they made common cause against the enemy, as did the Plug Uglies, Shirt Tails, and Chichesters. All of the Five Points gangsters commonly fought in their undershirts.

The Five Points gradually declined as an amusement center as the green groceries invaded the district and the gangs began to abuse their privileges as overlords of Paradise Square, and the Bowery became increasingly important as a place of recreation. As early as 1752, when the waters of the Collect still covered the site of the Tombs and flowed sluggishly through Canal street, the Bowery began to make some pretensions to being a street of pleasure by the opening of Sperry's Botanical Gardens, later Voxhaull's Gardens, at the upper end of the thoroughfare near Astor Place. Its claims were greatly enhanced in 1826 by the erection of the Bowery Theater on the site of the old Bull's Head Tavern, where George Washington had stopped to quench his thirst with Bowery ale on Evacuation Day in 1783. The new playhouse opened with a comedy, *The Road to Ruin*, but its first important production was in November, 1826, when Edwin Forrest played the title role in *Othello*. For many years it was one of the foremost theaters on the continent; its boards creaked beneath the tread of some of the greatest players of the time. It was then the largest playhouse in the city, with a seating capacity of 3,000, and was the first to be equipped with gas. The structure was burned three times between 1826 and 1838, and again caught fire some fifteen years before the Civil War, when the police, recently uniformed by order of Mayor Harper, appeared on the scene in all the glory of their new suits and glistening brass buttons. They ordered the spectators to make way for the firemen, but the Bowery gangsters jeered and laughed at them as liveried lackeys, and refused to do their bidding.

The thugs attacked with great ferocity when someone howled that the policemen were trying to imitate the English bobbies, and many were injured before they were subdued. So much ill-feeling arose because of this and similar incidents that the uniforms were called in, and for several years the police appeared on the streets with no other insignia than a star-shaped copper shield, whence came the names coppers and cops. After weathering many storms the theater was finally renamed the Thalia, and still stands in the shadow of the Third avenue elevated railroad, devoted to moving pictures and Italian stock, with occasional performances by travelling Chinese troupes.

Several other theaters soon followed the Bowery, among them the Windsor, which became famous for its performances of *Hands Across the Sea*, and for the remarkable acting of Johnny Thompson in *On Hand*. For many years these houses presented first-class plays and were frequented by the aristocracy of the city, but in time, as the character of the street changed and the dives and gangsters made it a byword from coast to coast, they offered blood and thunder thrillers of so distinct a type that they became known as Bowery plays, and could be seen nowhere else. Among them were *The Boy Detective, Marked for Life, Neck and Neck,* and *Si Slocum*. From these productions developed the "ten, twent', thirt' " melodrama which was so popular throughout the United States until its place was taken by the moving picture. The dress circles and first balconies of the early Bowery theaters, after the first citizens had abandoned them for the playhouses farther uptown and along Broadway, were generally filled with respectable German families from the Seventh Ward, who drank pink and yellow lemonade and noisily devoured Ridley's Old Fashioned Peppermint Kisses. But the pit and topmost galleries fairly swarmed with ragamuffins of all degrees and both sexes, who stamped and whistled and shouted "h'ist dat rag!" when the curtain failed to rise promptly on schedule time. "These places are jammed to suffocation on Sunday nights," wrote an author who visited the Bowery about the time of the Civil War. "Actresses too corrupt and dissolute to play elsewhere appear on the boards at the Bowery. Broad farces, indecent comedies, plays of highwaymen and murderers, are received with shouts by the reeking crowds which fill the low theaters. Newsboys, street-sweepers, ragpickers, begging girls, collectors of cinders, all who can beg or steal a sixpence, fill the galleries of these corrupt places of amusement. There is not a dance hall, a free-and-easy, a concert saloon, or a vile drinking-place that presents such a view of the depravity and degradation of New York as the gallery of a Bowery theater."

Within a few years after the erection of the first theater the Bowery was lined with playhouses, concert halls, saloons and basement dives, and huge beer gardens seating from 1,000 to 1,500 persons at long tables running lengthwise of an enormous room. As late as 1898 the Bowery had ninety-nine houses of entertainment, of which only fourteen were classed as respectable by the police, and there were six barrooms to a block. Now the street can muster a bare dozen theaters, devoted to burlesque, moving pictures, and Yiddish, Italian and Chinese drama. Some of the dives which dotted the Bowery before and after the Civil War have never been equalled, even by Prohibition speak-easies, for the frightful and deadly quality of their liquor. In many of the lower class places, in the early days, drinks were three cents each and no glasses or mugs were used. Barrels of fiery spirits stood on shelves behind the bar, and poured out their contents through lines of slender rubber hose. The customer, having deposited his money on the bar, took an end of the hose in his mouth, and was entitled to all he could drink without breathing. The moment he stopped for breath the watchful bartender turned off the supply, and nothing would start it again but another payment. Some of the Bowery bums became so expert at swallowing, and were able to hold their breaths for such a long period, that they could get delightfully drunk for three cents. One famous saloon, in Baxter street near the Bowery, provided and extensively advertised a rear chamber called the "velvet room." When a good customer was reduced to a nickel, he was given an extra large bowl of liquor and escorted with considerable ceremony into the "velvet room," where he was permitted to drink himself unconscious, and sleep until the effects of the potation wore off.

The most famous of the early Bowery beer halls was the Atlantic Gardens, next door to the old Bowery Theater and now a palace of the moving pictures. Upstairs and down it provided seats for more than a thousand, and two four-horse drays, working ten hours a day, were scarcely able to keep the customers supplied with beer fresh from the brewery. In this and other similar establishments there was music by pianos, harps, violins, drums and brasses; and dice, dominoes, cards, and sometimes rifles for target shooting were provided. Everything was free except the beer, which cost five cents for an enormous mug. Most of the gardens were operated by Germans, and at first were frequented by men and women of that nationality, who brought their families and spent the day quietly. Beer was served by girls from twelve to sixteen years of age, wearing short dresses and red-topped boots, which reached almost to the knees and had bells dangling from the tassels. The sale of the beverage was so profitable that the managers of the gardens bid against each other for the privilege of entertaining the large racial and political organizations, frequently paying as much as $500 to any association that would agree to hold an all-day picnic on their premises. For many years these gardens were entirely respectable, but low class thugs and hoodlums soon began to invade them, not to drink beer but to guzzle hard liquor from flasks, and in time they came to be the resorts of the gangsters and other criminals of the district, and the Bowery assumed the character which has made it one of the most renowned thoroughfares in the world.

The most important gangs of the early days of the Bowery district were the Bowery Boys, the True Blue Americans, the American Guards, the O'Connell Guards, and the Atlantic Guards. Their membership was principally Irish, but they do not appear to have been as criminal or as ferocious as their brethren of the Five Points, although among them were many gifted brawlers. The True Blue Americans were amusing, but harmless. They wore stovepipe hats and long black frock coats which reached flappingly to their ankles and buttoned close under the chin; their chief mission in life was to stand on street corners and denounce England, and gloomily predict the immediate destruction of the British Empire by fire and sword. Like most of the sons of Erin who have come to this country, they never became so thoroughly Americanized that Ireland did not remain their principal vocal interest. The other gangs were probably offshoots of the Bowery Boys, and commonly joined the latter in their fights with the roaring denizens of Paradise Square. Their exploits earned them no place of importance in gang history.

For many years the Bowery Boys and the Dead Rabbits waged a bitter feud, and a week seldom passed in which they did not come to blows, either along the Bowery, in the Five Points section, or on the ancient battleground of Bunker Hill, north of Grand street. The greatest gang conflicts of the early nineteenth century were fought by these groups, and they continued their feud until the Draft Riots of 1863, when they combined with other gangs and criminals in an effort to sack and burn the city. In these early struggles the Bowery Boys were supported by the other gangs of the Bowery, while the Plug Uglies, the Shirt Tails, and the Chichesters rallied under the fragrant emblem of the Dead Rabbits. Sometimes the battles raged for two or three days without cessation, while the streets of the gang area were barricaded with carts and paving stones, and the gangsters blazed away at each other with musket and pistol, or engaged in close work with knives, brickbats, bludgeons, teeth, and fists. On the outskirts of the struggling mob of thugs ranged the women, their arms filled with reserve ammunition, their keen eyes watching for a break in the enemy's defense, and always ready to lend a hand or a tooth in the fray.

Often these Amazons fought in the ranks, and many of them achieved great renown as ferocious battlers. They were particularly gifted in the art of mayhem, and during the Draft Riots it was the women who inflicted the most fiendish tortures upon Negroes, soldiers, and policemen captured by the mob, slicing their flesh with butcher knives, ripping out eyes and tongues, and applying the torch after the victims had been sprayed with oil and hanged to trees. The Dead Rabbits, during the early forties, commanded the allegiance of the most noted of the female battlers, an angular vixen known as Hell-Cat Maggie, who fought alongside the gang chieftains in many of the great battles with the Bowery gangs. She is said to have filed her front teeth to points, while on her fingers she wore long artificial nails, constructed of brass. When Hell-Cat Maggie screeched her battle cry and rushed biting and clawing into the midst of a mass of opposing gangsters, even the most stouthearted blanched and fled. No quarter was asked or given by the early gangsters; when a man fell wounded his enemies leaped joyfully upon him and kicked or stamped him to death. Frequently the police were unable to disperse the mob, and were compelled to ask the National Guard and the Regular Army for aid. The city soon became accustomed to regiments of soldiers marching in battle array through the streets to quell a gang riot. Occasionally the artillery was called out also, but generally the gangsters fled before the muskets of the infantrymen. Much of this work was done by the Twenty-seventh, later the Seventh, Regiment.

Little knowledge of the activities of most of the early Bowery gangs has survived, but the lore of the street is rich in tales of the Bowery Boys and the prowess of their mighty leaders. Sometimes this gang was called Bowery B'hoys, which is sufficient indication of its racial origin. It was probably the most celebrated gang in the history of the United States, but before the eminent Chuck Conners appeared in the late eighties and transformed the type into a bar fly and a tramp, the Bowery Boy was not a loafer except on Sundays and holidays. Nor was he a criminal, except on occasion, until the period of the Civil War. He was apt to earn his living as a butcher or apprentice mechanic, or as a bouncer in a Bowery saloon or dance cellar. But he was almost always a volunteer fireman, and therein lay much of the strength of the gang, for in the early days before the Civil War the firemen, most of them strong adherents of Tammany Hall, had much to say about the conduct of the city's government. Many of the most eminent politicians belonged to the fire brigade, and there was much rivalry between the companies, which gave their engines such names as White Ghost, Black Joke, Shad Belly, Dry Bones, Red Rover, Hay Wagon, Big Six, Yaller Gal, Bean Soup, Old Junk, and Old Maid. Such famous New York political leaders as Cornelius W. Lawrence, Zophar Mills, Samuel Willetts, William M. Wood, John J. Gorman and William M. Tweed were volunteer firemen. In still earlier days even George Washington was an ardent chaser after the fire engines, and for a short time during his residence in the metropolis was head of the New York department. Before the formation of a paid fire fighting force one of the great events of the year was the Fireman's Parade, and great crowds lined the sidewalks and cheered the red-shirted, beaver-hatted brawlers as they pulled their engines over the cobble-stones, while before them marched a brass band blaring away at *Solid Men to the Front,* a rousing tune which was a favorite for many years.

But the rivalry between the fire companies whose membership included men of substance was friendly if strenuous, while the Bowery Boy loved his fire engine almost as much as he did his girl, and considered both himself and his company disgraced if his apparatus was beaten to a conflagration. And the acme of humiliation was to roll to a fire and find that all of the fire plugs had been captured by other companies. To prevent this the Bowery Boy resorted to typically direct methods. When the fire alarm sounded he simply grabbed an empty barrel from a grocery store and hurried with it to the fire plug nearest the burning building. There he turned the barrel over the plug and sat on it, and defended it valorously against the assaults of rival firemen until his own engine arrived. If he succeeded he was a hero and his company had won a notable victory. Frequently the fight for fire plugs was so fierce that the Bowery Boys had no time to extinguish the flames.

The original Bowery Boy, who followed his chieftain in so many forays against the hated Dead Rabbits and other Five Points gangs, was a burly ruffian with his chin adorned by an Uncle Sam whisker—the type of American which is still portrayed by the English comic weeklies. On his head was a stovepipe hat, generally battered, and his trousers were tucked inside his boots, while his jaws moved constantly on a chew of tobacco as he whittled on a shingle with the huge knife which never left his possession. In later years, a little before the time of Chuck Conners, the type changed as new fashions in men's clothing appeared, and the Bowery Boy promenaded his favorite thoroughfare with his head crowned by a high beaver hat with the nap divided and brushed different ways, while his stalwart figure was encased in an elegant frock coat, and about his throat was knotted a gaudy kerchief. His pantaloons, out almost as full as the modern Oxford bags, were turned up over his heavy boots. The hair on the back of his head was clipped close and his neck and chin were shaven, while his temple locks were daintily curled and heavily anointed with bear's grease or some other powerful, evil-smelling unguent. His downfall had begun in those days, but he was still an unruly and belligerent citizen, and it was unwise to give him cause for offense.

Some of the most ferocious rough-and-tumble fighters that ever cracked a skull or gouged out an eyeball fought in the ranks of the Bowery Boys, and from their rough school emerged many celebrated brawlers and political leaders. Butcher Bill Poole, a famous gangster and ward heeler, owed allegiance to the Bowery Boys, and so did his murderer, Lew Baker, who shot him to death in Stanwix Hall in 1855.

But the greatest of the Bowery Boys, and the most imposing figure in all the history of the New York gangs, was a leader who flourished in the forties, and captained the gangsters in the most important of their punitive and marauding expeditions into the Five Points. His identity remains unknown, and there is excellent reason to believe that he may be a myth, but vasty tales of his prowess and of his valor in the fights against the Dead Rabbits and the Plug Uglies have come down through the years, gaining incident and momentum as they came. Under the simple sobriquet of Mose he has become a legendary figure of truly heroic proportions, at once the Samson, the Achilles, and the Paul Bunyan of the Bowery. And beside him, in the lore of the street, marches the diminutive figure of his faithful friend and coun- sellor, by name Syksey, who is said to have coined the phrase "hold de butt," an impressive plea for the remains of a dead cigar.

The present generation of Bowery riffraff knows little or nothing of the mighty Mose, and only the older men who plod that now dreary and dismal relict of a great street have heard the name. But in the days before the Civil War, when the Bowery was in its heyday and the Bowery Boy was the strutting peacock of gangland, songs were sung in honor of his great deeds, and the gangsters surged into battle shouting his name and imploring his spirit to join them and lend power to their arms. He was scarcely cold in his grave before Chanfrau had immortalized him by writing *Mose, The Bowery B'hoy*, which was first performed before a clamorous audience at the old Olympic Theater in 1849, the year of the Astor Place riot.

Mose was at least eight feet tall and broad in proportion, and his colossal bulk was crowned by a great shock of flaming ginger-colored hair, on which he wore a beaver hat measuring more than two feet from crown to brim. His hands were as large as the hams of a Virginia hog, and on those rare moments when he was in repose they dangled below his knees; it was Syksey's habit to boast pridefully that his chief- tain could stand erect and scratch his kneecap. The feet of the great captain were so large that the ordinary boot of commerce would not fit his big toe; he wore specially constructed footgear, the soles of which were copper plates studded with nails an inch long. Woe and desolation came upon the gangs of the Five Points when the great Mose leaped into their midst and began to kick and stamp; they fled in despair and hid themselves in the innermost depths of the rookeries of Paradise Square.

The strength of the gigantic Mose was as the strength of ten men. Other Bowery Boys went into battle carrying brickbats and the ordi- nary stave of the time, but Mose, when accoutered for the fray, bore in one hand a great paving stone and in the other a hickory or oak wagon tongue. This was his bludgeon, and when it was lost in the heat of battle he simply uprooted an iron lamp-post and laid about him with great zeal. Instead of the knife affected by his followers, he pinned his faith on a butcher's cleaver. Once when the Dead Rabbits over- whelmed his gang and rushed ferociously up the Bowery to wreck the Boys' headquarters, the great Mose wrenched an oak tree out of the earth, and holding it by the upper branches, employed it as a flail, smiting the Dead Rabbits even as Samson smote the Philistines. The Five Points thugs broke and fled before him, but he pursued them into their lairs around Paradise Square and wrecked two tenements before his rage cooled. Again, he stood his ground before a hundred of the best brawlers of the Points, ripping huge paving blocks from the street and sidewalk and hurling them into the midst of his enemies, inflicting frightful losses.

In his lighter moments it was the custom of this great god of the gangs to lift a horse car off the tracks and carry it a few blocks on his shoulders, laughing uproariously at the bumping the passengers received when he set it down. And so gusty was his laugh that the car trembled on its wheels, the trees swayed as though in a storm and the Bowery was filled with a rushing roar like the thunder of Niagara. Sometimes Mose unhitched the horses and himself pulled the street car the length of the Bowery at a bewildering speed; once, if the legend is to be credited, he lifted a car above his head at Chatham Square and carried it, with the horses dangling from the traces, on the palm of his hand as far as Astor Place. Again, when a sailing ship was becalmed in the East River and drifting dangerously near the treacherous rocks of Hell Gate, Mose pulled out in a rowboat, lighted his cigar, which was more than two feet long, and sent such mighty billows of smoke against the sails that the ship was saved, and plunged down the river as though driven by a hurricane. So terrific was the force of Mose's puffs, indeed, that the vessel was into the Harbor and beyond Staten Island before it would respond to the helm. Occasionally Mose amused himself by taking up a position in the center of the river and permitting no ship to pass; as fast as they appeared he blew them back. But Mose was always very much at home in the water; he often dived off at the Battery and came up on the Staten Island beach, a distance which is now traversed by ferry boats in twenty-five minutes. He could swim the Hudson River with two mighty strokes, and required but six for a complete circuit of Manhattan Island. But when he wanted to cross the East River to Brooklyn he scorned to swim the half mile or so; he simply jumped.

When Mose quenched his thirst a drayload of beer was ordered from the brewery, and during the hot summer months he went about with a great fifty gallon keg of ale dangling from his belt in lieu of a canteen. When he dined in state the butchers of the Center and Fly markets were busy for days in advance of the great event, slicing hogs and cattle and preparing the enormous roasts which the giant needs must consume to regain his strength; and his consumption of bread was so great that a report that Mose was hungry caused a flurry in the flour market. Four quarts of oysters were but an appetizer, and soup and coffee were served to him by the barrel. For dessert and light snacks he was very fond of fruit. Historians affirm that the cherry trees of Cherry Hill and the mulberry trees of Mulberry Bend vanished because of the building up of the city, but the legend of the Bowery has it that Mose tore them up by the roots and ate the fruit; he was hungry and in no mood to wait until the cherries and mulberries could be picked.

The political geniuses of Tammany Hall were quick to see the practical value of the gangsters, and to realize the advisability of providing them with meeting and hiding places, that their favor might be curried and their peculiar talents employed on election day to assure government of, by, and for Tammany. Many ward and district leaders acquired title to the green-grocery speakeasies in which the first of the Five Points gangs had been organized, while others operated saloons and dance houses along the Bowery, or took gambling houses and places of prostitution under their protection. The underworld thus became an important factor in politics, and under the manipulation of the worthy statemen the gangs of the Bowery and Five Points participated in the great series of riots which began with the spring election disturbances of 1834 and continued, with frequent outbreaks, for half a score of years. In this period occurred the Flour and Five Points riots, and the most important of the Abolition troubles, while there were at least two hundred battles between the gangs, and innumerable conflicts between volunteer fire companies.

During the summer of 1834 the opportunities for the gangs to engage in their natural employment were greatly increased by the appearance of two new political groups, the Native Americans and the Equal Rights Party. The latter was a disgruntled faction within Tammany Hall, and was vociferously in favor of equal rights for all citizens, and opposed to bank notes and the establishment of monopolies by legislation. The Native Americans deplored the election of foreigners to office, and vigorously demanded the repeal of the naturalization laws by which Tammany Hall had gained such an enormous following of Irish voters. The Native Americans took the place of the Whigs in some of the municipal elections, and both followed the example of Tammany and hired gangsters to blackjack their opponents and act as repeaters at the polls.

The Bowery gang known as the American Guards, the members of which prided themselves on their native ancestry, was soon devotedly attached to the Native Americans party, and responded joyfully to the appeals of its ward heelers and district leaders. During the summer of 1835, about a year after the election riots, bitter enmity developed between this gang and the O'Connell Guards, which had been organized under the aegis of a Bowery liquor seller, and was the particular champion of the Irish element of Tammany Hall. These gangs came to blows on June 21, 1835, at Grand and Crosby streets on the lower East Side. The fighting spread as far as the Five Points, where the gangsters of Paradise Square took a hand and the rioting became general throughout that part of the city. The Mayor and the Sheriff called out every watchman in the city, and the force managed to stop the fighting without the aid of soldiers, although several companies were mustered and remained in their armories overnight. Dr. W. M. Caffrey, a noted surgeon, was killed by a brickbat while trying to make his way through the mob to attend a patient, and Justice Olin M. Lowndes was seriously wounded when he entered the riot area with the police.

Several minor conflicts over the Abolition movement occurred late in 1833, and the homes of many prominent Abolitionists were bombarded with stones and bricks, but for the most part the anti-slavery agitation was obscured by the excitements of the spring election, for it was the first time that a mayor had been elected by direct vote and there was fierce fighting for three days between Tammany and the Whigs before the former was finally victorious. About the middle of 1834 the feeling against the Abolitionists, which was always very strong in the metropolis, once more flared into open violence, and on July 7 mobs attacked the Chatham street Chapel and the Bowery Theater, where Edwin Forrest was playing in *Metamora* for the benefit of the manager, an Englishman named Farren. When the police drove the rioters from the playhouse they roared down to Rose street, now a dingy thoroughfare in the gloomy shadow of Brooklyn Bridge, but then an important residential street lined with pretentious mansions. There they launched an assault against the home of Lewis Tappan, a prominent Abolitionist, and smashed the doors and windows with stones. Swarming into the building, they wrecked the interior and pitched the furniture into the street, where it was arranged in huge piles and oil poured over it. In throwing out the pictures which had adorned the walls one of the gangsters came across a portrait of George Washington, and another thug tried to snatch it from his arms. But the discoverer hugged it to his breast and shouted dramatically:

"It's Washington! For God's sake don't burn Washington!"

His cry was taken up in the street, and the mob began to shout in unison:

"For God's sake don't burn Washington!"

A line was formed, and the painting of the first President was passed tenderly down the stairs and into the street, where a group of huge bullies bore it aloft to a neighboring house. There it was installed upon the verandah and carefully guarded until the end of the riot. Sporadic outbreaks occurred during the next few days, and on July 10 a mob did great damage to residences and business houses in Spring, Catherine, Thompson, and Reade streets, while another great throng, composed almost entirely of Five Points gangsters, terrorized the area around Paradise Square. The rioters there appeared to be well organized, for runners were kept passing between the different gangs, and scouts patrolled the streets to give warning of the approach of the police and soldiers. The word spread that the gang chieftains had resolved to burn and loot every house around the Five Points that did not have a candle in a window, and soon the entire Paradise Square district blazed into illumination.

Nevertheless, a dozen buildings were sacked and set on fire, and by midnight the heavens glowed with the glare of the conflagration, while a dense pall of smoke hung low over that part of the city. Five houses of prostitution were burned, and the inmates, stripped and parcelled out among the gangsters, were shamefully mistreated. St. Philip's Negro Church in Center street was destroyed, as were three houses on the opposite side of the street, and one adjoining the church. Throughout the night the screams of tortured Negroes could be heard, and an Englishman who was captured by the thugs had both eyes gouged out and his ears torn off by the frenzied rioters. But at one o'clock in the morning, when the blare of bugles told of the coming of the military, the gang chieftains dispersed their thugs, and half an hour later the Five Points was quiet except for the tramping of the troops and the wailing of the unhappy victims who mourned beside the ruins of their homes. The next night the rioters wrecked a church in Spring street and barricaded the thoroughfare with furniture, but were routed by the Twenty-Seventh Regiment of Infantry, which destroyed the fortifications and chased the mob away without firing a shot.

The worries of the city authorities were enormously increased by the great fire of December 16–17, 1835, which raged for a day and a half with the thermometer at seventeen degrees below zero, and devastated thirteen acres in the heart of the financial district. The loss was more than $20,000,000. The conflagration started at No. 25 Merchant street and swept into Pearl street and Exchange Place, burned southward almost to Broad street, eastward to the East River, and from Wall street to Coenties Slip.[*] Every building on the south side of Wall street from William street to the East River was destroyed, and the flames were not checked until Marines from the Navy Yard dynamited the Dutch Church, the Merchants' Exchange and other buildings, and created a gap which the fire could not cross. Several hundred houses were burned, and at least fifty others were wrecked and looted by criminals, who also raided the great heaps of furniture, jewelry and clothing which were piled in the streets without adequate guard. Much valuable property was recovered by the police a week later in the hovels of the Bowery and Five Points. Many houses and stores were set on fire by the thugs, and one man who was caught applying the torch to a building at Broad and Stone streets was seized by a group of irate citizens and hanged to a tree. His body, frozen stiff, dangled for three days before the police found time to cut it down.

The fire was one of the direct causes of the panic of 1837, for the losses were so great that many banks suspended, and the insurance companies could not pay their policies in full. Consequently owners of business houses and factories were unable to obtain money with which to rebuild, and thousands who had been thrown out of employment by the disaster remained without work throughout the following summer. Early in September, 1836, flour was seven dollars a barrel, and within another month it had advanced to twelve, and commission merchants predicted that it would go to twenty before the end of the winter. Bread soon became a scarce article of diet among the poor, and in the slums of the Bowery and Five Points thousands were on the

---

[*]A few blocks north of the Battery. One story of the origin of the name is: In colonial times a Dutchman, named Coen, had a sweetheart, Antye. The slip was their trysting place, and the townspeople called it Coen's and Antye's Slip. From this came Coenties.

verge of actual starvation. In February, 1837, a report was circulated that there were only 4,000 barrels in the great depot at Troy, New York, instead of the customary 30,000, and the newspapers published the news with the largest headlines of the period, and in editorial articles denounced certain merchants who were said to be hoarding great quantities of flour and grain, waiting for the advance in price.

Great unrest prevailed, and many mass meetings were held, but there was no direct action until February 10, 1837, when a mob which had listened to inflammatory harangues in City Hall Park attacked the wheat and flour store of Eli Hart & Company, in Washington street between Dey and Cortlandt. Hart's watchmen retreated into the building, but neglected to bar the door, which soon gave way to the battering assault of the rioters. The mob rushed into the building and began throwing barrels of flour and sacks of wheat from the windows. Most of the casks were staved in when they struck the pavement, and the others were quickly smashed by the rioters, who had set up a sing-song shout of "here goes flour at eight dollars a barrel!" Five hundred barrels of flour and a thousand bushels of wheat in sacks had been destroyed when a large body of police appeared, supported by two companies of the National Guard. Fleeing before the muskets and nightsticks, the rioters streamed across the city and launched themselves against the store of S. H. Herrick & Company, near Coenties Slip. There they destroyed thirty barrels of flour and a hundred bushels of wheat before they were driven away.

The next day the price of flour increased $1 a barrel.

One of the first of the political leaders to discover that the gangsters could be employed to great advantage was Captain Isaiah Rynders, Tammany boss of the Sixth Ward, king of the Five Points gangsters and head of the notorious Empire Club at No. 25 Park Row, and owner of half a dozen Paradise Square green-groceries. Captain Rynders first appeared in New York in the middle thirties, after a brief career as a gambler and pistol-and-knife fighter along the Mississippi River. He was one of the most astute politicians who ever operated in the metropolis, although he sometimes permitted his love for the Irish and his hatred of the English to upset his judgment. Eventually he became United States Marshal, and for more than twenty-five years exercised considerable power in Tammany Hall, save for several years in the fifties when he became a renegade and espoused the cause of the Native Americans. For many years Captain Rynders made his head-quarters at Sweeney's House of Refreshment at No. 11 Ann street, a thoroughfare much frequented by volunteer firemen, but about 1843 he organized the Empire Club, which became the political center of the Sixth Ward and the clearing house of all gangster activities which had to do with politics. From it Rynders issued the commands and pulled the wires which kept his henchmen out of jail. With the aid of the gang chieftains and such gifted lieutenants as Dirty Face Jack, Country McCleester and Edward Z. C. Judson, better known as Ned Buntline, Captain Rynders kept the Sixth Ward under his political thumb and waxed rich and powerful. His control of the Five Points gangs was absolute, and he was frequently appealed to by the police to quell riots which the watchmen themselves could not stop.

Captain Rynders was an important figure in many of the Abolition disturbances, but his most notable exploit was performed in 1849, when he took advantage of the bitter professional jealousy between Edwin Forrest and William C. Macready, the eminent British actor, and became the principal instigator of the famous riots in Astor Place. Macready was driven from the stage of the Astor Place Opera House on May 7, 1849, by a mob which had gathered in response to fiery tirades of Captain Rynders and other agitators against the Briton, and their crafty manipulation of the racial prejudices of New York's large Irish population. Three days later, on May 10, Washington Irving, John Jacob Astor and other prominent citizens induced Macready to attempt another performance, and Captain Rynders immediately flooded the city with inflammatory handbills denouncing the English and calling upon the Americans to defend their country against foreign insult and oppression. That night a great mob of between 10,000 and 15,000 massed in Astor Place, and Macready again fled when the theater was bombarded with bricks and cobblestones and set on fire by gangsters who had been captured by the police and flung into the basement. The flames were extinguished before much damage was done.

The police were unable to control the mob even after Macready had left the theater and escaped to New Rochelle in disguise, and the Seventh Regiment was finally called into action. The soldiers were also attacked, and after they had been forced to fall back upon the sidewalk on the east side of the Opera House, and some of their muskets snatched from their hands, they fired several volleys into the mob, killing twenty-three persons and wounding twenty two. More than a hundred policemen and Guardsmen were injured by stones and bricks, and half a dozen of the latter were shot. Another attempt to wreck and burn the Opera House was made on the night of May 11, but the mob was cowed by additional troops and by artillery which had been planted to sweep Broadway and the Bowery. The excitement was intense for almost a week, and for several days a great crowd stood in front of the New York Hotel, where Macready had stopped, urging him to come forth and be hanged. But the actor boarded a train at New Rochelle within two hours after the rioting of May 10, and went to Boston. From there he sailed to England, and never again returned to this country.

The number of thugs who followed the great gang captains of the Five Points, the Bowery, and the Fourth Ward was enormously increased during the decade preceding the Civil War by the throngs of bruisers and bullies who swarmed into New York from other cities. By 1855 it was estimated that the metropolis contained at least thirty thousand men who owed allegiance to the gang leaders, and through them to the political leaders of Tammany Hall and the Know Nothing or Native American Party, who kept the political pot boiling furiously by their frantic and constant struggles for the privilege of plundering the public funds.

At every election gangs employed by the rival factions rioted at the polling places, smashing ballot boxes, slugging honest citizens who attempted to exercise the right of franchise, themselves voting early and often, and incidentally acquiring a contempt for the police and for constituted authority which was to have appalling consequences during the Draft Riots. The climax of the purely political rioting was reached in 1856, when Fernando Wood was elected to a second term as Mayor. Wood was bitterly opposed, not only by the Native Americans, who accused him of favoring the Irish and other foreign elements, but by the reformers as well, for he had shown himself a reckless and unprincipled official, and had thrown the city treasury wide open to the looting fingers of his henchmen. But he had the staunch support of all the lower strata of society, especially the saloon and gambling-house keepers, whose loyalty he had assured by preventing the enforcement of a Sunday closing law passed in 1855. He compelled every man on the police force to contribute to his campaign fund, one patrolman who at first refused to do so being kept on duty twenty-four hours without relief.

The Dead Rabbits, the largest and most powerful of the gangs, were enrolled under the Wood banner, as were most of the other bruisers of the Five Points and many of the most celebrated sluggers of the water front. The Bowery Boys and other gangs of the Bowery district were adherents of the Native Americans. The night before the election Mayor Wood issued an executive order sending a majority of the policemen off on furlough, with strict orders not to go near the polling places except to cast their votes. When the gangs began rioting they were confronted by small and ineffective detachments of patrolmen who were soon overwhelmed by sheer force of numbers and driven from the field. In the Sixth Ward, of which the Five Points was the heart, a crowd of Bowery gangsters made a surprise attack on the polling place and scattered the Dead Rabbit patrols, but the latter were quickly reinforced by thugs who swarmed from the dives and tenements of Paradise Square, and returned to the fray, armed with clubs, knives, axes, brickbats, and pistols. They soon defeated the Native American bullies, while half a dozen policemen added to the excitement by barricading themselves in a vacant house and firing an occasional shot through the windows. Throughout the day there were similar clashes in other wards, but Wood's gangsters proved the more efficient repeaters and the more ferocious battlers, and Tammany Hall carried the day, re-electing Wood with 34,860 votes to 25,209 for Isaac O. Barker, the Native American candidate. The count showed an enormous increase in the number of ballots cast over the previous election, and Wood's enemies charged that at least 10,000 of them were fraudulent. But there was no investigation.

In 1857, two years after Bill Poole had gone to his reward, New York passed through one of the most turbulent and disastrous twelve months in her history, beginning with appalling governmental corruption and ending with financial calamity, for this was the year of the great panic, and before the end of December more than a score of banks and almost a thousand business houses had failed with liabilities exceeding $120,000,000. During Fernando Wood's second administration as Mayor the police force had become so corrupt, and its organization so chaotic and inefficient, that the Legislature again intervened and relieved the city government of all control over the department. During the spring session several bills affecting the city charter were passed, the most important of which abolished the Municipal Police and the Police Board formed by the Act of 1853, and substituted a Metropolitan Police District comprising Manhattan, Brooklyn, and the small towns on Staten Island and on the mainland north of the Harlem River, all embraced within the counties of New York, Kings, Richmond and Westchester. The Governor was empowered to appoint five Commissioners, who were in turn to name a Superintendent of Police. The first Board was composed of Simeon Draper, James Bowen, James W. Nye, Jacob Cholwell and James S. T. Stranahan, all of whom had been more or less active in the various fights waged by the reformers against the political despoilers of the city. Frederick A.

Talmage, who had been Recorder during the Astor Place riots in 1849, became the first Superintendent of Police, accepting the post after several others had declined.

The new Police Board called upon Fernando Wood to disband the Municipal force and turn over all police property, but the Mayor refused, and would not submit even when the Supreme Court handed down a decision in May, 1857, affirming the constitutionality of the new law. He called upon the police force to stand by him, and when the question was put to a vote fifteen captains and eight hundred patrolmen, as well as Superintendent George W. Matsell, refused to acknowledge the authority of the Metropolitan Board, and decided to continue as members of the Municipal Police. The remaining officers and men, among them Captain George W. Walling, took the oath of allegiance to the new organization, which opened headquarters in White street and set about filling the places of the patrolmen who had remained loyal to the Mayor. Wood in turn appointed men to succeed those who had gone over to the Metropolitans. The trouble reached a crisis on June 16, when Daniel D. Conover went to City Hall to assume the office of Street Commissioner, to which he had been appointed by Governor King. The Mayor also claimed the power of appointment, and had named Charles Devlin, to whom it was charged he had sold the office for $50,000.

When Conover appeared he was forcibly ejected from the building by the Municipal Police, and immediately obtained two warrants for the Mayor's arrest, one charging him with inciting to riot and the other accusing him of violence against Conover's person. One of the warrants was given to Captain Walling, who went alone to City Hall and was admitted to Mayor Wood's private office, where the Mayor sat behind the desk clutching his ornate staff of office. Walling explained his errand, and when the Mayor vociferously refused to be placed under arrest the Captain calmly seized him by the arm and remarked that he would take him forcibly from the building, as he would any other person subject to a warrant. But more than three hundred Municipal Police had been stationed in City Hall in anticipation of trouble, and the Mayor was rescued before Captain Walling had dragged him beyond the door of the private office. Walling was then thrown into the street. He made several attempts to re-enter, but was prevented, and was still arguing with Captain Ackerman of the Municipals when a detachment of fifty Metropolitan policemen, under command of Coroner Perry and Captain Jacob Sebring, marched through Chambers street into City Hall Park to serve the second warrant obtained by Conover.

The Metropolitans presented an imposing appearance in their frock coats and plug hats, and with their new badges glistening in the sunshine, but they were no match for the throng of Municipals who swarmed from the building and attacked them. For more than a half hour the combat raged fiercely on the steps and in the corridors of City Hall, but at length the Metropolitans were pushed from the building and fled the scene in disorder. During the battle fifty-two policemen were injured, and one, Patrolman Crofut of the Seventeenth precinct, was so terribly beaten that he was ever afterward an invalid. They were carried into the offices of Recorder James M. Smith and their wounds treated by physicians, while the Mayor and his supporters gathered in the private offices, which had been barricaded, and jubilantly congratulated each other that the sacred person of the chief executive had been saved.

While the fighting was in progress Conover called upon Sheriff Westervelt to serve the warrants, and the Sheriff was advised by his lawyers that it was clearly his duty to do so. Accompanied by Conover and his attorney and bearing his staff of office, with his sword strapped to his waist and the official plug hat on his head, the Sheriff marched with great dignity up the steps of the City Hall and into the Mayor's offices, where Wood again angrily refused to submit to arrest. Meanwhile the Seventh Regiment of the National Guard, with flags flying and drums beating, was marching down Broadway to take a boat for Boston, where the troops were to be entertained by one of the Massachusetts regiments. A hundred yards from City Hall the members of the Metropolitan Police Board met the soldiers and informed the commander, Major-General Charles Sandford, that they had come to exercise the power granted to them by the Legislature of calling upon the National Guard whenever the peace and dignity of the city were threatened. They were unanimously of the opinion that such a time had arrived.

The Seventh Regiment was thereupon marched into the Park and City Hall surrounded, after which General Sandford and his staff held a conference with Sheriff Westervelt and the Police Commissioners. Then, with his sword clanking at his heels and a platoon of infantry with fixed bayonets surrounding him, the General strode fiercely into the building, where he informed Mayor Wood that he represented the military power of the Empire State and would tolerate no further resistance. Wood glanced out of the window, and seeing the Park filled with soldiers, accepted the warrants and submitted to arrest. Within an hour he was released on nominal bail, and so far as the records show was never brought to trial, the Civil Courts holding that the Governor had no right to appoint a Street Commissioner and that Devlin was entitled to the office. Several months later the policemen who had been injured in the clash between the Metropolitans and the Municipals brought suit against Wood and received judgment of $250 each. But the Mayor never settled, and the city finally paid the claims, together with the costs of the actions.

In the early autumn the Court of Appeals affirmed the decision of the Supreme Court and upheld the constitutionality of the new law, and within a few weeks the Mayor had disbanded the Municipals. But during the summer both police forces patrolled the city, and paid more attention to their private feud than to protecting the lives and property of the citizens. Whenever a Metropolitan arrested a criminal, a Municipal came along and released him, and the thug went about his business while the policemen fought. Aldermen and magistrates who supported the Mayor spent their days in the Metropolitan police stations, and whenever a prisoner was brought in they immediately released him on his own recognizance, while officials who favored the Metropolitan Board did the same at the Municipal stations. In consequence of this situation the gangsters and other criminals ran wild throughout the city, revelling in an orgy of loot, murder and disorder. Respectable citizens were held up and robbed in broad daylight on Broadway and other principal streets, while Municipal and Metropolitan policemen belabored each other with clubs, trying to decide which had the right to interfere. Gangs of thieves and rowdies invaded and plundered stores and other business houses, and stopped the stage coaches and compelled passengers to surrender their money and jewelry, while private residences had no protection save stout locks and the valour of the householders.

The gangs of the Five Points and the Bowery, by far the most turbulent of the city's inhabitants, took advantage of the opportunity to vent their ancient grudges against each other, and engaged in almost constant rioting. Scarcely a week passed without half a dozen conflicts, and once more, as during the great riot period of 1834, the National Guard regiments stood to arms and quelled the lawless elements with bayonet and saber. The most sanguinary of these battles occurred on July 4 and 5, 1857, when the dispute between the Mayor and the Metropolitan Board was at its height and the police organization was in a condition of utter chaos. Led by the Dead Rabbits and the Plug Uglies, all of the gangs of the Five Points with the exception of the Roach Guards began their celebration of the Fourth with a raid on the building at No. 42 Bowery, occupied by the Bowery Boys and the Atlantic Guards as a club-house. There was furious fighting, but the Bowery gangsters triumphed and drove their enemies back to their dens around Paradise Square. On this day the rioting spread as far as Pearl and Chatham streets, now the northern half of Park Row, and a few Metropolitan policemen who tried to interfere were badly beaten. The Municipals said it was not their fight, and would have no hand in any attempt to suppress the trouble.

Early the next morning the Five Points gangs, reinforced by the Roach Guards, marched out of Paradise Square and attacked a resort called the Green Dragon, in Broome street near the Bowery, a favorite loafing place of the Boys and other Bowery gangs. Carrying iron bars and huge paving blocks, the Five Pointers swarmed into the establishment before the Bowery thugs could rally to its defense, and after wrecking the bar-room and ripping up the floor of the dance hall, proceeded to drink all of the liquor in the place. News of the outrage reached the Bowery Boys, and they boiled furiously out of their holes, supported by the Atlantic Guards and the other gangsters who owed allegiance to them or loyalty to the Bowery. The gangs came together at Bayard street and immediately began the most ferocious free-for-all in the history of the city.

A lone policeman, with more courage than judgment, tried to club his way through the mass of struggling men and arrest the ringleaders, but he was knocked down and his clothing stripped from his body, and he was fearfully beaten with his own nightstick. He crawled through the plunging mob to the sidewalk, and, naked except for a pair of cotton drawers, ran to the Metropolitan headquarters in White street, where he gasped out the alarm and collapsed. A squad of policemen was dispatched to stop the rioting, but when they marched bravely up Center street the gangs made common cause against them, and they were compelled to retreat after a bloody encounter in which several men were injured. However, they rallied and finally fought their way into the center of the mob, where they arrested two men who seemed to be leaders. But again they were compelled to fall back, for the gangsters forced their way into the low houses which lined the Bowery and Bayard street, and after driving out the inhabitants, swarmed to the roofs and windows, whence they pelted the Metropolitans with stones and brickbats.

When the police had marched away without their prisoners, there was a breathing spell of a few moments, but the excitement grew more intense, and the Dead Rabbits attacked with great fury after a mob of wild-eyed, screaming Five Points hussies had rushed into their midst and taunted them with cowardice. Reinforcements from the dives of Paradise Square followed close on the heels of the women, and other thugs had arrived to swell the ranks of the heroes of the Bowery. It was estimated that from eight hundred to one thousand fighters were actively engaged, all armed with bludgeons, paving stones, brickbats, axes, pitchforks, pistols and knives. And from all parts of the city had hurried several hundred thieves and thugs who were members of none of the gangs. Attracted by the prospect of loot, and knowing that if the police were there at all they would be very busy with the rioters, these men attacked the residences and stores along the Bowery, and along Bayard, Baxter, Mulberry and Elizabeth streets, so that the owners had to barricade their buildings and protect their property with muskets and pistols. "Brick-bats, stones and clubs were flying thickly around," said the *New York Times* of July 6, 1857, "and from the windows in all directions, and men ran wildly about brandishing firearms. Wounded men lay on the sidewalks and were trampled upon. Now the Rabbits would make a combined rush and force their antagonists up Bayard street to the Bowery. Then the fugitives, being reinforced, would turn on their pursuers and compel a retreat to Mulberry, Elizabeth and Baxter streets."

Early in the afternoon Police Commissioner Simeon Draper dispatched another and larger force of policemen against the mob, and they marched in close formation to the scene of the riot, although assailed at every step. They cleared the street as they advanced, and forced scores of the Dead Rabbits and Bowery Boys into the houses and up the stairs to the roofs, clubbing them at every jump. One desperate gangster who refused to surrender was knocked off the roof of a house in Baxter street, and his skull was fractured when he hit the sidewalk. His enemies promptly stamped him to death. On another roof the police captured two of the leaders of the Dead Rabbits, and although the Five Points gangsters attacked with great fury managed to march their prisoners to the police station, escorted by a detachment of cheering Bowery Boys.

But no sooner had the police departed than the gangsters renewed their battle, and the rioting went forward with greater ferocity than ever. Barricades of carts and stones were piled up in the streets, and from behind these defenses the gangsters shot and hurled bricks and used their clubs. One giant member of the Dead Rabbits walked coolly along in front of his barricade and, although fired at repeatedly, used his pistol with such deadly accuracy that he killed two Bowery thugs and wounded two others. He was finally knocked unconscious by a small boy whose brother was fighting in the ranks of the Bowery Boys. This lad crept on his stomach along the barricade, and when he was close enough slammed a huge brickbat, about as heavy as he could lift, against the skull of the Dead Rabbit.

The police continued their efforts to disperse the battling gangs, but failed, and were compelled to retreat several times with heavy losses. Early in the evening the police authorities, in despair, sent for Captain Isaiah Rynders, political boss of the Sixth Ward and as such king of the Five Points gangsters, and implored him to stop the slaughter. But the rioters were in such a rage that they refused to obey his commands, and as he stood before their barricades haranguing them the Bowery Boys attacked and Captain Rynders was badly beaten before he could find refuge in the midst of his own henchmen. Realizing the futility of further appeal, he made his way to Metropolitan Police Headquarters and advised Commissioner Draper to call out the troops. Meanwhile the gangsters had set fire to two or three houses, and the fighting continued, while the independent thugs made life miserable for the householders who insisted on remaining in their homes within the battle area.

Commissioner Draper asked Major-General Sandford to order three regiments into action, but it was nine o'clock before the blare of bugles and the rattle of drums was heard and the soldiers, their bayonets glistening in the moonlight and the glare of the burning buildings, marched down White and Worth streets, supported by two police detachments of seventy-five men each, who ranged ahead of the troops and clubbed every gangster they could catch. Two regiments instead of three, the Eighth and the Seventy-first, had answered the call, and neither was up to full strength, but the display of force was sufficient to overawe the thugs, who abandoned the battlefield and slunk back to their dens. There was no more rioting, for the police and soldiers patrolled the district throughout the night and all the next day. During the two days' fighting eight men were killed and more than a hundred injured, of whom fifty were compelled to remain in hospitals for treatment. It is believed that many more dead and injured were carried away by their comrades, for several days after the fighting had ended it was reported that half a dozen new graves had been dug in the cellars and underground passageways of the Five Points and Paradise Square, and some of the most noted sluggers of both the Dead Rabbits and the Bowery Boys were no longer to be seen in their accustomed haunts.

On July 6 a wandering band of Bowery Boys engaged in a desperate fight with the Kerryonians in Center street, but were driven back to the Bowery and Chatham Square before the police could interfere. A few days later the excitement spread to the German settlements along the East Side, near the East River, and strong detachments of police were sent to Avenues A and B to quell outbreaks among the ambitious young hoodlums of that area, who desired to emulate the deeds of their Irish fellow citizens. For more than a week there was sporadic fighting whenever patrols of the Five Points gangsters came upon thugs from the Bowery, but the former bitterly resented the insinuations of the police and the newspapers that they were criminals. "We are requested by the Dead Rabbits," said *The Times*, "to state that the Dead Rabbit club members are not thieves, that they did not participate in the riot with the Bowery Boys, and that the fight in Mulberry street was between the Roach Guards of Mulberry street and the Atlantic Guards of the Bowery. The Dead Rabbits are sensitive on points of honor, we are assured, and wouldn't allow a thief to live on their beat, much less to be a member of their club."

Monk Eastman, Purveyor of Iniquities
by Jorge Luis Borges

Argentinean Jorge Luis Borges's (1899–1986) fiction blends fantasy, philosophy and poetry to offer readers art that is both strange and familiar. Borges's voice turns the story of real-life gangster Monk Eastman into something like a fairy tale.

Those of This America

Standing out sharply against a background of blue walls or open sky, two hoodlums dressed in close-fitting suits of sober black and wearing thick-heeled shoes dance a deadly dance—a ballet of matching knives—until a carnation starts from the ear of one of them as a knife finds its mark in him, and he brings the unaccompanied dance to a close on the ground with his death. Satisfied, the other adjusts his high-crowned hat and spends his final years recounting the story of this clean duel. That, in sum and substance, is the history of our old-time Argentine underworld. The history of New York's old underworld is both more dizzying and more clumsy.

Those of the Other

The history of the gangs of New York (revealed in 1928 by Herbert Asbury in a solid volume of four-hundred octavo pages) contains all of the confusion and cruelty of the barbarian cosmogonies, and much of

their giant-scale ineptitude—cellars of old breweries honeycombed
into Negro tenements; a ramshackle New York of three-story struc-
tures; criminal gangs like the Swamp Angels, who rendezvoused in a
labyrinth of sewers; criminal gangs like the Daybreak Boys, who
recruited precocious murderers of ten and eleven; loners, like the bold
and gigantic Plug Uglies, who earned the smirks of passersby with their
enormous plug hats, stuffed with wool and worn pulled down over
their ears as helmets, and their long shirttails, worn outside the
trousers, that flapped in the Bowery breeze (but with a huge bludgeon
in one hand and a pistol peeping out of a pocket); criminal gangs like
the Dead Rabbits, who entered into battle under the emblem of a dead
rabbit impaled on a pike; men like Dandy Johnny Dolan, famous for
the oiled forelock he wore curled and plastered against his forehead,
for his cane whose handle was carved in the likeness of a monkey, and
for the copper device he invented and used on the thumb for gouging
out an adversary's eyes; men like Kit Burns, who for twenty-five cents
would decapitate a live rat with a single bite; men like Blind Danny
Lyons, young and blond and with immense dead eyes, who pimped
for three girls, all of whom proudly walked the streets for him; rows of
houses showing red lanterns in the windows, like those run by seven
sisters from a small New England village, who always turned their
Christmas Eve proceeds over to charity; rat pits, where wharf rats were
starved and sent against terriers; Chinese gambling dives; women like
the repeatedly widowed Red Norah, the vaunted sweetheart of practically the entire Gopher gang; women like Lizzie the Dove, who
donned widow's weeds when Danny Lyons was executed for murder,
and who was stabbed in the throat by Gentle Maggie during an argument over whose sorrow for the departed blind man was the greater;
mob uprisings like the savage week of draft riots in 1863, when a
hundred buildings were burned to the ground and the city was
nearly taken over; teeming street fights in which a man went down as
at sea, trampled to death; a thief and horse poisoner like Yoske
Nigger. All these go to weave underworld New York's chaotic history.
And its most famous hero is Edward Delaney, alias William Delaney,

alias Joseph Marvin, alias Joseph Morris, alias Monk Eastman—boss of twelve hundred men.

The Hero

These shifts of identity (as distressing as a masquerade, in which one is not quite certain who is who) omit his real name—presuming there is such a thing as a real name. The recorded fact is, that he was born in the Williamsburg section of Brooklyn as Edward Osterman, a name later Americanized to Eastman. Oddly enough, this stormy underworld character was Jewish. He was the son of the owner of a kosher restaurant, where men wearing rabbinical beards could safely partake of the bloodless and thrice-cleansed flesh of ritually slaughtered calves. At the age of nineteen, about 1892, his father set him up in business with a bird store. A fascination for animals, an interest in their small decisions and inscrutable innocence, turned into a lifelong hobby. Years afterward, in a period of opulence, when he scornfully refused the Havana cigars of freckle-faced Tammany sachems or when he paid visits to the best houses of prostitution in that new invention, the automobile (which seemed the bastard offspring of a gondola), he started a second business, a front, that accommodated a hundred cats and more than four hundred pigeons—none of which were for sale to anyone. He loved each one, and often he strolled through his neighborhood with a happy cat under an arm, while several others trailed eagerly behind.

He was a battered, colossal man. He had a short, bull neck; a barrel chest; long, scrappy arms; a broken nose; a face, although plentifully scarred, less striking than his frame; and legs bowed like a cowboy's or a sailor's. He could usually be found without a shirt or coat, but not without a derby hat several sizes too small perched on his bullet-shaped head. Mankind has conserved his memory. Physically, the conventional moving-picture gunman is a copy of him, not of the pudgy, epicene Capone. It is said of Louis Wolheim that Hollywood employed him because his features suggested those of the lamented Monk Eastman.

Eastman used to strut about his underworld kingdom with a great blue pigeon on his shoulder, just like a bull with a cowbird on its rump.

Back in the mid-nineties, public dance halls were a dime a dozen in the city of New York. Eastman was employed in one of them as a bouncer. The story is told that a dance-hall manager once refused to hire him, whereupon Monk demonstrated his capacity for the work by wiping the floor with the pair of giants who stood between him and the job. Single-handed, universally feared, he held the position until 1899. For each troublemaker he quelled, he cut a notch in his brutal bludgeon. One night, his attention drawn to a shining bald pate minding its own business over a bock beer, he laid its bearer out with a blow. "I needed one more notch to make fifty," he later explained.

The Territory

From 1899 on, Eastman was not only famous but, during elections, he was captain of an important ward. He also collected protection money from the houses of prostitution, gambling dives, streetwalkers, pickpockets, and burglars of his sordid domain. Tammany politicians hired him to stir up trouble; so did private individuals. Here are some of his prices:

Ear chawed off	$15
Leg or arm broke	19
Shot in leg	25
Stab	25
Doing the big job	100 and up

Sometimes, to keep his hand in, Eastman personally carried out a commission.

A question of boundaries (as subtle and thorny as any cramming the dockets of international law) brought Eastman into confrontation with Paul Kelly, the well-known chief of a rival gang. Bullets and rough-and-tumble fighting of the two gangs had set certain territorial limits. Eastman crossed these bounds alone one early morning and was assailed by five of Kelly's men. With his flailing, apelike arms and blackjack, Monk knocked down three of the attackers, but he was ultimately shot twice in the stomach and left for dead. Eastman closed the hot wounds with thumb and index finger and staggered to Gouverneur Hospital. There, for several weeks, life, a high fever, and death vied for him, but his lips refused to name his would-be killer. When he left the hospital, the war was on, and, until the nineteenth of August, 1903, it flowered in one shoot-out after another.

The Battle of Rivington Street

A hundred heroes, each a bit different from his photograph fading in police files; a hundred heroes reeking of tobacco smoke and alcohol; a hundred heroes wearing straw boaters with gaily colored bands; a hundred heroes afflicted, some more, some less, with shameful diseases, tooth decay, complaints of the respiratory tracts or kidneys; a hundred heroes as insignificant or splendid as those of Troy or Bull Run—these hundred let loose this black feat of arms under the shadows of the arches of the Second Avenue elevated. The cause was the attempted raid by Kelly's gunmen on a stuss game operated by a friend of Eastman's on Rivington Street. One of the gunmen was killed, and the ensuing flurry of shots swelled into a battle of uncounted revolvers. Sheltered behind the pillars of the elevated structure, smooth-shaven men quietly blazed away at each other and became the focus of an awesome ring of rented automobiles loaded with eager reinforcements, each bearing a fistful of artillery.

What did the protagonists of this battle feel? First (I believe), the brutal conviction that the senseless din of a hundred revolvers was going to cut them down at any moment; second (I believe), the no less mistaken certainty that if the first shots did not hit them they were invulnerable. What is without doubt, however, is that, under cover of the iron pillars and the night, they fought with a vengeance. Twice the police intervened, and twice they were driven off. At the first glimmer of dawn, the battle petered out—as if it were obscene or ghostly. Under the great arches of the elevated were left seven critically wounded men, four corpses, and one dead pigeon.

The Creakings

The local politicians, in whose ranks Monk Eastman served, always publicly denied that such gangs existed, or else claimed that they were mere sporting clubs. The indiscreet battle of Rivington Street now alarmed them. They arranged a meeting between Eastman and Kelly in order to suggest to them the need for a truce. Kelly (knowing very well that Tammany Hall was more effective than any number of Colts when it came to obstructing police action) agreed at once; Eastman (with the pride of his great, brutish hulk) hungered for more blasting and further frays. He began to refuse, and the politicians had to threaten him with prison. In the end, the two famous gangsters came face to face in an unsavory dive, each with a huge cigar between his teeth, a hand on his revolver, and his watchful thugs surrounding him. They arrived at a typically American decision: they would settle their dispute in the ring by squaring off with their fists. Kelly was an experienced boxer. The fight took place in a barn up in the Bronx, and it was an extravagant affair. A hundred and forty spectators looked on, among them mobsters with rakish derbies and their molls with enormous coiffures in which weapons were sometimes concealed. The pair fought for two hours and it ended in a draw. Before a week was out, the shooting started up again. Monk was arrested for the nth time. With great relief, Tammany Hall washed their hands of him; the judge prophesied for him, with complete accuracy, ten years of prison.

Eastman vs. Germany

When the still puzzled Monk was released from Sing Sing, the twelve hundred members of his gang had broken up into warring factions.

Unable to reorganize them, he took to operating on his own. On the eighth of September, 1917, he was arrested for creating a disturbance in a public thoroughfare. The next day, deciding to take part in an even larger disturbance, he enlisted in the 106th infantry of the New York National Guard. Within a few months, he was shipped overseas with his regiment.

We know about various aspects of his campaign. We know that he violently disapproved of taking prisoners and that he once (with just his rifle butt) interfered with that deplorable practice. We know that he managed to slip out of the hospital three days after he had been wounded and make his way back to the front lines. We know that he distinguished himself in the fighting around Montfaucon. We know that he later held that a number of little dance halls around the Bowery were a lot tougher than the war in Europe.

The Mysterious, Logical End

On Christmas Day, 1920, Monk Eastman's body was found at dawn on one of the downtown streets of New York. It had five bullet wounds in it. Happily unaware of death, an alley cat hovered around the corpse with a certain puzzlement.

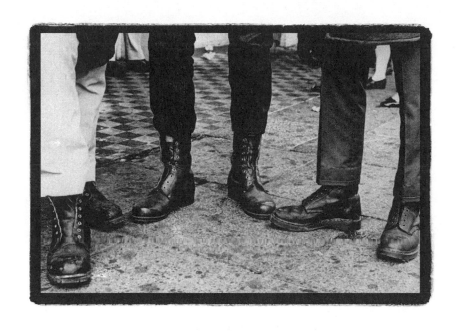

from A Clockwork Orange
by Anthony Burgess

Many people know Anthony Burgess's (1917–1993) tale of a dismal authoritarian future from Stanley Kubrick's 1971 film adaptation. But some of the story's thrill comes from reading the teenage narrator's speech—a blend of mangled Russian, cockney slang and wordplay that makes for a convincing gang lingo and an almost Joycean linguistic puzzle.

W hat's it going to be then, eh?'
   There was me, that is Alex, and my three droogs, that is Pete, Georgie, and Dim, Dim being really dim, and we sat in the Korova Milkbar making up our rassoodocks what to do with the evening, a flip dark chill winter bastard though dry. The Korova Milkbar was a milk-plus mesto, and you may, O my brothers, have forgotten what these mestos were like, things changing so skorry these days and everybody very quick to forget, newspapers not being read much neither. Well, what they sold there was milk plus something else. They had no licence for selling liquor, but there was no law yet against prodding some of the new veshches which they used to put into the old moloko, so you could peet it with vellocet or synthemesc or drencrom or one or two other veshches which would give you a nice quiet horrorshow fifteen minutes admiring Bog And All His Holy Angels And Saints in your left shoe with lights bursting all over

your mozg. Or you could peet milk with knives in it, as we used to say, and this would sharpen you up and make you ready for a bit of dirty twenty-to-one, and that was what we were peeting this evening I'm starting off the story with.

Our pockets were full of deng, so there was no real need from the point of view of crasting any more pretty polly to tolchock some old veck in an alley and viddy him swim in his blood while we counted the takings and divided by four, nor to do the ultra-violent on some shivering starry grey-haired ptitsa in a shop and go smecking off with the till's guts. But, as they say, money isn't everything.

The four of us were dressed in the heighth of fashion, which in those days was a pair of black very tight tights with the old jelly mould, as we called it, fitting on the crutch underneath the tights, this being to protect and also a sort of a design you could viddy clear enough in a certain light, so that I had one in the shape of a spider, Pete had a rooker (a hand, that is), Georgie had a very fancy one of a flower, and poor old Dim had a very hound-and-horny one of a clown's litso (face, that is), Dim not ever having much of an idea of things and being, beyond all shadow of a doubting thomas, the dimmest of we four. Then we wore waisty jackets without lapels but with these very big built-up shoulders ('pletchoes' we called them) which were a kind of a mockery of having real shoulders like that. Then, my brothers, we had these off-white cravats which looked like whipped-up kartoffel or spud with a sort of a design made on it with a fork. We wore our hair not too long and we had flip horrorshow boots for kicking.

'What's it going to be then, eh?'

There were three devotchkas sitting at the counter all together, but there were four of us malchicks and it was usually like one for all and all for one. These sharps were dressed in the heighth of fashion too, with purple and green and orange wigs on their gullivers, each one not costing less than three or four weeks of those sharps' wages, I should reckon, and make-up to match (rainbows round the glazzies, that is, and the rot painted very wide). Then they had long black very straight dresses, and on the groody part of them they had little badges of like silver with different malchicks' names on them—Joe and Mike and suchlike. These were supposed to be the names of the different malchicks they'd spatted with before they were fourteen. They kept looking our way and I nearly felt like saying the three of us (out of the corner of my rot, that is) should go off for a bit of pol and leave poor old Dim behind, because it would be just a matter of kupetting Dim a demi-litre of white but this time with a dollop of synthemesc in it, but that wouldn't really have been playing like the game. Dim was very very ugly and like his name, but he was a horrorshow filthy fighter and very handy with the boot.

'What's it going to be then, eh?'

The chelloveck sitting next to me, there being this long big plushy seat that ran round three walls, was well away with his glazzies glazed and sort of burbling slovos like 'Aristotle wishy washy works outing cyclamen get forficulate smartish'. He was in the land all right, well away, in orbit, and I knew what it was like, having tried it like everybody else had done, but at this time I'd got to thinking it was a cowardly sort of a veshch, O my brothers. You'd lay there after you'd drunk the old moloko and then you got the messel that everything all round you was sort of in the past. You could viddy it all right, all of it, very clear—tables, the stereo, the lights, the sharps and the malchicks—but it was like some veshch that used to be there but was not there not no more. And you were sort of hypnotized by your boot or shoe or a finger-nail as it might be, and at the same time you were sort of picked up by the old scruff and shook like it might be a cat. You got shook and shook till there was nothing left. You lost your name and your body and your self and you just didn't care, and you waited till your boot or your finger-nail got yellow, then yellower and yellower all the time. Then the lights started cracking like atomics and the boot or finger-nail or, as it might be, a bit of dirt on your trouser-bottom turned into a big big big mesto, bigger than the whole world, and you were just going to get introduced to old Bog or God when it was all over. You came back to here and now whimpering sort of, with your rot all squaring up for a boohoohoo. Now, that's very nice but very cowardly. You were not put on this earth just to get in touch with God. That sort of thing could sap all the strength and the goodness out of a chelloveck.

'What's it going to be then, eh?'

The stereo was on and you got the idea that the singer's goloss was moving from one part of the bar to another, flying up to the ceiling and then swooping down again and whizzing from wall to wall. It was Berti Laski rasping a real starry oldie called 'You Blister My Paint'. One of the three ptitsas at the counter, the one with the green wig, kept pushing her belly out and pulling it in in time to what they called the music. I could feel the knives in the old moloko starting to prick, and now I was ready for a bit of twenty-to-one. So I yelped: 'Out out out out!' like a doggie, and then I cracked this veck who was sitting next to me and well away and burbling a horrorshow crack on the ooko or ear-hole, but he didn't feel it and went on with his 'Telephonic hardware and when the farfarculule gets rubadubdub'. He'd feel it all right when he came to, out of the land.

'Where out?' said Georgie.

'Oh, just to keep walking,' I said, 'and viddy what turns up, O my little brothers.'

So we scatted out into the big winter nochy and walked down Marghanita Boulevard and then turned into Boothby Avenue, and there we found what we were pretty well looking for, a malenky jest to start off the evening with. There was a doddery starry schoolmaster type veck, glasses on and his rot open to the cold nochy air. He had books under his arm and a crappy umbrella and was coming round the corner from the Public Biblio, which not many lewdies used those days. You never really saw many of the older bourgeois type out after nightfall those days, what with the shortage of police and we fine young malchickiwicks about, and this prof type chelloveck was the only one walking in the whole of the street. So we goolied up to him, very polite, and I said: 'Pardon me, brother.'

He looked a malenky bit poogly when he viddied the four of us like that, coming up so quiet and polite and smiling, but he said: 'Yes? What is it?' in a very loud teacher-type goloss, as if he was trying to show us he wasn't poogly. I said:

'I see you have books under your arm, brother. It is indeed a rare pleasure these days to come across somebody that still reads, brother.'

'Oh,' he said, all shaky. 'Is it? Oh, I see.' And he kept looking from one to the other of we four, finding himself now like in the middle of a very smiling and polite square.

'Yes,' I said. 'It would interest me greatly, brother, if you would kindly allow me to see what books those are that you have under your arm. I like nothing better in this world than a good clean book, brother.'

'Clean,' he said. 'Clean, eh?' And then Pete skvatted these three books from him and handed them round real skorry. Being three, we all had one each to viddy at except for Dim. The one I had was called *Elementary Crystallography*, so I opened it up and said: 'Excellent, really first-class,' keeping turning the pages. Then I said in a very shocked type goloss: 'But what is this here? What is this filthy slovo? I blush to look at this word. You disappoint me, brother, you do really.'

'But,' he tried, 'but, but.'

'Now,' said Georgie, 'here is what I should call real dirt. There's one slovo beginning with an f and another with a c.' He had a book called *The Miracle of the Snowflake*.

'Oh,' said poor old Dim, smotting over Pete's shoulder and going too far, like he always did, 'it says here what he done to her, and there's a picture and all. Why,' he said, 'you're nothing but a filthy-minded old skitebird.'

'An old man of your age, brother,' I said, and I started to rip up the book I'd got, and the others did the same with the ones they had, Dim and Pete doing a tug-of-war with *The Rhombohedral System*. The starry prof type began to creech: 'But those are not mine, those are the property of the municipality, this is sheer wantonness and vandal work,' or some such slovos. And he tried to sort of wrest the books back off of us, which was like pathetic. 'You deserve to be taught a lesson, brother,'

I said, 'that you do.' This crystal book I had was very tough-bound and hard to razrez to bits, being real starry and made in days when things were made to last like, but I managed to rip the pages up and chuck them in handfuls of like snowflakes, though big, all over this creeching old veck, and then the others did the same with theirs, old Dim just dancing about like the clown he was. 'There you are,' said Pete. 'There's the mackerel of the cornflake for you, you dirty reader of filth and nastiness.'

'You naughty old veck, you,' I said, and then we began to filly about with him. Pete held his rookers and Georgie sort of hooked his rot wide open for him and Dim yanked out his false zoobies, upper and lower. He threw these down on the pavement and then I treated them to the old boot-crush, though they were hard bastards like, being made of some new horrorshow plastic stuff. The old veck began to make sort of chumbling shooms—'wuf waf wof'—so Georgie let go of holding his goobers apart and just let him have one in the toothless rot with his ringy fist, and that made the old veck start moaning a lot then, then out comes the blood, my brothers, real beautiful. So all we did then was to pull his outer platties off, stripping him down to his vest and long underpants (very starry; Dim smecked his head off near), and then Pete kicks him lovely in his pot, and we let him go. He went sort of staggering off, it not having been too hard of a tolchock really, going 'Oh oh oh', not knowing where or what was what really, and we had a snigger at him and then riffled through his pockets, Dim dancing round with his crappy umbrella meanwhile, but there wasn't much in them. There were a few starry letters, some of them dating right back to 1960, with 'My dearest dearest' in them and all that chepooka, and a keyring and a starry leaky pen. Old Dim gave up his umbrella dance and of course had to start reading one of the letters out loud, like to show the empty street he could read. 'My darling one,' he recited, in this very high type goloss, 'I shall be thinking of you while you are away and hope you will remember to wrap up warm when you go out at night.' Then he let out a very shoomny smeck—'Ho ho ho'— pretending to start wiping his yahma with it. 'All right,' I said. 'Let it go,

O my brothers.' In the trousers of this starry veck there was only a malenky bit of cutter (money, that is)—not more than three gollies—so we gave all his messy little coin the scatter treatment, it being henkorm to the amount of pretty polly we had on us already. Then we smashed the umbrella and razrezzed his platties and gave them to the blowing winds, my brothers, and then we'd finished with the starry teacher type veck. We hadn't done much, I know, but that was only like the start of the evening and I make no appy polly loggies to thee or thine for that. The knives in the milk-plus were stabbing away nice and horrorshow now.

The next thing was to do the sammy act, which was one way to unload some of our cutter so we'd have more of an incentive like for some shop-crasting, as well as it being a way of buying an alibi in advance, so we went into the Duke of New York on Amis Avenue and sure enough in the snug there were three or four old baboochkas peeting their black and suds on SA (State Aid). Now we were the very good malchicks, smiling good evensong to one and all, though these wrinkled old lighters started to get all shook, their veiny old rookers all trembling round their glasses and making the suds spill on the table. 'Leave us be, lads,' said one of them, her face all mappy with being a thousand years old, 'we're only poor old women.' But we just made with the zoobies, flash flash flash, sat down, rang the bell, and waited for the boy to come. When he came, all nervous and rubbing his rookers on his grazzy apron, we ordered us four veterans—a veteran being rum and cherry brandy mixed, which was popular just then, some liking a dash of lime in it, that being the Canadian variation. Then I said to the boy:

'Give these poor old baboochkas over there a nourishing something. Large Scotchmen all round and something to take away.' And I poured my pocket of deng all over the table, and the other three did likewise, O my brothers. So double firegolds were brought in for the scared starry lighters, and they knew not what to do or say. One of them got out 'Thanks, lads,' but you could see they thought there was something dirty like coming. Anyway, they were each given a bottle of Yank General, cognac that is, to take away, and I gave money for them to be delivered each a dozen of black and suds that following morning, they to leave their stinking old cheenas' addresses at the counter. Then with the cutter that was left over we did purchase, my brothers, all the meat pies, pretzels, cheese-snacks, crisps and chocbars in that mesto, and those too were for the old sharps. Then we said: 'Back in a minoota,' and the old ptitsas were still saying: 'Thanks, lads,' and 'God bless you, boys,' and we were going out without one cent of cutter in our cannans.

'Makes you feel real dobby, that does,' said Pete. You could viddy that poor old Dim the dim didn't quite pony all that, but he said nothing for fear of being called gloopy and a domeless wonderboy. Well, we went off now round the corner to Attlee Avenue, and there was this sweets and cancers shop still open. We'd left them alone near three months now and the whole district had been very quiet on the whole, so the armed millicents or rozz patrols weren't round there much, being more north of the river these days. We put our maskies on—new jobs these were, real horrorshow, wonderfully done really; they were like faces of historical personalities (they gave you the name when you bought) and I had Disraeli, Pete had Elvis Presley, Georgie had Henry VIII and poor old Dim had a poet veck called Peebee Shelley; they were a real like disguise, hair and all, and they were some very special plastic veshch so you could roll up when you'd done with it and hide it in your boot—then three of us went in, Pete keeping chasso without, not that there was anything to worry about out there. As soon as we launched on the shop we went for Slouse who ran it, a big portwine jelly of a veck who viddied at once what was coming and made straight for the inside where the telephone was and perhaps his well-oiled pooshka, complete with six dirty rounds. Dim was round that counter skorry as a bird, sending packets of snoutie flying and cracking over a big cut-out showing a sharp with all her zoobies going flash at the customers and her groodies near hanging out to advertise some new brand of cancers. What you could viddy then was a sort of a big ball rolling into the inside of the shop behind the curtain, this being old Dim and Slouse sort of locked in a death struggle.

Then you could slooshy panting and snoring and kicking behind the curtain and veshches falling over and swearing and then glass going smash smash smash. Mother Slouse, the wife, was sort of froze behind the counter. We could tell she would creech murder given one chance, so I was round that counter very skorry and had a hold of her, and a horrorshow big lump she was too, all nuking of scent and with flipflop big bobbing groodies on her. I'd got my rooker round her rot to stop her belting out death and destruction to the four winds of heaven, but this lady doggie gave me a large foul big bite on it and it was me that did the creeching, and then she opened up beautiful with a flip yell for the millicents. Well, then she had to be tolchocked proper with one of the weights for the scales, and then a fair tap with a crowbar they had for opening cases, and that brought the red out like an old friend. So we had her down on the floor and a rip of her platties for fun and a gentle bit of the boot to stop her moaning. And, viddying her lying there with her groodies on show, I wondered should I or not, but that was for later on in the evening. Then we cleaned the till, and there was flip horrorshow takings that nochy, and we had a few packs of the very best top cancers apiece, then off we went, my brothers.

'A real big heavy great bastard he was,' Dim kept saying. I didn't like the look of Dim; he looked dirty and untidy, like a veck who'd been in a fight, which he had been, of course, but you should never *look* as though you have been. His cravat was like someone had trampled on it, his maskie had been pulled off and he had floor-dirt on his litso, so we got him in an alleyway and tidied him up a malenky bit, soaking our tashtooks in spit to cheest the dirt off. The things we did for old Dim. We were back in the Duke of New York very skorry, and I reckoned by my watch we hadn't been more than ten minutes away. The starry old baboochkas were still there on the black and suds and Scotchmen we'd bought them, and we said: 'Hallo there, girlies, what's it going to be?' They started on the old 'Very kind, lads, God bless you, boys,' and so we rang the collocoll and brought a different waiter in this time and we ordered beers with rum in, being sore athirst, my brothers, and whatever the old ptitsas wanted. Then I said to the old baboochkas: 'We haven't been out of here, have we? Been here all the time, haven't we?' They all caught on real skorry and said:

'That's right, lads. Not been out of our sight, you haven't. God bless you, boys,' drinking.

Not that it mattered much, really. About half an hour went by before there was any sign of life among the millicents, and then it was only two very young rozzes that came in, very pink under their big copper's shlemmies. One said: 'You lot know anything about the happenings at Slouse's shop this night?'

'Us?' I said, innocent. 'Why, what happened?'

'Stealing and roughing. Two hospitalizations. Where've you lot been this evening?'

'I don't go for that nasty tone,' I said. 'I don't care much for these nasty insinuations. A very suspicious nature all this betokeneth, my little brothers.'

'They've been in here all night, lads,' the old sharps started to creech out. 'God bless them, there's no better lot of boys living for kindness and generosity. Been here all the time they have. Not seen them move we haven't.'

'We're only asking,' said the other young millicent. 'We've got our job to do like anyone else.' But they gave us the nasty warning look before they went out. As they were going out we handed them a bit of lip-music: brrrrzzzzrrrr. But, myself, I couldn't help a bit of disappointment at things as they were those days. Nothing to fight against really. Everything as easy as kiss-my-sharries. Still, the night was still very young.

When we got outside of the Duke of New York we viddied, by the main bar's long lighted window, a burbling old pyahnitsa or drunkie, howling away at the filthy songs of his fathers and going blerp blerp in between as it might be a filthy old orchestra in his stinking rotten guts. One veshch I could never stand was that. I could never stand to see a moodge all filthy and rolling and burping and drunk, whatever his age might be, but more especially when he was real starry like this one was. He was sort of flattened to the wall and his platties were a disgrace, all creased and untidy and covered in cal and mud and filth and stuff. So we got hold of him and cracked him with a few good horrorshow tolchocks, but he still went on singing. The song went:

> And I will go back to my darling, my darling,
> When you, my darling, are gone.

But when Dim fisted him a few times on his filthy drunkard's rot he shut up singing and started to creech: 'Go on, do me in, you bastard cowards, I don't want to live anyway, not in a stinking world like this one.' I told Dim to lay off a bit then, because it used to interest me sometimes to slooshy what some of these starry decreps had to say about life and the world. I said: 'Oh. And what's stinking about it?'

He cried out: 'It's a stinking world because it lets the young get on to the old like you done, and there's no law nor order no more.' He was creeching out loud and waving his rookers and making real horrorshow with the slovos, only the odd blurp blurp coming from his keeshkas, like something was orbiting within, or like some very rude interrupting sort of a moodge making a shoom, so that this old veck kept sort of threatening it with his fists, shouting: 'It's no world for any old man any longer, and that means that I'm not one bit scared of you, my boyos, because I'm too drunk to feel the pain if you hit me, and if you kill me I'll be glad to be dead.' We smecked and then grinned but said nothing, and then he said: 'What sort of a world is it at all? Men on the moon and men spinning round the earth like it might be midges round a lamp, and there's not no attention paid to earthly law nor order no more. So your worst you may do, you filthy cowardly hooligans.' Then he gave us some lip-music—'Prrrrzzzzrrrr'—like we'd done to those young millicents, and then he started singing again:

> O dear dear land, I fought for thee
> And brought thee peace and victory—

So we cracked into him lovely, grinning all over our litsos, but he still went on singing. Then we tripped him so he laid down flat and heavy and a bucketload of beer-vomit came whooshing out. That was disgusting so we gave him the boot, one go each, and then it was blood, not song nor vomit, that came out of his filthy old rot. Then we went on our way.

It was round by the Municipal Power Plant that we came across Billyboy and his five droogs. Now in those days, my brothers, the teaming up was mostly by fours or fives, these being like auto-teams, four being a comfy number for an auto, and six being the outside limit for gang-size. Sometimes gangs would gang up so as to make like malenky armies for big night-war, but mostly it was best to roam in these like small numbers. Billyboy was something that made me want to sick just to viddy his fat grinning litso, and he always had this von of very stale oil that's been used for frying over and over, even when he was dressed in his best platties, like now. They viddied us just as we viddied them, and there was like a very quiet kind of watching each other now. This would be real, this would be proper, this would be the nozh, the oozy, the britva, not just fisties and boots. Billyboy and his droogs stopped what they were doing, which was just getting ready to perform something on a weepy young devotchka they had there, not more than ten, she creeching away but with her platties still on, Billyboy holding her by one rooker and his number-one, Leo, holding the other. They'd probably just been doing the dirty slovo part of the act before getting down to a malenky bit of ultra-violence. When they viddied us a-coming they let go of this boo-hooing little ptitsa, there being plenty more where she came from, and she ran with her thin white legs flashing through the dark, still going 'Oh oh oh'. I said, smiling very wide and droogie: 'Well, if it isn't fat stinking billygoat Billyboy in poison. How art thou, thou globby bottle of cheap stinking chip-oil? Come and get one in the yarbles, if you have any yarbles, you eunuch jelly, thou.' And then we started.

There were four of us to six of them, like I have already indicated, but poor old Dim, for all his dimness, was worth three of the others in sheer madness and dirty fighting. Dim had a real horrorshow length of oozy or chain round his waist, twice wound round, and he unwound this and began to swing it beautiful in the eyes or glazzies. Pete and Georgie had good sharp nozhes, but I for my own part had a fine starry horrorshow cut-throat britva which, at that time, I could flash and shine artistic. So there we were dratsing away in the dark, the old Luna with men on it just coming up, the stars stabbing away as it might be knives anxious to join in the dratsing. With my britva I managed to slit right down the front of one of Billyboy's droog's platties, very very neat and not even touching the plott under the cloth. Then in the dratsing this droog of Billyboy's suddenly found himself all opened up like a pea-pod, with his belly bare and his poor old yarbles showing, and then he got very very razdrag, waving and screaming and losing his guard and letting in old Dim with his chain snaking whissssssshhhhhhhhh, so that old Dim chained him right in the glazzies, and this droog of Billyboy's went tottering off and howling his heart out. We were doing very horrorshow, and soon we had Billyboy's number-one down underfoot, blinded with old Dim's chain and crawling and howling about like an animal, but with one fair boot on the gulliver he was out and out and out.

Of the four of us Dim, as usual, came out the worst in point of looks, that is to say his litso was all bloodied and his platties a dirty mess, but the others of us were still cool and whole. It was stinking fatty Billyboy I wanted now, and there I was dancing about with my britva like I might be a barber on board a ship on a very rough sea, trying to get in at him with a few fair slashes on his unclean oily litso. Billyboy had a nozh, a long flick-type, but he was a malenky bit too slow and heavy in his movements to vred anyone really bad. And, my brothers, it was real satisfaction to me to waltz—left two three, right two three—and carve left cheeky and right cheeky, so that like two curtains of blood seemed to pour out at the same time, one on either side of his fat filthy oily snout in the winter starlight. Down this blood poured in like red curtains, but you could viddy Billyboy felt not a thing, and he went lumbering on like a filthy fatty bear, poking at me with his nozh.

Then we slooshied the sirens and knew the millicents were coming with pooshkas pushing out of the police-auto-windows at the ready. That little weepy devotchka had told them, no doubt, there being a box for calling the rozzes not too far behind the Muni Power Plant. 'Get you soon, fear not,' I called, 'stinking billygoat. I'll have your yarbles off lovely.' Then off they ran, slow and panting, except for Number One Leo out snoring on the ground, away north towards the river, and we went the other way. Just round the next turning was an alley, dark and empty and open at both ends, and we rested there, panting fast then slower, then breathing like normal. It was like resting between the feet of two terrific and very enormous mountains, these being the flat blocks, and in the windows of all of the flats you could viddy like blue dancing light. This would be the telly. Tonight was what they called a worldcast, meaning that the same programme was being viddied by everybody in the world that wanted to, that being mostly the middle-aged middle-class lewdies. There would be some big famous stupid comic chelloveck or black singer, and it was all being bounced off the special telly satellites in outer space, my brothers. We waited panting, and we could slooshy the sirening millicents going east, so we knew we were all right now. But poor old Dim kept looking up at the stars and planets and the Luna with his rot wide open like a kid who'd never viddied any such thing before, and he said:

'What's on them, I wonder. What would be up there on things like that?'

I nudged him hard, saying: 'Come, gloopy bastard as thou art. Think thou not on them. There'll be life like down here most likely, with some getting knifed and others doing the knifing. And now, with the nochy still molodoy, let us be on our way, O my brothers.' The others smecked at this, but poor old Dim looked at me serious, then up again at the stars and the Luna. So we went on our way down the alley, with the worldcast blueing on on either side. What we needed now was an auto, so we turned left coming out of the alley, knowing right away we were in Priestley Place as soon as we viddied the big bronze statue of some starry poet with an apey upper lip and a pipe stuck in a droopy old rot. Going north we came to the filthy old Filmdrome, peeling and dropping to bits through nobody going there much except malchicks like me and my droogs, and then only for a yell or a razrez or a bit of in-out-in-out in the dark. We could viddy from the poster on the Filmdrome's face, a couple of fly-dirted spots trained on it, that there was the usual cowboy riot, with the archangels on the side of the US marshal six-shooting at the rustlers out of hell's fighting legions, the kind of hound-and-horny veshch put out by Statefilm in those days. The autos parked by the sinny weren't all that horrorshow, crappy starry veshches most of them, but there was a newish Durango 95 that I thought might do. Georgie had one of these polyclefs, as they called them, on his keyring, so we were soon aboard—Dim and Pete at the back, puffing away lordly at their cancers—and I turned on the ignition and started her up and she grumbled away real horrorshow, a nice warm vibraty feeling grumbling all through your guttiwuts. Then I made with the noga, and we backed out lovely, and nobody viddied us take off.

We fillied round what was called the backtown for a bit, scaring old vecks and cheenas that were crossing the roads and zigzagging after cats and that. Then we took the road west. There wasn't much traffic about, so I kept pushing the old noga through the floorboards near, and the Durango 95 ate up the road like spaghetti. Soon it was winter trees and dark, my brothers, with a country dark, and at one place I ran over something big with a snarling toothy rot in the headlamps, then it screamed and squelched under and old Dim at the back near laughed his gulliver off—'Ho ho ho'—at that. Then we saw one young malchick with his sharp, lubbilubbing under a tree, so we stopped and cheered at them, then we bashed into them both with a couple of half-hearted tolchocks, making them cry, and on we went. What we were after now was the old surprise visit. That was a real kick and good for smecks and lashings of the ultra-violent. We came at last to a sort of a village, and just outside this village was a small sort of a cottage on its own with a bit of a garden. The Luna was well up now, and we could viddy this cottage fine and clear as I eased up and put the brake on, the other three giggling like bezoomny, and we could viddy the name on the gate of this cottage veshch was HOME, a gloopy sort of name. I got out of the auto, ordering my droogs to shush their giggles and act like serious, and I opened this malenky gate and walked up to the front door. I knocked nice and gentle and nobody came, so I knocked a bit more and this time I could slooshy somebody coming, then a bolt drawn, then the door inched open an inch or so, then I could viddy this one glaz looking out at me and the door was on a chain. 'Yes? Who is it?' It was a sharp's goloss, a youngish devotchka by her sound, so I said in a very refined manner of speech, a real gentleman's goloss:

'Pardon, madam, most sorry to disturb you, but my friend and me were out for a walk, and my friend has taken bad all of a sudden with a very troublesome turn, and he is out there on the road dead out and groaning. Would you have the goodness to let me use your telephone to telephone for an ambulance?'

'We haven't a telephone,' said this devotchka. 'I'm sorry, but we haven't. You'll have to go somewhere else.' From inside this malenky cottage I could slooshy the clack clack clacky clack clack clackity clack-clack of some veck typing away, and then the typing stopped and there was this chelloveck's goloss calling: 'What is it, dear?'

'Well,' I said, 'could you of your goodness please let him have a cup of water? It's like a faint, you see. It seems as though he's passed out in a sort of a fainting fit.'

The devotchka sort of hesitated and then said: 'Wait' Then she went off, and my three droogs had got out of the auto quiet and crept up horrorshow stealthy, putting their maskies on now, then I put mine on, then it was only a matter of me putting in the old rooker and undoing the chain, me having softened up this devotchka with my gent's goloss, so that she hadn't shut the door like she should have done, us being strangers of the night. The four of us then went roaring in, old Dim playing the shoot as usual with his jumping up and down and singing out dirty slovos, and it was a nice malenky cottage, I'll say that. We all went smecking into the room with a light on, and there was this devotchka sort of cowering, a young pretty bit of sharp with real horrorshow groodies on her, and with her was this chelloveck who was her moodge, youngish too with horn-rimmed otchkies on him, and on a table was a typewriter and all papers scattered everywhere, but there was one little pile of paper like that must have been what he'd already typed, so here was another intelligent type bookman type like that we'd fillied with some hours back, but this one was a writer not a reader. Anyway, he said:

'What is this? Who are you? How dare you enter my house without permission.' And all the time his goloss was trembling and his rookers too. So I said:

'Never fear. If fear thou hast in thy heart, O brother, pray banish it forthwith.' Then Georgie and Pete went out to find the kitchen, while old Dim waited for orders, standing next to me with his rot wide open. 'What is this, then?' I said, picking up the pile like of typing from off of the table, and the horn-rimmed moodge said, dithering:

'That's just what I want to know. What *is* this? What do you want? Get out at once before I throw you out.' So poor old Dim, masked like Peebee Shelley, had a good loud smeck at that, roaring like some animal.

'It's a book,' I said. 'It's a book what you are writing.' I made the old goloss very coarse. 'I have always had the strongest admiration for them as can write books.' Then I looked at its top sheet, and there was the name—A CLOCKWORK ORANGE—and I said: 'That's a fair gloopy title. Who ever heard of a clockwork orange?' Then I read a malenky bit out loud in a sort of very high type preaching goloss: '— The attempt to impose upon man, a creature of growth and capable of sweetness, to ooze juicily at the last round the bearded lips of God, to attempt to impose, I say, laws and conditions appropriate to a mechanical creation, against this I raise my sword-pen—' Dim made the old lipmusic at that and I had to smeck myself. Then I started to tear up the sheets and scatter the bits over the floor, and this writer moodge went sort of bezoomny and made for me with his zoobies clenched and showing yellow and his nails ready for me like claws. So that was old Dim's cue and he went grinning and going er er and a a a for this veck's dithering rot, crack crack, first left fistie then right, so that our dear old droog the red—red vino on tap and the same in all places, like it's put out by the same big firm—started to pour and spot the nice clean carpet and the bits of his book that I was still ripping away at, razrez razrez. All this time this devotchka, his loving and faithful wife, just stood like froze by the fireplace, and then she started letting out little malenky creeches, like in time to the like music of old Dim's fisty work. Then Georgie and Pete came in from the kitchen, both munching away, though with their maskies on, you could do that with them on and no trouble, Georgie with like a cold leg of something in one rooker and half a loaf of kleb with a big dollop of maslo on it in the other, and Pete with a bottle of beer frothing its gulliver off and a horrorshow rookerful of like plum cake. They went haw haw haw, vid-dying old Dim dancing round and fisting the writer veck so that the writer veck started to platch like his life's work was ruined, going boo hoo hoo with a very square bloody rot, but it was haw haw haw in a muffled eater's way and you could see bits of what they were eating. I didn't like that, it being dirty and slobbery, so I said:

'Drop that mounch. I gave no permission. Grab hold of this veck here so he can viddy all and not get away.' So they put down their fatty pishcha on the table among all the flying paper and they clopped over to the writer veck whose horn-rimmed otchkies were cracked but still hanging on, with old Dim still dancing round and making ornaments shake on the mantelpiece (I swept them all off then and they couldn't shake no more, little brothers) while he fillied with the author of *A Clockwork Orange,* making his litso all purple and dripping away like some very special sort of a juicy fruit. 'All right, Dim,' I said. 'Now for the other veshch, Bog help us all.' So he did the strong-man on the devotchka, who was still creech creech creeching away in very horror-show four-in-a-bar, locking her rockers from the back, while I ripped away at this and that and the other, the others going haw haw haw still, and real good horrorshow groodies they were that then exhibited their pink glazzies, O my brothers, while I untrussed and got ready for the plunge. Plunging, I could slooshy cries of agony and this writer bleeding veck that Georgie and Pete held on to nearly got loose howling bezoomny with the filthiest of slovos that I already knew and others he was making up. Then after me it was right old Dim should have his turn, which he did in a beasty snorty howly sort of a way with his Peebee Shelley maskie taking no notice, while I held on to her. Then there was a changeover, Dim and me grabbing the slobbering writer veck who was past struggling really, only just coming out with slack sort of slovos like he was in the land in a milk-plus bar, and Pete and Georgie had theirs. Then there was like quiet and we were full of like hate, so smashed what was left to be smashed—typewriter, lamp, chairs—and Dim, it was typical of old Dim, watered the fire out and was going to dung on the carpet, there being plenty of paper, but I said no. 'Out out out out,' I howled. The writer veck and his zheena were not really there, bloody and torn and making noises. But they'd live.

So we got into the waiting auto and I left it to Georgie to take the wheel, me feeling that malenky bit shagged, and we went back to town, running over odd squealing things on the way.

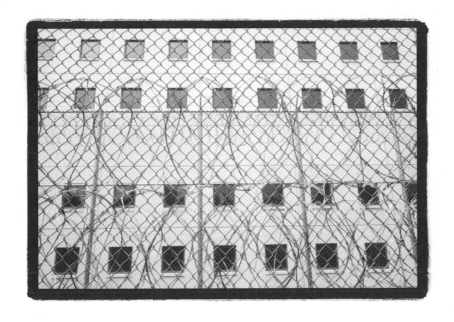

Capone's Revenge
by Jeffrey Toobin

This 1994 New Yorker article by Jeffrey Toobin profiled a prosecutor accused of using dubious methods to destroy Chicago's infamous El Rukn gang.

One by one, this winter and spring, the members of the El Rukn street gang have been returning to federal court in Chicago, going back to the courtrooms where, in a wave of prosecutions that started in 1989, their long reign over the city's South Side was emphatically brought to an end. For nearly three decades, the El Rukn gang—which one judge called "the most infamous gang of organized criminals that Chicago has seen since the days of Al Capone"—had terrorized the city's black neighborhoods. The El Rukns (who were once known as the Blackstone Rangers) murdered one another and their rivals, and they murdered witnesses and the relatives of witnesses to keep the law at bay. They established nationwide networks for dealing in heroin, cocaine, and marijuana. They maintained sway over their turf with extortion and, when necessary, bribery of public officials, including a judge.

Prosecutors in Chicago had chased the El Rukns for years, and one man finally brought them down—William R. Hogan, Jr., an Assistant

United States Attorney for the Northern District of Illinois. Hogan made the El Rukn case by working hard—in one sixteen-month stretch he took just ten days off—and by assembling a comparably dedicated team of a few junior colleagues, Chicago police officers, and federal agents. But Hogan's greatest gift may have been a more specialized skill. He demonstrated a remarkable ability to recruit El Rukns to his side—to "flip" them, as prosecutors put it. All Hogan's El Rukn trials featured, at their center, gang members who entered into plea bargains and then testified against their former colleagues. The strategy was a brilliant success. By late 1992, Hogan's investigation had netted fifty-four convictions, with many defendants facing decades or life in prison. The Department of Justice viewed the case—and Hogan—as a model for the nation. Three months after Los Angeles was shaken by riots in April of 1992, Hogan was dispatched there with the assignment of organizing a comparable attack on that city's notorious Bloods and Crips.

These days, however, the El Rukns are returning to court for a reason that could scarcely have been imagined when Hogan was convicting them: they are being released. They are being released because of what may be one of the most significant cases of prosecutorial misconduct in the history of the justice Department—prosecutorial misconduct by Bill Hogan. The convictions have evaporated because of accusations that Hogan's cooperating witnesses were given drugs and alcohol and allowed to have sex in prison and in the prosecutors' offices, and that the prosecutors condoned these practices and then covered them up. Unable to retry many of the cases, because its star witnesses have been revealed as liars and drug abusers, the United States Attorney's Office is now presenting defendants with astonishingly generous plea bargains. To name a few: C. D. Jackson, facing a life sentence for narcotics trafficking, was allowed in January to plead to the misdemeanor of marijuana possession and was released; and for Thomas Burnside, facing a hundred and sixty years, and Codell Griffin, facing eighty, both for narcotics conspiracy, the government moved to dismiss all charges.

The El Rukn case has brought to the fore a growing but largely unexplored peril of modern law enforcement. In recent years, prosecutors have shifted from charging individuals with isolated crimes to bringing down entire criminal organizations—Mafia families, Asian drug tongs, Jamaican posses, and urban street gangs. These cases, it turns out, are difficult, if not impossible, to try without the assistance of members of the organizations involved. But the alliance between prosecutors and turncoats—who are known, variously (and appropriately), as cooperators, accomplices, snitches, informants, flippers, rats, and scumbags—is fraught with hazards. Ironically, the greatest danger is not that what seem to be polar opposites—prosecutors and criminals—might never find a way to work together. Rather, it is just the reverse—that the good guys and the bad guys may fall in love.

The El Rukn cases have turned into a tragedy for the city of Chicago, for an eminent United States Attorney's Office, and, most especially, for Bill Hogan. As a result of findings by the judges trying the cases, and notwithstanding a stellar record, Hogan was placed on paid administrative leave last July and made the subject of an investigation by the Justice Department's Office of Professional Responsibility, or O.P.R. For the past ten months, this consummate investigator has looked on as his colleagues, his targets, and even his ex-wife have been summoned in the course of the O.P.R. probe. For ten months, he has not been allowed to work in the office that was all but his permanent residence for the previous eight years. Yet Hogan's ordeal may be only beginning. Later this month, when O.P.R. is expected to make its final report to Attorney General Janet Reno, Hogan will learn whether he is to be cleared, disciplined, fired, or even, potentially, prosecuted as a criminal himself for his role in the El Rukn case.

The United States Attorney's Office for the Northern District of Illinois has long ranked among the most illustrious prosecutors' offices in the nation. Former United States Attorneys there include James R. Thompson, who was the governor of Illinois from 1977 to 1991; Samuel K. Skinner, a Cabinet member and the White House chief of staff for President George Bush; and Dan K. Webb, who conducted the Iran-Contra prosecution of John Poindexter. Indeed, one might argue that the Northern District is responsible for much of the public mythology surrounding American prosecutors. Eliot Ness made his tax-evasion case against Al Capone there, and Scott Turow, an Assistant United States Attorney there from 1978 to 1986, drew on his experiences to create the Kindle County district attorney's office of his novel "Presumed Innocent" and its sequels. Against the often sleazy world of Cook County politics, the Northern District stood for incorruptibility, competence, and prosecutorial panache.

In August of 1986, Bill Hogan, who was then a fairly junior Northern District prosecutor with a growing reputation, was invited to a conference of prosecutors in New Haven. Hogan learned that federal agents in New England believed that a drug ring there was laundering its profits through fast-food restaurants that were owned by a Chicago businessman named Noah Robinson. There was even a rumor in Robinson's home town, Greenville, South Carolina, that he had commissioned a hit team from the Blackstone Rangers to kill one Leroy (Hambone) Barber. The news piqued Hogan's interest. Robinson had long drawn attention in the Northern District because he was rich, flamboyant, and shady—and because he was Jesse Jackson's half brother.

Hogan thought the Barber murder might be the wedge that allowed the Northern District to take on the gang, now known as the El Rukns, once and for all. (El Rukn is a corner of an Islamic shrine in Mecca.) An earlier investigation had resulted in the conviction of the gang's leader, Jeff Fort, but Hogan knew that Fort's organization was still thriving on the street. Leftover wiretaps from the Fort investigation were an enormous potential resource, and Hogan assigned a paralegal named Corinda Luchetta to catalogue hundreds of hours' worth of tapes and parcel them out to thirty secretaries to make transcripts. But because Fort had devised a code that was so elaborate that it practically amounted to a separate language, what Hogan really needed was a flipper—someone who could translate the gibberish on the tapes.

His big break came on July 11, 1988, when Chicago police picked up an El Rukn general named Henry Leon Harris in a rooming house and told him he was going to be charged in connection with the Barber murder in South Carolina. By the time the squad car reached the station house, Harris had confessed to his own role and had told the officer that Fort and Robinson had indeed ordered the hit. Hogan had his flipper.

This past February, I wrote to Henry Harris at the witness-protection unit of the latest of the maximum-security prisons where he has lived for the past six years. In the weeks since, he has telephoned me regularly. Harris, who is now thirty-four, told me that when he was thirteen, in his home town of Milwaukee, he joined the gang that became the El Rukns and rose through the ranks until he was named a general, in 1983, and placed in charge of the gang's far-flung narcotics operation. (His progress may have been accelerated when he married Jeff Fort's younger sister.) The reason he decided to cooperate with the prosecution could not have been clearer: Harris wrote in his notes just after he was arrested in connection with the conspiracy to murder Barber, "I'm looking at the hot chair as I write this."

Harris is a professional criminal, and he is also charming, witty, and a fine raconteur, who speaks with a mixture of regret and pride about his days with the El Rukns. "We were planning the international black crime syndicate," Harris told me on the phone one afternoon. "We pushed the button on people, on high people! There were people who were out to get former President Reagan. That's right—a couple of people were planning on killing Reagan." In his many hours with Hogan, Harris sometimes wrapped a towel around his neck, to create a persona he called "the Professor," and regaled Hogan with tales of the El Rukns' exploits. "Bill Hogan was a damned good guy," Harris said. "He had a lot of potential as a gang-crime prosecutor. It was, like, running through his blood to get these guys off the streets. Hogan was on a mission. I spent almost six or seven hours a day with Bill for three or four years. I was doing tapes, man, nothing but tapes—listening, transcribing hundreds of hours' worth."

The volume of tapes and documents was such that Hogan had to leave his office in the courthouse and set up Corinda Luchetta and the rest of his team in a suite of offices across South Dearborn Street, on the thirty-ninth floor of the Kluczynski Building. "Bill used to stop by his office at seven-thirty every morning, but he really worked in the Kluczynski," a former senior member of the United States Attorney's Office staff recalled. "Hogan had a space behind a combination lock where they had the run of the turf up there. That kind of stuff really matters. Day to day, they were not visible to anybody. They became a separate world." In that separate world, Harris was soon joined by several other El Rukns, who had also decided to flip: Harry Evans, a three-hundred-pound diabetic with chronic renal failure; Earl Hawkins, an El Rukn triggerman, who had received a death sentence from an Illinois state court; and Eugene Hunter, another admitted murderer. As Hogan learned what was on the tapes and mined his flippers' recollections, the scope of his case kept growing.

It grew to vast, virtually unprecedented size. On October 27, 1989, the federal grand jury that Hogan was supervising returned a pair of indictments—one of them was three hundred and five pages long and weighed almost four pounds—that charged Noah Robinson and sixty-four El Rukn members and associates with a panoply of crimes over a twenty-four-year period. In a news conference at the courthouse, United States Attorney Anton Valukas said that the indictments charged that "these defendants sought to obtain and maintain control of drug territories through a systematic process of murder, narcotics distribution, terrorism, robberies, extortions, intimidations, fraud, bribery, kidnapping, and obstruction of justice." The charges included twenty murders and seven attempted killings. Near the bottom of a front-page Chicago *Tribune* story announcing the indictment, it was noted that Valukas praised the work of Hogan, "who had spearheaded the three-year investigation."

Bill Hogan has always had goals, and until the El Rukn cases unravelled around him he had methodically accomplished them. He was born forty-two years ago, the son of a businessman and a homemaker, and grew up in a small stucco house in the pleasant Chicago suburb of Winnetka. "Bill's the oldest of eight kids," a longtime friend of his, Mike O'Rourke, said recently. "What else do you need to know?" At Loyola Academy, he made the Chicago Catholic League's all-star football team as a center and a linebacker, and he was elected to the Torch Club honor society. Tall, blond, lean, and well-muscled, Hogan radiated laconic confidence. "Just before our senior prom, Bill banged up his knee and he was in the hospital," O'Rourke recalled. "A bunch of us just bagged the prom and spent the night keeping him company. People looked up to him, wanted to be around him."

Hogan won a football scholarship to Holy Cross, but he lost it when his knee gave out, and in 1970 he married his high-school sweetheart and returned home. Their first child, Sheila Jane, was born the next year. These detours might well have thrown a less focussed young man permanently off track. Without the scholarship, Hogan was forced to paint houses to pay his way through Loyola University night school, in Chicago. But even with the new financial burdens—a son, Billy, quickly followed—Hogan never faltered in articulating and acting upon a clear plan for his future. "We were in a bar called the P.M. Club one day, and Bill said to me, 'Mikey, tell me if you think I'm crazy, but I'm going to transfer to the University of Illinois, and then I'm going to go to law school,'" O'Rourke said. "He was under such pressure at that time, with the kids and money issues. But I knew he would do it. He's a guy who, once he sets his mind to something, he's absolutely tenacious, just relentless. Do not mess with Hogan." Hogan finished law school, as predicted, right on schedule.

Law school produced a new set of goals. At Loyola University School of Law, Hogan took a trial-practice class with several adjunct professors who had been Assistant United States Attorneys in Chicago. "He saw those guys and he just knew from then on what he wanted to do," his friend Alexander Vesselinovitch said. Shortly after law school, Hogan and Vesselinovitch became law clerks for Charles Kocoras, a newly appointed federal judge in Chicago, and the exposure to the rough-and-tumble of the courthouse only deepened Hogan's desire to be a prosecutor. "When we finished our clerkship, there were no openings in Chicago, so Bill said, 'Where can I be an A.U.S.A.?' " Vesselinovitch said. "It turned out there was an opening in Seattle." With his marriage unravelling, Hogan moved west.

He was an immediate success as a prosecutor. He loved the work and excelled at it. After conducting a complex environmental investigation and then winning a monthlong trial against members of the Bandidos motorcycle gang, Hogan was poised for long-term success in Seattle. But his goal remained Chicago. Part of the reason was personal. "A lot of guys, when they get divorced, they kind of forget about their kids, but Bill always stayed close to his," Hogan's friend Patrick Keeley said. "Seattle was never going to work for him, because he couldn't be near them." And there remained the passion to become an Assistant United States Attorney in the Northern District of Illinois. After almost three years on the job in Seattle, Hogan finally obtained the job offer. He returned to Chicago and started work in the United States Attorney's Office in 1985. "It was the only job I ever wanted," Hogan said later.

Once again, he stood out. Because of his tenure in Seattle, he had more experience than most new Northern District Assistant United States Attorneys, so he was able to investigate and try complex cases from the start. His reputation in the Chicago legal community soared. "I told him for years that he could triple his income overnight by going into private practice," Keeley says. "But Bill's focus in life is to do what is right. Monetary and financial issues are so far down the list that they don't even become a factor. The guy is actually very much a liberal in his politics, and he saw these cases as an opportunity to help the community."

In Seattle, Hogan had married again, but the marriage ended quickly after he returned to Chicago. The focus of his life outside the courthouse remained his children. He was especially close to his daughter, a tall, blond, athletic kid much like him—a gymnast and soccer player and, in the summers, a lifeguard on Lake Michigan. In the fall of 1989, Sheila went away for her freshman year at the University of Illinois. The next March, she made a quick trip home to Chicago before making a spring-break pilgrimage to Florida. She mentioned to her mother that she had some bruises on one leg that did not seem to be healing. Her mother asked her to check with a doctor before she left. The diagnosis was acute leukemia. Sheila Hogan died three weeks later. She was eighteen. Almost all the lawyers at the United States Attorney's Office attended her funeral. "Everyone has a way of dealing with tragedy," Vesselinovitch said. "Bill worked. To say he threw himself into his work is an understatement. After Sheila's death, he worked his tail off in the El Rukn case. He thought the case could make a difference in the community that was beneficial." A year after his daughter's funeral, Bill Hogan's first El Rukn trial began.

It was Hogan's headstrong, driven nature that allowed him to pull the El Rukn case together. It was this single-mindedness that likewise allowed him to carry on after Sheila's death. But as the trials in the El Rukn case began, that strength looked less like a positive attribute and more like a fatal flaw. Hogan's troubles had their start with the judges. "One of the first rules you learn as a lawyer—defense or prosecutor— is don't piss off the judge," Robert Loeb, a defense lawyer for one of the El Rukns, said. "Hogan made a cardinal mistake. He decided to go toe to toe with these judges."

First, Hogan alienated Judge Marvin E. Aspen by insisting that his major indictment, which charged thirty-seven defendants, be tried in a single megatrial. In a caustic opinion, Aspen severed the case into smaller trials. (There would ultimately be seven different El Rukn trials.) But Hogan's relationship with Aspen was downright cordial compared with his dealings with the other main judge in the El Rukn cases, James F. Holderman. Before being appointed to the bench, in 1985, at the age of thirty-eight, Holderman, like Hogan, had been a senior trial prosecutor in the Northern District. Warm and friendly off the bench, Holderman is subject to fits of rage in court that baffle even his admirers. Pacing behind his big leather chair, his chubby face growing red, Holderman can turn into a scary, almost irrational figure—as Bill Hogan witnessed again and again. Hogan's conflicts with Holderman began over small issues like scheduling, but they escalated until it was clear that the judge completely distrusted the prosecutor. "Mr. Hogan, at the end of the day yesterday, you insisted upon further reasons why I don't believe you," Holderman said during the trial. "You have provided a further reason. You don't do things when you say you are going to do them, you make statements that are presented as true when, in fact, they are not—"

"Judge, that's—" Hogan sputtered.

"You have stated that certain notes exist, and then later you say they do not . . . I could go on, but I will not, because I have wasted enough time dealing with your problems."

The run-ins with the judges did not prevent Hogan from winning his cases. He was working very hard. Because of the severances, there was sometimes more than one trial going on at the same time. One morning in October of 1991, as Hogan was giving his rebuttal summation in a trial before Judge Holderman, he learned that in another El Rukn case his colleagues had run out of evidence that they could present without him. So, after speaking to the jury for an entire morning in front of Holderman, Hogan headed for the other trial and spent the afternoon putting Earl Hawkins, one of the flippers, through his paces there.

Hogan was winning his cases because his flippers were brilliant, convincing witnesses. They had to be. There was precious little physical evidence or eyewitness testimony tying the defendants to the murders in these cases. The evidence consisted largely of the recollections of the cooperators Henry Harris and Harry Evans of conversations and events that stretched back nearly a quarter century. Hogan's summations amounted to passionate defenses of their veracity. They were criminals and drug abusers, he said, but they had reformed. In one case, Hogan picked up a catchphrase that a defense attorney named Marianne Jackson had used in her summation to disparage Harris and company.

"Miss Jackson talked about 'Who you are speaks so loud I can't hear what you say.' I disagree with that," Hogan told the jury. "And I think that you should, too. What they said is as important as who they are. They were able to say what they did because of who they are. They were able to tell you about the things that they have done through twenty years, and the people that they did them with, because of who they are. And they were able to tell you about the defendants in this courtroom, because they did them with the defendants in this courtroom. There is an old proverb that says, 'Show me your friends, and I will show you who you are.' These men, the government witnesses who took the stand in this case, ladies and gentlemen, spent twenty years, day in, day out . . . sitting around with these three men in small rooms . . . plotting murder, selling narcotics."

In the end, as Hogan told the jury, it was his own integrity, as much as that of his witnesses, that was on the line: "If you believe the arguments that you heard from these defense lawyers, you have to believe that the government, the federal government . . . the Assistant United States Attorneys who investigated this case for the last number of years . . . deliberately colluded with . . . Earl Hawkins, Harry Evans, Eugene Hunter, and Henry Harris in order to present this evidence to you." Hogan met the argument with a challenge. "If you believe that, which has been the tenor of these arguments for the last several hours here, then I do invite you to acquit these defendants. Because if you believe that, then they have no business being in this courtroom, because there is in fact something wrong, very desperately wrong, with the system of justice that has brought them to this courtroom." All the defendants were convicted.

During that trial, in 1991, Marianne Jackson heard a rumor that the El Rukn cooperating witnesses were still using narcotics in prison, so she issued a subpoena to the Metropolitan Correctional Center for Harris's and Evans's urinalysis records. One record, produced late in the trial, showed that each of the two witnesses had failed one test, in 1989. Their urine showed the presence of morphine, which can indicate heroin use. This was a potentially significant—even an explosive—piece of evidence. It showed that the government's top witnesses were not reformed drug abusers, as they had testified. Rather, it showed that they were still using drugs after their arrests, and thus cast doubt on their over-all credibility. Hogan, however, cleverly defused the importance of the failed drug tests. He called an official of the M.C.C. to testify that his records showed that neither Harris nor Evans had been disciplined for using drugs in prison. Because there was no record of discipline, the official stated, the use of morphine must have been medically authorized. The testimony was ambiguous, but the defense attorneys succeeded in persuading Judge Holderman to hold a post-trial hearing about the drug tests.

Just as that hearing was getting started, in the fall of 1992, what turned out to be the most significant event in the collapse of the El Rukn cases was taking place six hundred miles away, in a restaurant at the edge of Georgetown, in Washington, D.C. There, on the night of September 17, 1992, Lawrence Rosenthal, a former Assistant United States Attorney in the Northern District, had a casual dinner at the Sequoia restaurant with Michael Shepard, a former colleague, who was on assignment in the capital. Shepard happened to mention Holderman's hearing, of which Rosenthal had been unaware. They're looking into whether the El Rukn witnesses used drugs, Shepard said.

Wait a second, Rosenthal replied. He knew something about that. It was back in 1989, just before Hogan indicted the case. Somehow, Rosenthal got a memo from the M.C.C. which showed that some El Rukn witnesses had failed their urine tests. Rosenthal said he walked the memo over to Hogan's office and mentioned it to him. As Rosenthal later testified, he told Hogan, "I thought this would be a real problem for the investigation and asked him . . . what he was going to do about it," and Hogan responded that "it was not a problem, it was nothing to worry about." Rosenthal recalled that he had repeated to Hogan that the memo would be a problem, that it would have to be turned over to the defense. And Rosenthal went on, "At that point it was clear to me from Mr. Hogan's demeanor that he was not interested in having any type of extended discussion on this, that he had discussed this all that he cared to, and the conversation ended."

This was a bombshell, and Shepard knew it. Since the Supreme Court's 1963 decision in Brady v. Maryland, prosecutors have had the duty to disclose to defense attorneys any exculpatory information about their clients. So-called Brady material also includes information that undermines the credibility of government witnesses, such as a failed drug test by an incarcerated cooperator. The Rosenthal-Hogan conversation established that Hogan had known about the failed drug test in 1989—before the indictments and the trials. The defense had learned of the failed drug tests only through a subpoena to the M.C.C. in 1991. The obvious implication was that Hogan had simply decided not to tell the defense about the failed tests, because such information would damage his case. Shepard alerted the Northern District prosecutors conducting the hearing, and they called Rosenthal in to testify before Holderman. They also called in Hogan, who at that point was on assignment in Los Angeles.

Hogan's testimony was, as many recalled it later, pure Bill Hogan. Rosenthal had testified to the effect that the conversation with Hogan was brief, and that Hogan had been preoccupied with his work on the El Rukn indictment. It would have been entirely understandable if Hogan had simply said that he did not remember Rosenthal's saying anything to him. But Hogan was emphatic. He testified that the conversation that Larry Rosenthal described "simply did not occur." Holderman thereupon ordered the United States Attorney's Office to scour its files to determine whether the "Rosenthal memorandum" could be found, and it was found, with papers from one of Rosenthal's old cases. It showed that Harris and Evans had failed the drug tests uncovered by Marianne Jackson's subpoena. Hogan swore that he had never seen the memo before. The Rosenthal memorandum acquired a nickname—"the smoking gun."

Holderman was enraged, and he dramatically expanded the scope of his hearings. He wanted to know everything about how the cooperating witnesses had been treated in the course of the investigation.

There was, it turned out, more evidence relating to drug use by the cooperators. Five prisoners at the M.C.C. testified that they knew that Harris and Evans had used drugs in prison. Equally damaging was a memo that turned up from an agent of the Bureau of Alcohol, Tobacco, and Firearms who had been charged with guarding the cooperators while they were meeting with the prosecutors on the thirty-ninth floor of the Kluczynski Building. The memo indicated that Hogan's thirty-ninth-floor office suite functioned like a frat house. El Rukn witnesses, the agent wrote at the time, had "unlimited access to telephone service," and even answered the phones themselves, saying, "A.T.F." The cooperators, he continued, "offered agents an opportunity to watch pornographic videos from a collection kept in task-force work spaces." At one point, the witnesses apparently stole prosecution documents, including Hogan's outline of his proposed prosecution of the case, and took them back to the M.C.C. to study. Holderman also learned that Hogan had a nickname on the thirty-ninth floor—"the Imam," which was the El Rukns' term for Jeff Fort, the commander of the gang.

Harris and Evans were called back to the stand, and Holderman found out that the cooperators also had been allowed to have sex with visitors. "They allowed us to have sex with our wives," Henry Harris told me, expanding on his testimony. "Everybody knew it. We called it office sex. We didn't know nothing 'bout it, and the A.T.F. agents were the ones who taught us. 'Go and lay your coat on the floor and get you some.' That's what they said to us. And we did." Harris and Hunter had occasional beers. Visitors were not checked for contraband when they arrived. Once, when Harry Evans's mother came to see him, he removed his shoe and passed it to her, saying, "Look at my gym shoe, Mom." She did, and passed it back. It was around this time that fellow-inmates said Evans often looked stoned.

The eccentric side to Henry Harris's character, which was well hidden during his trial testimony, came to the fore during his post-trial testimony. For example, he portrayed his failed drug tests as part of a conspiracy in the M.C.C. to incriminate him. "I was set up by the

Bureau of Prisons," he told me. "I threatened to blow the whistle on an organized-crime community that they were running right there in the prison, so they dirtied up my urine." Harris also testified to an unusually close relationship with Hogan and his junior trial partner Ted Poulos. In a cross-examination, Harris recalled that, to take Harris's mind off his troubles in prison, Poulos "asked me to put together two essays, because I was in school then," and Harris went on to say, "He asked me to put together an essay concerning Abraham Lincoln's second inaugural address. And he wanted me to explain it from A to Z to him in writing."

A defense attorney, Richard S. Kling, followed up. Kling asked, "Mr. Harris, have you sent other essays to the United States Attorney's Office regarding your perspectives on life?"

"My perspectives on life?" Harris responded.

"You sent Mr. Poulos an evaluation of Abraham Lincoln's second inaugural address."

"Yes," Harris said. "And I sent him a complete essay concerning Abraham Lincoln. He didn't know Abraham Lincoln was black until I told him, you know, so—by the fact I went through the whole research for him and listed books and stuff where he can check things out and find out."

"You learned Abraham Lincoln was black?" Kling asked.

"Yes, sir."

"How—would you tell us how it is that you learned Abraham Lincoln was black?"

"Research, sir," Henry Harris replied. "Reading books, sir."

Harris, who was the government's most important witness in the El Rukn cases, was revealed as a drug user, a liar, and, it appeared, a nut. Evidence at the hearing established that the cooperators mingled freely, with few restrictions on their ability to line up their stories. (The theft of the prosecution memorandum would, in any event, have given the cooperators a handy script.) None of the privileges the cooperators received, such as the sex and the beer, had been disclosed to the defense attorneys, so they had had no opportunity to cross-examine the cooperators about them. And, of course, their failed drug tests had not been reported. As the hearing continued, Holderman just took to shaking his head in despair. Then he asked Corinda Luchetta, Hogan's paralegal, to take the stand.

Luchetta seems to have been a lonely young woman whose work habits were nearly as obsessive as Hogan's. She had gone to law school at night and was admitted to the bar in November of 1990, but she was so deeply committed to the El Rukn case that she decided to see it through to the end, even though doing so meant staying on as a paralegal. Another reason that Luchetta remained on the job may have been that the case gave her an opportunity to make friends.

The cooperators leaned on Luchetta and confided in her. One cooperator asked Luchetta if she would bring him a box of Ex-Lax at the M.C.C. She did. (Another inmate testified that visitors to the M.C.C. provided drugs to Harris and Evans in balloons or condoms, and that the inmates would swallow those and "then request Ex-Lax in order to quickly pass the condoms and/or balloons.") At another point, Henry Harris volunteered to Luchetta that he had refused to submit a urine specimen for a drug test at the M.C.C., because he was "too tired." (At the M.C.C., refusal to take a urine test is viewed as equivalent to failing it.) And on December 17, 1991, Luchetta unwound in a telephone call with Eugene Hunter, one of the cooperators, who was being held at the M.C.C. (Luchetta was apparently unaware that such phone calls were routinely tape-recorded.)

"Well, Corinda, I'll—I talked to you last weekend," Hunter said. "I thought you woulda took my advice. But my advice goes in one ear, out the other. . . . "

"What advice? Did you give me some?" Luchetta asked.

"Yeah . . . you know, I'm going to be very direct and very respectful at the same time. You need to go out and get laid—good."

"Yeah, I know, I know, I know, I know." Luchetta went on to say that she had a problem she wanted to discuss with Hunter—her feelings for Earl Hawkins, another El Rukn cooperator and convicted murderer. As

Luchetta reported it to Hunter, a friend had said to her "that this is just a physical thing." She went on, "It—see, what I don't understand is I feel weird about it. I mean, normally I can handle just being attracted to somebody. . . . But I feel weird about it because of who he is." Luchetta then said that "the Imam"—Hogan—had just come by to invite her to the office Christmas party, but "I'd rather think about Earl, anyway."

"So, just out of curiosity," Hunter asked, "what would you like to do to Earl?"

Luchetta laughed. "Ten minutes in a locked room. That's all it would take."

"All right, Rindy," Hunter said, changing the subject. "We done had enough business for the day. You have to tell me my bedtime stories for the night."

"Tell you a bedtime story? Gee."

"Yeah, I have tension, too. You know?"

"You poor thing."

"And you help me release my tension."

"I don't know, Eugene," Luchetta said. "Oh, let me see, what kind of a story can I tell you?" She asked him to describe the visiting room of a prison, where she might visit him, then asked, "What would you have me do first?"

"I just want to look."

"Look but don't touch," Luchetta said. "I don't think so."

"You sit on my lap. . . . Um huh. Just sitting down and standing up."

"Yeah, I gotcha," Luchetta said, laughing. "I know the anatomy well enough for one of those virgin Catholic girls."

Hunter then inquired, "So now that you've got everything up in the air, will you help me get it down?"

"Oh, gosh, let me see," Luchetta mused. "I've always wanted to, like, stop an elevator between floors."

"Um huh."

"And just stand someone up against the wall."

The conversation continued for a while longer, and Hunter said, "You know, talking to you sometimes, I get—I have orgasms."

Luchetta laughed.

"Real ones," Hunter went on. "Today I have one."

"It's very flattering, Gene."

The courtroom was very quiet as the Luchetta-Hunter tape was played. Actually, it is not clear precisely what rule, if any, was broken by this conversation between a prosecution paralegal and a confessed murderer. It was inappropriate, bizarre, and embarrassing, but not, perhaps, illegal. Yet, turning up, as it did, near the end of the hearings, the tape must have looked to Holderman like the last straw, the final, and clearest, indicator that this prosecution was out of control—that the prosecution and its witnesses had ceased operating at some distance from one another, and that their alliance was an unholy one.

Because Hogan was a witness in the post-trial hearings, he could not represent the government, and the Northern District prosecutors who took over, led by a lawyer named Barry Rand Elden, made a key strategic decision, despite heated objections by Hogan. Once the Rosenthal memo surfaced, the government decided to forgo the argument that there had been no prosecutorial misconduct. Since Rosenthal obviously had known about the failed drug test, and since he was a prosecutor, the government's theory went, "the government" had known about it and had failed to disclose it to the defense. Instead of arguing that no misconduct had taken place, Elden moved to a fallback position. Even assuming that the government had neglected to disclose the failed drug tests, office sex, and alcohol use, Elden argued, the convictions should still not be reversed. Elden said that Hogan had disclosed to the defense that his cooperators were murderers, drug dealers, and, before their arrests, drug abusers. The disclosure of the prison drug tests would have made no difference. Hogan's dereliction was therefore harmless error.

While waiting for Holderman's decision, in early 1993, Hogan had one more duty to fulfill—perhaps his most important one. In a case peripherally related to the other El Rukn prosecutions, Thomas J.

Maloney, who had been a Cook County Circuit Court judge for thirteen years, was charged with accepting bribes to fix five cases, including three murder cases, and Hogan was acting as prosecutor in the trial of Maloney. As it happened, one of the cases was a prosecution of the El Rukn cooperator Earl Hawkins. Maloney was the first judge in the history of Illinois ever prosecuted for fixing a murder trial, and the case was a difficult one. Perhaps aware that he was being investigated, Maloney at one point had returned the bribe money, and Hawkins had been convicted and sentenced to death. "Bill was under enormous pressure," Scott Mendeloff, who tried the Maloney case with Hogan, later told me. "He was exhausted to start with, because he had tried six El Rukn cases in the previous year and a half. We had evidence that was strong but not a slam dunk by any stretch of the imagination. We had very tough defense attorneys. And Bill had just finished the post-trial hearings with Holderman, and he had the spectre of losing his job and his law license. It was just crushing pressure, and Bill tried the Maloney case magnificently—like I've never seen someone try a case." On April 16, 1993, Judge Maloney was convicted of fixing all three murder cases.

Seven weeks later, Judge Holderman issued his opinion on the post-trial hearing. He found that Hogan had engaged in extensive prosecutorial misconduct, had lied on the witness stand about his meeting with Rosenthal, and had "deliberately suppressed" his knowledge of "continuing criminal conduct of illegal acquisition, possession and use of drugs over a prolonged period . . . within the prosecutor's office and aided by the government's permissiveness." Holderman found that these errors were not harmless and that all the convictions had to be reversed, because the cooperators' veracity was so important to the government's case. "The only conclusion that can be drawn is that Hogan suppressed the Brady information in bad faith to improve, unconstitutionally, the government's chances of victory," Holderman wrote. Ten days later, on June 14, 1993, Judge Suzanne B. Conlon, a judge in another of the El Rukn cases, and with whom Hogan had also clashed, reversed the El Rukn convictions over which she had presided, because of the prosecution's "failure to comply with basic constitutional and ethical discovery obligations."

Hogan had one hope left. Judge Aspen had yet to rule on the misconduct motion in his trial. The Holderman and Conlon rulings could be attributed, at least in part, to the extremely bad chemistry that had developed between Hogan and those judges. Even though Hogan had clashed with Aspen over the severance issues, the prosecution he conducted under Aspen had passed without major conflict between them. What was more, the defendants in Aspen's case were the worst of the El Rukn defendants—the generals, and also Noah Robinson. Surely, Hogan and his supporters thought, Aspen—levelheaded, fair-minded, responsible—would never let those people go.

Hogan had to wait all summer to find out. On September 20, 1993, Aspen ruled. "This is the most painful decision that this court has ever been obliged to render, making the crafting of this opinion a sad and difficult undertaking," the hundred-and-eighty-one-page opinion began. "Mindful of the consequences of our ruling, we would have preferred to have been able to reach a result other than what must be. . . .

"The consequences of our ruling today are tragic in many respects. It is a tragedy that the convictions of some of the most hardened and anti-social criminals in the history of this community must be overturned.

"It is tragic that the United States of America has squandered millions of taxpayer dollars and years of difficult labor by the courts, prosecutors, and law-enforcement officers in the investigation and trial of these botched prosecutions.

"It is tragic that the hard-earned and well-deserved reputations for professionalism of the United States Attorney's Office for the Northern District of Illinois have been so unfairly tainted by the actions of so few.

"It is a personal tragedy for the lead El Rukn prosecutor who, in seeking to attain the laudable goal of ridding society of an organization of predatory career criminals, was willing to abandon fundamental notions of due process of law and deviate from acceptable standards of prosecutorial conduct."

• • •

When I met with Bill Hogan in Chicago over two days this spring, he looked physically transformed from the man who had tried the El Rukn cases. Tropical sun had bleached his blond hair to the color of straw, and it flopped down well over his collar. His skin was ruddy and tanned, his belly was flat, and his arms were thickly muscled. Two rope bracelets encircled his right wrist. But for the Marlboro Lights he was chain-smoking, Hogan might have been an especially well-preserved, if rather grim, beach bum.

"After I was suspended last July, the Office of Professional Responsibility told me they wanted to interview me in September, then it was October, then December," Hogan told me. "All I was wanting was to get the hell out of Dodge."

Hogan went to the Virgin Islands alone, and there he met up with a group of expatriate Europeans. "Just before I came back here, we figured we'd take a long sail from the Caribbean to Fort Lauderdale, just take a handful of days," Hogan said. "There were four of us on this thirty-six-foot boat." Three days into the open sea, they were caught up in hurricane-force winds. "We had forty hours of sixty-knot winds, lost our mainsail, came goddam close to being killed." Hogan tells the story without self-pity, but the message is clear: Just my luck. He arrived back in Chicago, by airplane, in the last week of February.

Hogan now spends most of his days in the office of his lawyer, a genial law-school chum named Shelly B. Kulwin. Hogan speaks calmly and cogently about his predicament. He has a trial lawyer's low, sonorous voice, with just a long-vowelled hint of Chicago, which used to remind juries of his local roots. He knows that the public picture of him is that of a lawless vigilante. Indeed, with the exception of a balanced story by Michael Abramowitz in the magazine *Chicago*, the local press has done little but repeat the judges' accusations against him. He is quick to cite the few bright spots that remain in the El Rukn story. Judge Aspen's decision (but not Holderman's) is being appealed. Several defendants (including Noah Robinson) are serving lengthy prison terms for crimes unrelated to these cases, so they cannot be released immediately. The judge in one El Rukn case (albeit one that Hogan did not try) has declined to reverse the convictions from that trial. Still, on his own behavior Hogan is adamant.

"Do I regret my actions in this case?" he said. "Not a bit. Not one iota. I don't want to sound arrogant, but I am extraordinarily proud of my work here and the results we achieved and how we achieved them. I never, ever, ever would have compromised my efforts here in order to win, and I didn't." The Office of Professional Responsibility has asked Hogan not to discuss the details of the case publicly, but in a brief that he and Kulwin filed, Hogan offered a thoughtful, considered response to every accusation. He never knew that Harris and Evans were using drugs at the M.C.C. He never knew that Harris refused to take a drug test. (He says Luchetta never told him.) He never knew that any of the cooperators had sex in the office. The A.T.F. agent who wrote the memo about it, Hogan notes, later admitted that he may have overreacted. Hogan never gave any cooperator a beer. And no, Hogan insists, Larry Rosenthal never mentioned the so-called smoking-gun memo to him. "Leopards don't change their spots," he said. "I've been a prosecutor for nearly twelve years, and I was never—not once—accused of any kind of misconduct. And now they say I just all of a sudden did all these improper things. It makes no sense. It couldn't happen and it didn't happen. I was not some wild-eyed zealot who was desperate to rid the earth of this scourge. I was very professional and I did the job the way it's supposed to be done."

In our conversation, Hogan seemed less than persuasive only once—when I asked him about Henry Harris. "Henry is a very multifaceted person, a very interesting guy," Hogan said. "He used drugs for years, but he's got a tremendous memory. He's not crazy, but he can seem pretty wacky." In consequence of the misconduct findings, Harris has moved to have his guilty plea set aside, on the ground that the prosecutors broke promises to him—specifically, that Hogan had told Harris that he would get less than twenty years in prison. One of the many ironies of the El Rukn case is that the cooperators may wind up worse off than anyone else. According to Harris's plea bargain, he must serve a minimum of twenty years, but the people he testified against may go free. Hogan and the Northern District, of course, insist that Harris was promised no better deal than the twenty-year minimum.

Harris (who is now hedging on Lincoln's race) told me, "The government has the nerve to respond that Hogan said he ain't made me any promises. If he didn't make me any promises, why did I plead guilty? If he didn't make any promises, why did six El Rukns plead out to all these murders? I mean, people don't just walk into court and plead to thirty different murders because they feel like it. We all expected to get something from it, and we're getting nothing, man. See, when I tell on sixty-five black men the government says I'm telling the truth, but when I talk about a few white prosecutors they say it's not so. You tell me, how can that be?"

It's a good question. All deal-makers obviously want the best deal they can get. But perhaps the message of the El Rukn case is that there are some people with whom prosecutors should never make deals, even if it costs them the opportunity to make megacases. Every time the government puts someone on the witness stand, it identifies with him, vouches for him, stands by him. After all, as the proverb that Hogan quoted says, "show me your friends and I will show you who you are." Perhaps when prosecutors make friends with the Henry Harrises of the world that is what they become. And perhaps, ultimately, Hogan was not the right man to make this case. The judges' case against him is largely one of willful blindness—that Hogan must have known that his cooperators were abusing drugs, and that he could not have missed the shenanigans on the thirty-ninth floor. But the combination of Hogan's obsessive focus on his own goals and his endless overwork may indeed have blinded him; he simply may not have seen what he should have.

Hogan, of course, would be neither the first nor the only prosecutor to make a deal with the Devil. Indeed, as he and his lawyer acidly point out, it was Hogan's superiors in the office who negotiated the details of Harris's and the other El Rukns' plea bargains. It was the same superiors who allowed him to shoulder such an enormous burden of trials virtually by himself, the same superiors who were so eager to share in the credit as the convictions in the El Rukn cases were first coming in; and the same superiors who decided not to defend Hogan's good faith in the post-trial hearings. Of late, Hogan hears little from these superiors.

I noticed a small change in Hogan over the two days I saw him. The first day, he was confident, poised, almost serene. The second day, his tan looked to be fading, and as he sat before a thick stack of documents from the case he seemed to be sensing anew the size of his troubles. His son, Billy, has just graduated from college in Michigan. Hogan lives alone in a small apartment downtown. He receives a paycheck, but he may not have a job. As he well knows, the Office of Professional Responsibility has lately been much criticized as a paper tiger, unwilling to take on prosecutors. What better case for O.P.R. to prove its mettle than one in which three judges have already found serious misconduct?

When I asked Hogan what he thought he would do after the O.P.R. report came out, he told me, "When I was twelve, I had a teacher in the seventh grade who distributed books that people could read for extra credit. He gave me some books by a guy named Kenneth Roberts, who's pretty much forgotten now, but who wrote a whole series of historical novels in the thirties and forties. They were about a town he called Arundel, in Maine, between the French and Indian War and the War of 1812. I must have read a dozen of these books, and as a result I sort of decided that I wanted to do two things. I decided I wanted to become a lawyer. They were really putting the country together in those books, and I saw what a big role the law had, and I just knew that was what I would do with my life. The other thing I wanted to do was sail around the world, and that's what I'm going to do after the report. There's nothing holding me here."

Editor's note: In 1998, the judge hearing the O.P.R.'s case against Bill Hogan determined that Hogan was guilty of no wrongdoing, and ordered him reinstated as a U.S. Attorney.

Young Convicts
by James T. Farrell

Novelist James T. Farrell (1904–1979) became famous during the 1930s for his realistic depictions of life in Chicago's toughest neighborhoods. Best-known for his fictional trilogy Studs Lonigan, *Farrell also wrote short stories such as this one.*

They were the children of Slavic immigrants and lived in the manufacturing district around Thirty-fifth and Morgan. Their fathers worked in the factories located in the area. Their sisters, even before they started to bloom and lose their gawky pre-puberty figures, also joined the ranks of those who trooped to the factories at six and seven in the morning. At six, seven, eight o'clock, rain or shine, morning after morning, their fathers, mothers, older brothers, sisters, all became part of the long line plodding to work.

There were six kids in this gang. Tony, the eldest, was a boy of twelve, and Stanley, the youngest, was eight. They all liked candy. They liked to go to the movies, especially on Saturday afternoons, when the serial was shown. They liked serials and movies of that type best because there was danger and adventure, shooting, robbing, train wrecks, bandits, outlaws, Indians, Mexicans, battles. And they scarcely ever had money for candy or for movies.

But they liked candy and they liked movies. And they liked to do dangerous, brave things, to pull off stunts like those pulled off by the older fellows in the neighborhood. They wanted to fight and steal, and then brag about it, just as they heard their older brothers bragging. They could be heroes just like the older boys. And when they could steal, they could have money for candy and the movies.

Home to each of the kids in the gang was much the same. A wooden shack, one or two stories high, with an outside privy that smelled you out every time you wanted to take a leak. Three, four, five rooms, generally dirty, full of rags, papers, the smell of kerosene lamps. Dark bedrooms, old beds, dirty sheets, two, three, four, and five sleeping together in the same bed, and on cold nights there was always a fight for the blankets. A mother and a father who were generally overtired from work, and from raising a family. And the mother and father didn't speak English. They were greenhorns. And once every week, two weeks, three weeks, the mother and father would get drunk. They would curse and fight, throwing things at one another, shouting, even brandishing knives and cutting one another up, until the police came with a paddy wagon. These kids' homes were alike.

They didn't like school very much. They didn't like their studies, and in the classroom they groaned, twisted, squirmed, itched, dreamed of high deeds like those of the movie heroes and villains in the Saturday-afternoon serials, like those of the older fellows, like those of Al Capone. In school, they waited for the end of class. They were afraid of their teachers, and they neither liked nor trusted them. The teachers, some of them young girls from good families who were waiting until they found a husband, did not like the bad boys much either. Sometimes, in the hallways, the kids would hear one teacher tell another that she wished she would be transferred to another school where there was a better class of pupils than these incorrigible Polacks and Bohemians.

Often, they didn't learn their lessons. They bummed from school regularly, and went scavenging through vacant lots and streets, keeping their eyes peeled for the overworked truant officers. Or they went to the railroad yards with sacks and wagons for coal that was needed at home. In fact, they learned to steal in the railroad yards. The parents would send them out at night to get coal, and they'd go down to the yards and get it, one kid getting up in a car and throwing chunks down to the others. From the railroad yards they went to the stockyards, going over the fences and leaving with anything removable that could perhaps be sold. They stole everything they could, and finally stealing got to be a nightly occupation.

They knew about hold-ups. They knew that some of the older guys in the district had pulled off hold-ups, and that made them heroes. So they determined that they too would be heroes and pull hold-ups. That would get money for candy and movies. And they would be living like the heroes they saw in the movies. One night, Tony, the gang leader, picked out the Nation Oil filling station on Thirty-fifth Street. They played across the street from the station for two nights. They goofed about, ran, played tag by a closed factory, getting a line on what time the station closed and what time the cop on the beat passed by after it had closed. When they were sure of their time and their layout, they went to work. Young Stanley tossed a house brick through a side window. Tony then stood on a box, put his hand through the broken glass, and unlatched the window. He went in, followed by the others. The money was in the safe, and that could not be touched. So they tore the telephone box from the wall and scooted with it. They broke it open in a vacant lot and divided the nickels that were in it. The loot was three dollars, and, although it was to be divided evenly, Stanley was cheated out of a quarter.

Successful in their raid on the filling station, they made other raids. They robbed every filling station in the district, always running off with the telephone box, and they enjoyed the fruits of their robbery in candy, cigarettes, and movies. Tony liked it. He bossed his gang with an iron hand. Night after night he drove them in raid after raid. If they complained, he kicked them in the pants and slapped their faces. If they talked back to him, he cracked them. He saw himself as a young Al Capone. He dreamed of shootings, gang fights, submachine guns, robberies, money, automobiles, everything the gangsters had in the movies, everything Al Capone had in real life. And he always planned out the raids, instructing each kid in what he should do, going to the place in advance to get the lay of the land. He always had money and gave some of it away to younger kids, to girls whom he would try to bribe in order to get them alone with him in basements. He hung around the corners and the poolrooms late at night, watching the older fellows. He imitated them in walking, talking, gestures, held his cigarettes as they did, borrowed all their remarks. He pushed and pressed his gang constantly, always discovering new places to rob. One night they robbed a chain restaurant. Stanley threw a brick through the back window, and they entered and ran off with the cash in the till. Two nights later, they returned to the Nation Oil Company's filling station and again ran off with the telephone box full of nickels. This time they noticed that the attendant had gone home, leaving his safe open. In it, they saw bills, many of them, dollars and dollars, more money than they had ever seen before. They were so surprised by the sight of the money, so afraid, that they did not take it, satisfying themselves with only the small change in the safe. And on the night after this robbery they returned to the chain restaurant. They were caught by a watchman and a city policeman.

They were brought before Judge Katherine Henderson in the Juvenile Court; she was a woman jurist who was known beyond the city for her good work. The court was crowded with its usual array of young culprits and harassed, shamed parents. The boys had to wait their turn, and they sat with other boys, cowed and meek, and with their shabbily dressed immigrant parents. Nearly all those waiting to be tried were the children of working people, most of them of immigrants. Some were released, some placed on probation, some sentenced to the Juvenile Detention Home. Judge Henderson spoke crisply, hastily, perfunctorily, often in a scolding tone. She hurried through case after case, disposed of it, making instant decisions, bawling out parents, often telling immigrant fathers and mothers that they were responsible for the delinquent conduct of their children.

Judge Henderson just didn't have the time. The cases had to be disposed of. Tomorrow there would be the same number. The juvenile problem was insoluble. There was no settlement of it. The same boys were warned, but they were brought back. Parents were warned, but they were helpless. There was nothing to do but rush through from case to case, let so many off, put so many on probation, send so many to the Detention Home. Day after day, this must go on. The law must be upheld. There was no time for her to delay, study, probe into the causes of these delinquencies. All she could do was reach out and try, and hope that a few boys would be rescued from crime, and a few girls from the life of a prostitute. That was what she did. Lectures, warnings, scoldings, questions, sentences. Next. Next. Next. All morning. Next. All afternoon. Next. Tomorrow. More. Next.

Tony and the gang were called up. The bailiff rounded them up and prodded them in the back, his language curt and sharp. He shoved them up to the bar of justice. Judge Henderson read the papers on the case, closed her lips as she read, nodded her gray head. She raised her brows. Her benign face showed worry. She seemed to be wondering and thinking. She looked down sharply at the six boys before her. Their heads dropped. They were afraid to look her in the eye, just as they feared looking teachers, or policemen, in the eye. Her gaze shifted. She stared at their parents, who stood silently behind the boys. She asked each of the boys what his name was. The first answered that he was Clement Comorosky. Where was his mother? He shook his head. Again she asked where his mother was. Again he shook his head. More stridently, she asked where his father and mother were. He said that both were working and could not come down. Stanley's mother then spoke in Polish. An interpreter was called, and she spoke to him. He told the judge that the woman had said that the father and mother of the Comorosky boy worked in a factory and were afraid to stay out because they were too poor, and needed the day's wages, and they were afraid that if they didn't report for work they might be laid off. Please, she would take their place.

"All right. Now, do you boys know what you did?" the judge asked.

None of them answered. They stood with averted eyes.

"Can any of you talk? Can you talk?" she asked, sweeping her eyes from one to another, fixing them on Clement, who was ten years old.

He nodded his head affirmatively.

"Do you know that it's a crime to break into other people's homes and stores and to take things that don't belong to you?"

"I'm sorry . . . ma'am," Clement said.

"How long have you been doing this!"

"Just this time," Clement said.

She looked through the papers before her and called out Stanley's name.

"You were here before, and I told you that I didn't want to see you brought back. And why don't you go to school?"

He looked at her with large-eyed awe.

"Are your parents here?"

A small Slavic woman said that she was his mother; her face was lined, and an old black shawl covered her head. The judge asked her if she ever tried to keep her boy in at night. She shook her head, and said that she tried, but that he went out anyway. The judge looked down at Stanley, glowering.

"And what did you do?"

"Me? I thrun the brick through de window."

Many who heard him smiled. The judge continued to question them in a brusque manner which inspired fear. Their answers came slowly. They were evasive. They did not understand all of her questions. She became more brusque. She seemed annoyed. She listened, with increasing irritation, while the watchman who caught the boys gave his testimony. Then the gas station attendant testified that twice the station had been broken into, and the telephone box had been ripped off the wall on each occasion. The restaurant manager gave testimony also.

"You boys have to learn that you can't go on breaking into places and stealing money. That is not right, and it is not permitted. Do you hear me?"

Six heads nodded.

"Well, why did you do it?"

Her additional questions brought out the fact that Tony was the leader and inspiration of the gang, that Stevie Lozminski was his lieutenant, and that the raids and burglaries had been committed under their direction. Both had been in the court before for truancy and burglary, and the truant officer testified that all her efforts to do anything that would keep them in the classroom, where they belonged, were fruitless. Their teachers and the principal of the school had turned in written reports describing them as incorrigible. The judge continued her brusque questioning, directing some of it at the parents, who stood in silent awe and fear. She lectured the parents about taking care of their offspring and insisted that the interpreter translate her remarks so that they would surely be understood. Tony, Stevie, and Clement were all sentenced to six months in the Juvenile Detention Home, and the others were put on probation. The mothers cried. They looked with bewildered grief at the judge, their pleading eyes almost like those of sick animals. The boys were pulled from their parents' arms and taken off. Two of the mothers cried.

The next case, that of a colored boy caught stealing, was called.

The mill of the court continued.

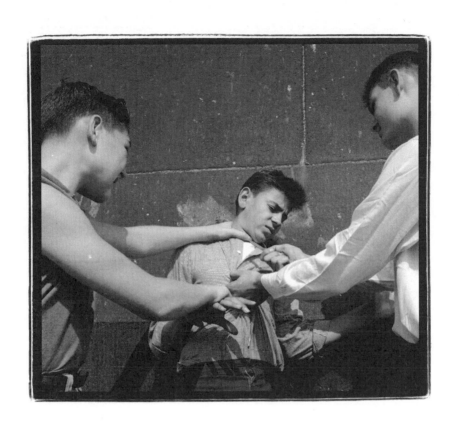

from Down These Mean Streets
by Piri Thomas

Some kids don't exactly choose to join a gang—they are violently drafted into the ranks when they come of age. Author and poet Piri Thomas (born 1928) in this passage from his autobiography, describes being "jumped in" by a local gang after his family moved into a new neighborhood in New York City during the early 1940s.

We were moving—our new pad was back in Spanish Harlem—to 104th Street between Lex and Park Avenue.

Moving into a new block is a big jump for a Harlem kid. You're torn up from your hard-won turf and brought into an "I don't know you" block where every kid is some kind of enemy. Even when the block belongs to your own people, you are still an outsider who has to prove himself a down stud with heart.

As the moving van rolled to a stop in front of our new building, number 109, we were all standing there, waiting for it—Momma, Poppa, Sis, Paulie, James, José, and myself. I made out like I didn't notice the cats looking us over, especially me—I was gang age. I read their faces and found no trust, plenty of suspicion, and a glint of rising hate. I said to myself, *These cats don't mean nothin'. They're just nosy.* But I remembered what had happened to me in my old block, and that it had ended with me in the hospital.

This was a tough-looking block. That was good, that was cool; but my old turf had been tough, too. *I'm tough,* a voice within said. *I hope I'm tough enough. I am tough enough. I've got* mucho corazón, *I'm king wherever I go. I'm a killer to my heart. I* not only can *live, I will* live, *no punk out, no die out, walk bad; be down, cool breeze, smooth.* My mind raced, and thoughts crashed against each other, trying to reassemble themselves into a pattern of rep. I turned slowly and with eyelids half-closed I looked at the rulers of this new world and with a cool shrug of my shoulders I followed the movers into the hallway of number 109 and dismissed the coming war from my mind.

The next morning I went to my new school, called Patrick Henry, and strange, mean eyes followed me.

"Say, pops," said a voice belonging to a guy I later came to know as Waneko, "where's your territory?"

In the same tone of voice Waneko had used, I answered, "I'm on it, dad, what's shaking?"

"Bad, huh?" He half-smiled.

"No, not all the way. Good when I'm cool breeze and bad when I'm down."

"What's your name, kid?"

"That depends. 'Piri' when I'm smooth and 'Johnny Gringo' when stomping time's around."

"What's your name now?" he pushed.

"You name me, man," I answered, playing my role like a champ.

He looked around, and with no kind of words, his boys cruised in. Guys I would come to know, to fight, to hate, to love, to take care of. Little Red, Waneko, Little Louie, Indio, Carlito, Alfredo, Crip, and plenty more. I stiffened and said to myself, *Stomping time, Piri boy, go with heart.*

I fingered the garbage-can handle in my pocket—my homemade brass knuckles. They were great for breaking down large odds into small, chopped-up ones.

Waneko, secure in his grandstand, said, "We'll name you later, *panín.*"

I didn't answer. Scared, yeah, but wooden-faced to the end, I thought, *Chevere, panín.*

It wasn't long in coming. Three days later, at about 6 p.m., Waneko and his boys were sitting around the stoop at number 115. I was cut off from my number 109. For an instant I thought, *Make a break for it down the basement steps and through the back yards—get away in one piece!* Then I thought, *Caramba! Live punk, dead hero. I'm no punk kid. I'm not copping any pleas.* I kept walking, hell's a-burning, hell's a-churning, rolling with cheer. *Walk on, baby man, roll on without fear. What's he going to call?*

"Whatta ya say, Mr. Johnny Gringo?" drawled Waneko.

Think, man, I told myself, *think your way out of a stomping. Make it good.* "I hear you 104th Street coolies are supposed to have heart," I said. "I don't know this for sure. You know there's a lot of streets where a whole 'click' is made out of punks who can't fight one guy unless they all jump him for the stomp." I hoped this would push Waneko into giving me a fair one. His expression didn't change.

"Maybe we don't look at it that way."

Crazy, man. I cheer inwardly, the cabrón *is falling into my setup. We'll see who gets messed up first, baby!* "I wasn't talking to you," I said. "Where I come from, the pres is president 'cause he got heart when it comes to dealing."

Waneko was starting to look uneasy. He had bit on my worm and felt like a sucker fish. His boys were now light on me. They were no longer so much interested in stomping me as in seeing the outcome between Waneko and me. "Yeah," was his reply.

I smiled at him. "You trying to dig where I'm at and now you got me interested in you. I'd like to see where you're at."

Waneko hesitated a tiny little second before replying, "Yeah."

I knew I'd won. Sure, I'd have to fight; but one guy, not ten or fifteen. If I lost I might still get stomped, and if I won I might get stomped. I took care of this with my next sentence. "I don't know you or your boys," I said, "but they look cool to me. They don't feature as punks."

I had left him out purposely when I said "they." Now his boys were in a separate class. I had cut him off. He would have to fight me on his own, to prove his heart to himself, to his boys, and most important, to his turf. He got away from the stoop and asked, "Fair one, Gringo?"

"Uh-uh," I said, "roll all the way—anything goes." I thought, *I've got to beat him bad and yet not bad enough to take his prestige all away.* He had *corazón.* He came on me. *Let him draw first blood,* I thought, *it's his block.* Smish, my nose began to bleed. His boys cheered, his heart cheered, his turf cheered. "Waste this chump," somebody shouted.

Okay, baby, now it's my turn. He swung. I grabbed innocently, and my forehead smashed into his nose. His eyes crossed. His fingernails went for my eye and landed in my mouth—crunch, I bit hard. I punched him in the mouth as he pulled away from me, and he slammed his foot into my chest.

We broke, my nose running red, my chest throbbing, his finger— well, that was his worry. I tied him up with body punching and slugging. We rolled onto the street. I wrestled for acceptance, he for rejection or, worse yet, acceptance on his terms. It was time to start peace talks. I smiled at him. "You got heart, baby," I said.

He answered with a punch to my head. I grunted and hit back, harder now. I had to back up my overtures of peace with strength. I hit him in the ribs, I rubbed my knuckles in his ear as we clinched. I tried again. "You deal good," I said.

"You too," he muttered, pressuring out. And just like that, the fight was over. No more words. We just separated, hands half up, half down. My heart pumped out, *You've established your rep. Move over, 104th Street. Lift your wings, I'm one of your baby chicks now.*

Five seconds later my spurs were given to me in the form of introductions to streetdom's elite. There were no looks of blankness now; I was accepted by heart.

"What's your other name, Johnny Gringo?"

"Piri."

"Okay, Pete, you wanna join my fellows?"

"Sure, why not?"

But I knew I had first joined their gang when I cool-looked them on moving day. *I was cool, man,* I thought. *I could've wasted Waneko any time. I'm good, I'm damned good, pure* corazón. *Viva me!* Shit, I had been scared, but that was over. I was in; it was *my* block now.

Not that I could relax. In Harlem you always lived on the edge of losing rep. All it takes is a one-time loss of heart.

Sometimes, the shit ran smooth until something just had to happen. Then we busted out. Like the time I was leaning against the banister of my stoop, together with Little Louie, Waneko, Indio, and the rest of the guys, and little Crip, small, dark and crippled from birth, came tearing down the block. Crip never ran if he could walk, so we knew there was some kind of trouble. We had been bragging about our greatness in rumbles and love, half truths, half lies. We stopped short and waited cool-like for little Crip to set us straight on what was happening.

"Oh, them lousy motherfuckers, they almost keeled me," he whined.

"Cool it, man," Waneko said, "what happened?"

"I wasn't doin' nothing, just walking through the fuckin' Jolly Rogers' territory," Crip said. "I met a couple of their broads, so friendly-like, I felt one's *culo* and asked, 'How about a lay?' Imagine, just for that she started yelling for her boys." Crip acted out his narrow escape. We nodded in unimpressed sympathy because there wasn't a mark on him. A stomping don't leave you in walking condition, much less able to run. But he was one of our boys and hadda be backed up. We all looked to Waneko, who was our president. "How about it, war counselor?" he asked me.

We were ready to fight. "We're down," I said softly, "an' the shit's on."

That night we set a meet with the Jolly Rogers. We put on our jackets with our club name, "TNT's." Waneko and I met Picao, Macho, and Cuchee of the Jolly Rogers under the Park Avenue bridge at 104th Street. This was the line between their block and ours. They were Puerto Ricans just like we were, but this didn't mean shit, under our need to keep our reps.

"How's it going to be?" I asked Macho.

Picao, who I dug as no heart, squawked out, "Sticks, shanks, zips—you call it."

I looked at him shittily and said, "Yeah, like I figured, you ain't got no heart for dealing on fists alone."

Macho, their president, jumped stink and said, "Time man, we got heart, we deal with our *manos*. Wanna meet here ten tomorrow night?"

"Ten guys each is okay?"

"That's cool," Macho said and turned away with his boys. The next night we got our boys together. They were all there with one exception— Crip. He sent word that he couldn't make our little 10 p.m. get-together. His sister, skinny Lena, was having a birthday party. We took turns sounding his mother for giving birth to a *maricón* like him.

Our strategy was simple. We'd meet in the Park Avenue tunnel and each gang would fight with its back to its own block to kill any chance of getting sapped from behind. Our debs sat on the stoops watching for the fuzz or for any wrong shit from the Jolly Rogers.

It got to 10 p.m. and we dug the Jolly Rogers coming under the Park Avenue tunnel. We walked that way too. Macho had heart; he didn't wait for us in the tunnel; he came with his boys right into our block. My guts got tight, as always before a rumble, and I felt my breath come in short spurts. I had wrapped handkerchiefs around each hand to keep my knuckles from getting cut on any Jolly Roger's teeth. We began to pair off. I saw Giant, a big, ugly Jolly Roger, looking me over.

"Deal, motherfucker," I screamed at him.

He was willing like mad. I felt his fist fuck up my shoulder. I was glad 'cause it cooled away my tight guts. I side-slipped and banged my fist in his guts and missed getting my jaw busted by an inch. I came back with two shots to his guts and got shook up by a blast on the side of my head that set my eyeballs afire. I closed on him and held on, hearing the noise of pains and punches. Some sounded like slaps, others hurt dully. I pushed my head into Giant's jaw. He blinked and swung hard, catching my nose. I felt it running. I didn't have a cold, so it had to be blood. I sniffed back hard and drove rights and lefts and busted Giant's lip open. Now he was bleeding too. *Chevere.*

Everybody was dealing hard. Somebody got in between me and Giant. It was Waneko, and he began dealing with Giant. I took over with the Jolly Roger he'd been punching it out with. It was Picao. He had been fighting all along—not too hard, I suspected. I got most happy. I'd been aching to chill that *maricón*. He didn't back down and we just stood there and threw punches at each other. I felt hurt a couple of times, but I wanted to put him out so bad, I didn't give a fuck about getting hurt. And then it happened—I caught Picao on his chin with an uppercut and he went sliding on his ass and just lay there.

I felt king-shit high and I wanted to fight anybody. I had the fever. I started for Giant, who was getting wasted by Waneko, when one of our debs opened up her mouth like an air-raid siren. "Look out, ya gonna get japped," she shouted.

We saw more Rogers coming from Madison Avenue. They were yelling their asses off and waiving stickball bats.

"Make it," Waneko shouted. "Them *cabrones* wanna make a massacre!"

Everybody stopped fighting and both gangs looked at that wasting party tearing up the street toward us. We started cutting out and some of the Rogers tried grabbing on to some of us. Waneko pulled out a blade and started slashing out at any J.R. he could get to. I tore my hand into my back pocket and came out with my garbage-can-handle brass knucks and hit out at a cat who was holding on to one of my boys. He grabbed at a broken nose and went wailing through the tunnel.

We split, everybody making it up some building. I felt bad those *cabrones* had made us split, but I kept running. I made it to number 109 and loped up the stairs. "*Adiós*, motherfuckers," I yelled over my shoulder. "You *cabrones* ain't got no heart!" I crashed through my apartment door with thanks that Momma had left it open, 'cause two or three Jolly Rogers were beating the air inches behind me with stick-ball bats.

"*Qué pasa?*" yelled Momma.

The Jolly Rogers outside were beating their stickball bats on the door for me to come out if I had any heart. I hollered to them, "I'm coming out right now, you motherfuckers, with my fucking piece!" I didn't have one, but I felt good-o satisfaction at hearing the cattle stampede down the stairs.

"What happened, *muchacho?*" Momma asked, in a shook-up voice.

I laughed. "Nothing, Moms, we was just playing ring-a-livio."

"What about your nose, it got blood on it," said Sis.

I looked bad at her. "Bumped it," I said, then turning to Momma, I asked, "Say, Moms, what's for dinner? Je-sus, I'm starvin'."

from Land of Opportunity
by William M. Adler

After fleeing the poverty of rural Arkansas, brothers Billy Joe and Larry "Marlow" Chambers made fortunes during the 1980s selling crack on the streets of Detroit . William M. Adler's 1995 book about the Chambers family describes an operation that combined aspects of a well-run business and a vicious street gang.

On the first Sunday of 1986, *The Detroit News* discovered crack. Its front-page story began:

A superpotent, highly addictive—and medically dangerous—new form of cocaine has begun turning up in Metro Detroit in a big way.

Called "crack," it comes in small chunks rather than a powder. It is sometimes referred to as a "fast food" drug because it is made on short order and priced to appeal to teen-agers.

"We started getting an increasing volume of calls about crack on the hot line about four months ago," Dr. Arnold Washton, research director of the nationwide 800-COCAINE help line, said last week. "The three areas we're getting the most calls from are New York, Los Angeles and Detroit.

"Of late, the volume of calls from Detroit is nearly that
of New York."

Headlined "ADDICTIVE NEW 'CRACK' COCAINE SWEEPS DETROIT," the story
was the first in either of the city's daily newspapers to mention crack.
By then crack was hardly news to most Detroiters; for more than a year
the trade had dominated the economy of the east side. By early 1986,
Billy and Larry had already developed into something like folk
heroes—the Lee Iacoccas of the crack business—for street kids and
even for some adults. Between them, they employed scores of east-side
residents, with separate payrolls approaching a hundred thousand dollars a week. In front of one woman's house one afternoon, an eight-
year-old and a nine-year-old were playing "BJ and Larry." "I'm Larry,"
declared the younger. "No you're not," the older kid said. "You're BJ
and *I'm* Larry."

By early 1986, Larry operated a handful of crack houses in the neighborhood. He wanted to expand, but he believed that to open individual
houses scattered around the east side could become an organizational
nightmare. He was searching for a single, large outlet that could serve as
his flagship; by the beginning of 1986 he had found it.

The prewar building at 1350 East Grand Boulevard was a handsome
but tired red brick structure. Its name, The Broadmoor, was carved in
granite above the arched entrance. The elevator no longer worked, the
hallways were narrow, dark, and grimy, the heating fickle. The building
was horseshoe-shaped and four stories high. It was managed by a man
who Larry believed would likely be receptive to payoffs—the man's
sister dated one of Larry's lieutenants. An absentee landlord owned the
building, and commandeering it would not require extensive tenant
displacement: of its fifty-two apartments, all but a half dozen or so
were vacant.

The Broadmoor was decades past its prime. From the antiquated
building, though, which became known simply as "The Boulevard,"
Larry and his lieutenants were constructing a state-of-the-art crack
empire so chillingly efficient it was as if they were stealing chapters

from the textbook of business culture. "They were skilled entrepreneurs; they had every major business technique going for them," says William R. Coonce, the chief of the U.S. Drug Enforcement Administration in Detroit.

Sometime around the appearance of the first crack headline, the building manager spied a suspicious fellow in the lobby. "He wasn't dressed too clean and was kind of wild-looking," the manager, a man named David Havard, would later recall. Havard asked him what he was doing there; the reply was unsatisfactory. "I knew he was lying and I told him to get the hell out."

The next day the man returned with two others: Larry Chambers and Roderick Byrd, who was working as a location scout for Larry. Byrd, a college-educated Detroit native, dated Havard's sister; he had heard about the building from her. Havard answered the knock at the door. "We are working out of your building and we would like to hire your services so we won't have no trouble with the police and you," one of the three—Havard does not recall which—told Havard. Larry and his cohorts had just opened a "dime house"—ten-dollar rocks— in Apartment 101, down the hall from the manager's apartment.

As building manager, the thirty-six-year-old Havard earned two hundred and fifty dollars a week, plus free rent and telephone service. He had lived at The Boulevard since 1982, when he followed a girlfriend there. At the time, the building retained some luster. Its marble-tiled lobby still shone under fluorescent lights, the grounds were well kept, and fully half the units were occupied. There was little trouble even from the one tenant who sold drugs—heroin—from his second-floor apartment.

Havard had become the building's handyman shortly after he moved in. He was receiving General Assistance, state welfare payments for able-bodied adults, and needed additional off-the-books income. He painted apartments, changed the locks, shored up plumbing and wiring. He did good work, and the owner came to depend on him; soon he was promoted to building manager.

Havard had learned general maintenance skills from his father, a Ford worker. He began life on the west side of Detroit, but at the age of six or seven left for California with his mother following his parents' divorce. She died when he was eleven and his father reclaimed him and his three siblings, bringing them back to Detroit. David attended school through the ninth grade and had done handyman work ever since. He has the large, meaty hands of a plumber, a stubbly black-and-white beard, a stooped gait, and a mouth mostly devoid of teeth.

Havard quickly agreed to Larry's offer of a six-hundred-dollar weekly starting salary in exchange for allowing Larry continued use of Apartment 101 and, as business warranted, the use of additional apartments. "They told me all I needed to do was keep the building quiet, keep the riffraff out, and occasional other things like putting up gates and being on call for quick repairs or maintenance." After a couple of months on the job, Havard says, Larry "kicked me up to a thousand a week."

Two or three more months went by. One day Larry knocked again on Havard's door. It was opened by a short heavyset white woman, Havard's girlfriend. Patricia Middleton, who was thirty, had lived at The Boulevard since November of 1984, seven months after arriving in Detroit from a small town in southwestern Michigan. She and Havard struck up a romance (he and his previous girlfriend had since parted company), and in the spring of 1985, in April or early May, she moved into his rent-free apartment.

Pat Middleton was born in Indiana but raised across the state line on a farm in New Buffalo, Michigan, a town of twenty-eight hundred people near the Indiana border and the southernmost shores of Lake Michigan. Her parents divorced when she was five. She lived with her mother, who cleaned trailer homes and collected welfare to support Pat and four other children.

From an early age Pat figured she could do as well on her own. She ran away frequently, the last time to Indiana to be with a boyfriend. She was sixteen. When her mother finally found her, she placed Pat in a foster home. At seventeen she married. By the time she was twenty she had three children. By then, though, her marriage was over. Her husband was abusive, she says, and she was in no position to provide care for her children; she surrendered custody to a foster home and divorced her husband.

It was the summer of 1975. Pat Middleton was free of familial obligation, ready for a fresh start. One night she attended a traveling carnival. On a whim she asked for a job. She was hired to sell tickets and spent the summer on the road. She settled in the fall back in southwestern Michigan, in Paw Paw, where she met a man named Tom Middleton and "married his ugly butt." They stayed together nearly five years before she called it quits. "I got fed up and moved to Detroit," she says. "I had lived in small towns all my life and I wanted a big town I could get lost in."

She found an apartment on the city's west side and a job on the east side, as a waitress at a Big Boy restaurant on Jefferson Avenue at East Grand Boulevard. It made more sense, though, to live nearer her job. Her daily bus rode past the stately building at 1350 East Grand Boulevard. The afternoon she noticed the sign advertising a move-in special— 1ST MO. RENT FREE, $200/1-BR—she hopped off the bus, knocked on the manager's door, and signed a lease for a first-floor apartment. Half a year later, she moved in with the manager, David Havard.

It was July of 1986 when Pat Middleton opened the door to her apartment to find Larry Chambers standing there. Larry asked if Havard was home. "I said no and he said he wanted to talk to me," she recalls. "He asked me if I wanted to make some money." Larry told her he would pay her eight hundred dollars a week to pick up money from four other houses he operated in the neighborhood. Middleton told him no, that she "didn't think I wanted to get involved." In that case, she says Larry told her, he would "arrange for David to have an accident." Middleton changed her mind.

Within the week, Middleton went to work as a courier. Between two and four times a week, she would pick up the money—always folded once and wrapped in rubber bands in hundred-dollar bundles and packaged in brown paper bags—from houses on Field, Canton, and Helen streets, and from a four-family flat down East Grand Boulevard. She aroused no suspicion: "I was white and chunky," she says. "I wore my Big Boy uniform and drove my AMC Concord. Police left me alone." On her first outing, Middleton picked up forty or fifty thousand dollars. On weekends, she picked up as much as two hundred thousand. She was assigned a route: "I would leave from 1350 and go to the other boulevard [house] and then I would go to Field and over on Helen and Canton." The workers at those locations would put the money in small paper bags and mark their house on the bags. She in turn placed those bags in a larger, brown grocery bag and put them in the trunk of the Concord. After her final stop, she would meet Larry at a predetermined drop-off point. Sometimes it would be a parking lot across from Chene Park, off Jefferson, or at any of a number of motels along Jefferson.

Two to three weeks after Apartment 101 was in business, Larry opened apartments on The Boulevard's upper three floors as well. In all, he opened outlets in five apartments: one on the first floor, two on the second, and one on the third and fourth floors. Each outlet offered a different-sized rock; three-dollar rocks were available on the first floor; five- and eight-dollar rocks from the second-floor units; ten-dollar rocks on the third; and twenty-dollar "boulders" on the fourth. (Later, the fourth-floor house was closed and moved down a flight; the climb was too much and Larry wanted an entire floor "clean" of crack to which his staff could flee if a raid occurred.)

From the beginning, the business was an unqualified success, raking in some sixty-five thousand dollars every weekday and close to a hundred thousand on weekend days. Larry borrowed some of Billy's successful marketing tools. He hired neighborhood kids to distribute handwritten coupons and fliers: BUY ONE, GET ONE FREE, or BUY NINE AND GET TENTH FREE. And he developed a customer incentive program to spur sales. He awarded to regulars who recruited a first-time buyer an amount of crack equal to the new customer's purchase.

The building operated around the clock, likely humming at any hour. During the week, business was generally slow in the morning. Traffic picked up around noon and stayed steady until about six p.m. It slackened until one a.m., when the bar closings brought a surge of customers for the next three hours or so.

On Fridays through early Sunday mornings, the place positively roared. "It was like a merry-go-round on the weekends; it was jammed all the time," says Pat Middleton. "On Fridays, there was probably three hundred or four hundred people that would come there. A lot of it was repeat, the same people, they would go off and come back and go off and come back." One regular customer always arrived in a stretch limousine. He would send his driver in to buy five hundred dollars worth at a time. Another was a bus driver who would pull over and run in; there were doctors, a lawyer, and other professionals. And there were lots of hard-luck customers: a pregnant teenager (of whom David Havard says "I'd kick her out whenever I saw her"); people with no money who were so desperate for their next hit they would seek to barter anything and everything they had. "Men would come in with clothes from their girlfriends or wives, or gold or diamonds or furniture, appliances, VCRs, cars—*anything*," recalls Havard.

Larry encouraged barter. Anything of value, no matter how harmful the consequences for his vulnerable patrons, he considered legal tender. He established these rates: a new nineteen-inch color television was worth five five-dollar rocks; a handgun no more than six rocks; an Uzi no more than twenty rocks; a black-and-white TV one or two rocks. The value of jewelry varied. "One guy gave me a almost new nineteen-inch color TV for three dime bags," Havard says. Other men would offer sex with their teenage daughters in exchange for rocks. Still another died of an overdose in the building. Havard says he did "everything I could to wake him up: put ice under his genitals, slapped him." A crew disposed of the body in a Dumpster.

Unparalleled customer service was a point of pride with Larry. When customers who did not wish to defer their pleasure requested a "smokehouse"—an on-site facility to sample their purchases—he added one on the first floor. (Among the habitués was Danny Chambers. Although Larry tried to keep his brother out, Danny would often linger for three or four days in the smokehouse.) He furnished it with a couch, coffee tables, and a radio. And he beneficently dispensed crack pipes and shots of rum on the house. Then, in response to male customers' demands for in-house sex and to female customers who craved crack but had no money, Larry converted an apartment to a brothel, or "pussy house." The apartment was spartan: a bed frame, box springs, and mattress.

"Didn't no matter if it was noon or midnight," says Billy, who visited The Boulevard but owned no part of the business. "You could get dope, liquor, pussy, and never leave. We used to joke about doing TV commercials. Larry wanted to call it Marlow's One-Stop."

A customer who approached the iron gate of The Boulevard was greeted by an Uzi-toting doorman; only he could unlock the gate's deadbolt. Larry wanted his doormen to project warmth, and to treat the customer, no matter how pathetic, with respect. As he explained to one doorman: "When a crackhead comes to you and his woman is on his back, his babies don't have no Pampers, he hasn't eaten in two days, and he's about to spend his last five dollars on crack, you have to make him feel good about spending his money."

The customer was asked what size unit he wished to purchase. Like a ticket-taker at the multiplex cinema, the doorman would direct the customer accordingly: *"Dime rock? Third floor, first gate." "Nick? Right around the corner."* Once at the proper "house," the customer would slip his money through the gate to one of the two sellers. Like a waiter wheeling a sample dessert tray, the seller would produce a silvery saucer with representative rocks. Upon making his or her selection, the customer would be escorted by an armed guard to the exit or to one of the building's other houses. (Some customers were left to find their own way. They often mistook Pat Middleton and David Havard's barred first-floor residence for a crack house. Eventually, Havard tacked up a sign on the door: THIS IS THE MANAGER'S APARTMENT, THIS IS NO DOPE HOUSE.)

There were staircases at both ends of the lobby. Posted on the landings between the first and second floor at both ends were "watchouts." Peering out the windows, they could observe the side streets, as well as the front and back of the building. Their assignment was to keep an eye out for police and "stick-up guys." There were also watchouts stationed on the nearby street corners. All were equipped with walkie-talkies. And when Larry himself showed up, his street crew served as Larry's security detail: they "swept the block" before he got out of his car. "Made sure it was cool," says a doorman, "like he was J. Edgar Hoover."

Larry says the police were not difficult to spot. "Everyone knew they only had two raid vans, a blue and a brown one. Even the little kids on the street knew it: 'Here come the van! Here come the van!' "

Larry put his crew through mock raid practices, like fire drills or the old nuclear-preparedness duck-and-cover drills in school. He assigned roles to each of his workers; Larry usually reserved for himself the part of the bad cop. "Thing is," says a doorman called Pork Chop, "he was meaner than the polices. He had one of them big black [flash]lights like they bust you face with. He used to get off tellin' you 'Assume the position' and TV shit like that."

In the event of an actual raid, watch-outs were taught to first alert the rest of the staff and to hide all crack and firearms in the hallways or the elevator shaft, and then to shepherd everyone to the fourth floor, where no business was conducted. This was done because Larry knew if the police found the dope or guns, they could not charge anyone with possession; the goods were stashed in a common area of the building rather than on an individual's person. After the raid, the watch-outs would then retrieve the goods.

Police raided The Boulevard for the first time about two months after it opened under Larry's management. David Havard had just walked out of the smokehouse when he heard the police yell "RAID!" He ran back in. When the door opened the first thing he saw was a shotgun. He was led to the hallway and instructed to lie on the floor, belly-up, hands outstretched. While he answered questions about where he lived and worked, why he was there, who worked for whom, and so forth, what struck him was not fear of arrest, but barely concealed laughter. All around him, practically stepping over him as if he were a drunk splayed on the sidewalk, was a steady stream of customers. Outside the building was a fleet of marked police cars; inside, Havard says, "looked like a schoolhouse, there were so many people in there."

Larry was not there, but he received word immediately via beeper. "We practiced what to do," Larry says. "A watch-out beeped [my number] and then hit 1350 (the building's street number) and then 11, the code for a raid, and I knew without even having to talk to anyone what was going down. And so I'd beep my van crew." The crew, with a fully equipped van, was always on call. Larry: "They'd pull up to the house, make sure the cops were gone, and put up new gates, clean up the place, do whatever repairs were necessary to open the place back up as quick as possible." Usually within an hour of a raid, the crew had the building reopened. After the first raid, Larry instituted combat pay for anyone caught in subsequent raids.

The jobs required sustained concentration and discipline. Employees worked twelve-hour shifts. There were normally about fourteen workers per shift: two sellers in each of the four apartments, a doorman, a couple of guards, and two to four watch-outs. On busy weekends and holidays, Larry summoned additional help. There were no breaks, but couriers delivered fast food regularly, usually from the nearby McDonald's. Neither sleeping nor drinking was permitted on the job. Larry frequently dropped by in the middle of the night to assure himself that the crew was alert and sober.

Larry rewarded the staff for the hard work. Watch-outs, many of whom were no older than fourteen or fifteen, were at the bottom of the pecking order. Even so, their entry-level jobs were critical to the unimpeded flow of commerce, and they were paid well: three hundred dollars a week. Doormen and guards earned between four and six hundred a week, and the sellers, cooped up behind locked gates, made eight hundred a week. Workers were penalized fifty dollars weekly if they were late for a shift; a second late arrival cost a week's pay. Larry's lieutenants, like Rod Byrd, who were in charge when Larry was elsewhere, received two thousand dollars weekly. Bonuses were paid to any employee who remained in the building for an entire pay period—a week.

For the employees who lived virtually in the streets anyway, the extra compensation was easy money. In Patricia Middleton they had a surrogate mother, a "den mother anyway," as she puts it. Middleton saw to it that they had enough to eat and drink, and that they wore clean clothes. "I bought trunk loads of food; I fed the kids in my apartment," she says. "Chicken, pork chops, they ate well. Marlow gave me five hundred dollars to put a second fridge in. I kept it full of pop for the kids." On laundry day, every employee would stuff his dirty clothes in a duffel bag. One worker would carry the bags out to Middleton's car, another would bring them in. And Middleton acted as the in-house banker, storing cash for anyone who asked in a lockbox in her apartment.

In addition to those who worked in Larry's crack houses, he employed a "support staff" that numbered as high as twenty-five. Some of the positions were typical of any sizable crack distributor: "cooks" to process the cocaine powder into crack and "cut-up girls" (or, as the police would come to call them, "rockettes") to carve the crack into retail-size units.

But Larry went a step further than most dealers, his brother Billy included. He recognized the need to monitor developments in the outside world that could affect his livelihood. He hired one young woman named "Baby Godmother" whose sole responsibility was to read the *Free Press* and the *News* every day for reports of drug-related indictments, arrests, murders, and so forth. She briefed Larry every afternoon, but none too thoroughly. "She was no good reader," Larry says with a laugh. And he hired "female spies" to "cozy up" to other dealers. "I had their hair dipped professionally," Larry says, "dressed them real well. I wanted to know where they [rival dealers] was opening up, who was working for them, and did they have any spies in my organization." And he hired "courtroom watchers"—two women who attended the trials of other dealers. Larry received daily briefings with particular attention paid to the testimony of government informants.

He also initiated a "job hotline," which amounted to authorizing certain employees to beep him with a special code amended for job inquiries. Larry: "Someone would call and say, 'Hey, I'm ready to work again,' and if, let's say, the house on Helen was just hit, I'd say, 'Well, the workers over there just went to jail and we have an opening there. Do you want it? How soon can you be there?' "

Saturday was payday at The Boulevard. Workers lined up in the hallway outside the manager's apartment. Inside, at the kitchen table, sat Larry's girlfriend, Belinda Lumpkin, and another man named Larry, who served as Belinda's bodyguard. Belinda was known as the "paymaster." She would arrive with an oversized leather briefcase, the kind with folding flaps trial lawyers favor. In it was the cash for the week's payroll, which usually amounted to around fifty thousand dollars, a ledger book, and photo albums containing a Polaroid shot of every employee. On the bottom border of each picture was the employee's name and work site: "Stacy, 1350." By the time Belinda was ready, there would be thirty or forty young men in line, sometimes as many as sixty. They came not only from The Boulevard but from the four other houses in the neighborhood Larry operated—the payroll was centralized.

The process took a couple of hours. Patricia Middleton stood at the door and let in the workers one at a time. The kids who worked at The Boulevard were paid first. "In-house first!" Middleton would bellow. She shut the door behind each one and escorted him into the kitchen. Belinda consulted her record, counted out loud the money, and handed it to Larry. Larry counted it and paid the worker. He always told each employee to count it then and there. One day a worker claimed he received less than he was entitled to. "You shorted me," he told Belinda. "No, we didn't short you," Belinda replied, noting that he was an hour and a half tardy one day. "You got deducted for being late."

Inevitably there were other employee-relations conflicts. Once a young man pushed a much smaller boy out of the pay line. Middleton told him to "knock it off."

"Fuck you, you fat white bitch," he retorted. Rod Byrd, Larry's chief of staff, handled the incident with dispatch. "Go on home," he told the aggressor. "You're not getting paid this week."

Conflicts were not always resolved peaceably. Toward the end of June of 1986, one foolhardy worker named Keith sought to capitalize on the heavy traffic in The Boulevard by establishing his own, unaffiliated sales outlet on the third floor. Larry was not keen on the competition. "This was a guy I tried to help," Larry recalls. Keith was in his early to middle twenties, about five feet six, and wore his hair in a Jheri curl. "He was homeless and broke and I gave him a job and a place to live right there at 1350. And he starts rolling right out of my place. I warned him three times, but he wouldn't stop."

They were on the third floor one night when the last of a series of heated arguments boiled over. Larry cornered Keith against the window at the end of a hallway. He gave Keith a choice: jump or be pushed. Keith froze; Larry grabbed him and shoved him through the windowpane. Keith was fortunate; it had poured the previous night and he landed on soggy grass. After a minute or so, he picked himself up and limped away. Larry never saw him again.

Larry's reputation for offering high-quality crack was as important to him as, say, Frank Perdue's reputation for selling tender chickens. Quality control was everything. Once a young employee violated his customers' trust by selling soap chunks in place of crack. Larry expressed his displeasure with a public flogging. He had arrived at the building that day dressed in what were commonly referred to as his "ass-kicking clothes": blue jeans, gym shoes, and a long overcoat; in the coat he hid a pistol. He announced that all his workers should follow him. He headed up the stairs, pausing near the well to pick up a broken chair in the lobby. Pat Middleton saw that he was angry and turned back toward her apartment. "No. *Everybody*," he barked.

Larry led the group to a second-floor apartment where the boy was working. Larry took a leg off the chair and slugged the boy with it eight or ten times, striking him in the back, legs, and shoulders. The boy was screaming, begging Larry to stop. Larry responded, "That'll teach all of you and make you understand that no one will ever sell soap for crack."

Stories of Larry's ruthlessness were legend—and countless. A sampling: "Once he told a girl 'no' about something she asked him for," says David Havard. "She asked him again, and he knocked her out. Punched her right in the jaw."

"I once saw him almost kill this guy they call Shake N Bake," says a young woman who did not want her name used; she worked for Larry as a cut-up girl. "The guy insulted Marlow—called him a 'bitch'—and Marlow told his boys to beat him up. They used bats, two-by-fours, busted bottles over his head." She adds: "Another time he choked this girl off her feet." Tiger Alexander (who worked variously for both Larry and Billy): "He [Larry] used to carry a mini-steel baseball bat, and if you came up ten dollars short, he'd hit you ten times."

Larry did not always mete out the discipline himself. He employed a team of enforcers, the Wrecking Crew, when additional muscle was necessary or he simply could not be present for the prescribed beating. Terry Colbert, the fellow whose father first put Billy Joe in business, says a man who sold for Larry out of a house on Montclair Street once "came up a hundred dollars short. . . . After Marlow checked it out, he left, and five minutes later three cars pull up and beat up the guy pretty bad. His head was all busted, you know, his brain was almost about to come out of his head and they took him out in the back of the alley, threw him by a Dumpster, and just left him there." Colbert continues: "I didn't see him die, but I heard that he was dead."

At The Boulevard one day, a member of the Wrecking Crew asked David Havard if he could borrow the baseball bat Havard kept in his apartment. He explained that a salesman on the third floor was skimming money. The Wrecking Crew member went upstairs, crushed the young man's skull, walked him to a nearby store, and called an ambulance. On another occasion, Havard says he saved the life of a young woman who had sold as crack a bogus substance—and kept the cocaine for resale elsewhere. He says the Wrecking Crew had her tied up in the lobby when he walked in. He pleaded for her life. "I told them, 'Look, instead of killing her, do something for yourselves. Take her in the pussy house and make her give all of you head.' "

Viciousness came naturally to Larry, but he was as capable of an impulsive flicker of charm as he was a flash of anger. Unlike Billy, though, whose unrestrained ardor for young women resulted in multiple simultaneous short- and long-term couplings, Larry was less likely to act on his romantic impulses. (Though of course he did so when courting Belinda Lumpkin.) Instead, his charm was more likely to surface when women interested him as potential employees.

One afternoon in August of 1986, fourteen-year-old Cindy Davis was clowning around with some girlfriends down the block from her family's Dickerson Street home when Larry drove by. He was with a friend named William (Jack) Jackson. "He"—Larry—"asked us do we want to make a video," Cindy recalls. "They seemed like nice guys and we didn't have anything better to do so we got in their car and they took us to Knodell"—Larry's initial base of operations.

"A guy was there they call Buzz. He told us, 'If y'all cut this stuff up, you'll get some money.' I said, 'How much?' He told us a hundred each.

"So we stayed there, I'll say less than a hour, and they took us around to [the house on] Buffalo. And we got there and started dancing and made videos of us dancing. It was fun because everyone just sat around and tripping out. When they brought us home, they asked us did we want to keep on and did we know anyone else who could help out."

Later that afternoon, Cindy's sister Janice was killing time at home. Her summer vacation was at an end and in a few days the seventeen-year-old would be heading back to Southeastern High for her senior year. Cindy burst through the door waving a fistful of cash. "I made a hundred dollars! All I had to do was cut up some coke and put it in a few bags, cut up a few ounces, and they gave me a hundred dollars!"

"Who?"

"I don't even know their names," Cindy replied. "But they need some more cutters. Would you want to go with me?"

Around four the next afternoon, Janice accompanied Cindy and two of their friends back to Buffalo Street to a two-story house with a basement. It turned out that one of the guys who had cruised by Dickerson Street lived there. His name was Marlow, they learned, and he shared the house with his girlfriend, Belinda. Through a side door by the driveway, the four young women went directly down to the basement. The furnishings were utilitarian: a couch, a television, and a glass table. Neither Larry nor Belinda was there, but "Jack" Jackson was seated on the couch with two other fellows. On the table were large rocks of crack cocaine.

"Hey, Jack," one of Cindy's friends said by way of introducing Janice, "we got you another worker."

"That's good. We got plenty to do today. We need twenty thousand dimes and ten thousand nickels." The girls explained to Janice the uncomplicated procedure. They gave her a supply of razor blades and five- and ten-dollar rock samples. "You roll your sleeves up. That's it. Start cutting. That's it," Janice says.

There was a little more to it. To ward off the chemical odor, the girls wore cloth "doctor masks" and to protect their fingers they wore Band-Aids or rubber thimbles. They were to count the rocks, put them in a plastic sandwich Baggie in quantities of a hundred or five hundred or a thousand, and indicate on a scrap of paper the amount therein. The Baggies were placed on the middle of the table and ultimately put in canvas bags—five thousand nickels or two thousand dimes to a bag.

Nothing was wasted. During the course of cutting thousands of rocks, there would accumulate a good amount of shavings. This excess was called "shake." At the end of the workday, says Cindy, "one girl would collect the shake and cook it up in a Vision pot with a little baking soda." Once it hardened, the girls cut that too. They worked four or five hours that afternoon and Jack gave them each a hundred dollars. "See you tomorrow," he told them as their cab arrived.

The girls returned the following day, and it was then that Janice met Larry. He came downstairs and pointed to one girl's rock pile. "Look at her, she is cutting boulders," Janice recalls Larry saying. He came over, picked up a rock, and trimmed it to his specifications. At the end of the second day, Jack told the girls, "I want y'all to start working and we will pay you by the week."

Janice says she never questioned the morality of working for a crack dealer. "I was thinking I always been broke, I always had to work." Janice had worked previously for minimum wage at a McDonald's and in the kitchen at Manoogian Mansion, the mayor's residence. "I was thinking about he [Larry] had some fast money. I don't have to work and I can still go to school and get my hair done. That's all I was thinking about."

Classes were starting, and to Janice and Cindy rock-cutting seemed the ideal after-school job. For three or four hours a weekday (and sometimes a full Saturday) they were to earn three hundred and fifty dollars a week, plus generous perks: cab fare when necessary, a meals stipend, a fifty-dollar bonus for each new worker recruited. (There were many bonuses paid. "Girls used to come up to us in school and get on their hands and knees and *beg* us to get them in," Cindy says.) Additionally, the boys in the crew were instructed to take the girls on shopping sprees at the mall from time to time. And to pay for their hair care.

Most days, the girls would go straight home after school and await a phone call from Jack. He "knew what time we got out of school," Janice says, "and most of the time, he made sure we got a way from school. And the boys would come pick us up and drop us off at home." Other days, if the girls knew the job site in advance, they would catch a cab to work directly from school. The cut house shifted with the ease of a floating crap game. It might be a duplex on Rosemary Street one day, an apartment at Newport and Forest the next, a house on Knodell or French Road off Gratiot the following. Why? "To be cautious," Janice explains. "Just in case somebody was wondering why is there a large amount of girls going in there all the time and coming back out." A place that had been a stash house one week before might now be a cut house. Or a former cut house might have been converted to a sell house. "We would never usually know where we were going," Cindy says. "We'd just go wherever."

The cut-up crew made Larry nervous. He could not keep a steady eye on them himself. He worried that the teenage girls would scare easily and snitch, or maybe they would steal and sell the rocks for themselves. He had no way of telling if a few rocks were missing from every key they cut. One day, convinced they were ripping him off, he ordered one shift of cut-up girls at the Knodell house to strip. "We was upstairs and he had 'em to take off everything but their bras and panties," says Tiger Alexander, who happened by at the time. "Then they go downstairs and work half naked. He made sure they wasn't gonna smuggle none out."

But even such drastic measures could not satisfy Larry; he wanted to bypass the cut-up girls completely. The challenge was to come up with a means to mass-produce crack cocaine—to cook and cut the rocks in one labor-saving procedure. Larry spent days experimenting in the kitchen of his Buffalo Street house—an inventor possessed. Finally he emerged with a prototype: a two-foot by two-foot Plexiglas sheet permeated with holes drilled precisely the circumference of a five-dollar rock. The idea was to pour the heated liquid crack mixture over the sheet, allow it to cool, and then punch the prefab rocks out of each hole. Unfortunately for Larry, the design was flawed; the liquid did not conform to the holes, it dripped through. "I never got around to perfecting it," Larry says, "but I was getting close. I even called the government about a patent."

Stuck for the time being (patent pending) with the cut-up girls, he issued them three principal rules: "Don't tell people where you work"; "Don't tell who you work for"; and, "Don't give out any phone numbers." If caught in a raid, the girls were instructed to "play dumb." "We would just say we don't know [who we worked for]," Janice says. "Big Man, give a name, Tony or whatever. That's who we were working for. This is our first time ever coming. We just came to make extra money or something."

Death in Venice
by Mike Sager

Gangs played a key role as dealers during the crack boom of the 1980s. But reporter Mike Sager discovered another side to the story when he hung out with one of the oldest gangs in Venice, California for this 1988 Rolling Stone article.

L il' Gato and Tequila are hanging with Yogi, all three sitting on his bed. The room is dark, narrow, smoky. A towel is jammed against the bottom of the door.

"I forgot to tell you," says Yogi, "Big Gato called."

"Yeah?" says Lil' Gato.

"He asked what have we done to pay back Culver City."

"Pay 'em back for what?"

"You know, man. The drive-by at the park. Those *vatos* who shot at us."

Lil' Gato chews his thumb. He thinks. The TV screen flickers, the radio plays rap, a table fan moves air back and forth. After a minute, he knocks his girl, Tequila, on the knee. "When this happen?" he asks.

Tequila's eyes pan slowly toward his face. She is wearing a necklace of hickeys, a black miniskirt, a pair of three-inch heels she bought two weeks ago on her fourteenth birthday. Her hair is shoulder length, crowned at the front with a stiff, thick pompadour four inches high, a

tiara of bangs combed skyward and encased in Aqua Net. She blinks.
She shrugs.

Lil' Gato chews his thumb some more. The skin at the tip, just below
the nail, is burned and crusty, a condition the homeboys call Bic thumb.
Like Yogi, he is nineteen. He is wearing a nylon sweat suit and high-top
Adidas. His hair is black, clipped short and oiled straight back from a
widow's peak. His lashes are long and curly, his eyes are bloodshot, a
front tooth is missing. He was arrested first when he was six, for stealing
a TV from his grammar school. Last year, he was arrested eleven times
for using heroin and two times for using PCP, a drug he likes because
"when you do it, it be hard for you to walk and think."

As days in the neighborhood go, this one started off pretty well. At
ten this morning, Lil' Gato and Tequila ran into a crack dealer they
know. He gave them some "love," free drugs, the dregs of last night's
stash: a couple of five- and ten-dollar rocks and a lot of crumbs. They
went immediately to Yogi's and smoked it all in fifteen minutes.

Now they need more.

Especially Lil' Gato. Sitting on the edge of the bed, Lil' Gato is a
ramrod. His mouth is pulled back in a tight grimace, and above his lip,
among the faint stirrings of a mustache, are little drops of sweat. His
teeth are clenched, and you can see the strain in the muscles of his jaw
and in the cords of his neck, upon which is tattooed, in big blue letters, the logo of his gang, V-13.

Lil' Gato plucks an ice cube from his glass. He holds it up, regards
it in the light, turns it over, then over again. "Wouldn't you like a rock
this size?" he says.

"Yea-ah!" says Yogi.

"What would you say this was, a fifty?"

"A righteous five-oh," says Yogi.

Lil' Gato loses himself in his daydream, and hope pops like a flash-
bulb in his eyes, and then the light recedes, and his attention drifts to
the carpet. There are lots of little white pieces of paper and lint and
cloth and cigarette ash down there. To him, each piece looks like a
rock. Could be a rock. He has an urge to reach down with his index

finger. He knows there are no rocks on the carpet; he's too methodical to have dropped anything, but it doesn't matter, because something strong makes him want to get down on his hands and knees on the filthy rug in the dark, narrow room and touch each little piece of paper and lint and cloth and ash and test its composition. There are no crumbs. He knows that, but it doesn't matter. Just a few minutes ago, he tried to smoke a sesame seed in a pipe made of aluminum foil.

"So what are we going to do about Culver City?" asks Yogi. "Big Gato say that if we down for the neighborhood, we got to pay them back."

Lil' Gato looks up from the floor. He's remembering something. The neighborhood. The gang. The tradition. He and Yogi are members of V-13, the Venice Gang, among the oldest of the 400 gangs in Los Angeles. Theirs is a gang with history. For more than thirty years, Chicano homeboys have claimed this neighborhood, one square mile of palm trees and poverty in the middle of Venice, California, a little piece of barrio in the heart of the California lifestyle.

Ten years ago, when Yogi and Lil' Gato were just coming up, war was raging in the neighborhood; V-13 was battling all the gangs that surrounded it. The Venice gang fought the Shoreline Crips, Santa Monica, Culver City, anyone, everyone. In March 1979, the *Los Angeles Times* devoted a special section to the unrest in Venice, or more specifically in Oakwood, as their barrio is officially named. DEATH, DAILY VIOLENCE BECOME WAY OF LIFE FOR NEIGHBORHOOD, said the lead headline, one of twelve screamers in the twelve-page pullout. The Los Angeles police department's now-famous CRASH unit (Community Resources Against Street Hoodlums) cut its teeth here, back when it numbered 21 instead of the present 143. The National Guard walked the streets for a period, too, and a whole generation of Venice homeboys went to jail, or became addicted to heroin, or died.

These days, Venice still gets its CRASH sweeps, low-key Tuesday- and Thursday-night affairs, and the pop of automatic-weapons fire is still part of the everyday soundtrack of squealing tires, cursing homeboys, laughing children, thumping rap. But aside from Popo, the homeboy who lost his cool during a burglary and slit the throat of L.A. city councilwoman Ruth Galanter, Venice hasn't been in the news at all.

South-central L.A. is where the action is now. There, black gangs like the Bloods and the Crips have begun a reign of entrepreneurial terror that has turned the L.A. gang culture inside out. For thirty years, the poor and the powerless of Southern California have banded together in gangs to fight for the safety of their neighborhoods, for some measure of self-respect. In those days, the Chicanos owned the streets of L.A., and gangs like Venice were strong and proud. Today, everything is different. Gangs are no longer about turf and respect. Instead, they are about drugs and money.

Last year, there were 387 reported gang killings in Los Angeles County, a good many of them in the district called South Central, sixty percent of them claiming the lives of innocent bystanders. This year, according to the L.A. County Sheriff's Department, that total could rise to as many as 450. Following the death last January of a twenty-seven-year-old woman who was caught in the cross fire of a gang fight outside a tony restaurant in Westwood Village, the L.A. County Board of Supervisors appropriated $1.5 million to halt the epidemic of gang violence. Since then, the police have been working overtime, battering doors, arresting hundreds, seizing ounce after ounce of crack. The press, for its part, has made sure the public has kept in step along the way, providing bang-bang footage from a war where the front lines are America's own streets.

Behind the lines of the drug war, in the Venice barrio, crack is doing to V-13 what the police and the National Guard and other gangs have been trying to do for years. If horrible can get worse, that is what has happened to Venice. Spend time there, and what you see is the real raw footage, the daily pictures of lives being burned through a tinfoil tube.

The drive-by happened two nights ago, on Tuesday, at the park.

Yogi and Lil' Gato and Tequila were there and so were their friends Wormy and Linda and a couple other *vatos* and *heinas*. They were kickin' it, hanging out on a field behind Broadway Elementary, in the middle of their neighborhood, on their own turf. Someone had bought a *pisto*, a bottle of Colt 45, and someone had *yeska*, Mexican pot. Everyone was shermed out, high on *frios*, which are menthol cigarettes dipped in a bottle of liquid PCP. Some of them were shermed worse than others, and three or four of them were prone. Yogi and Lil' Gato and Panther were taking turns crouching behind a wall, doing blasts, taking hits of crack.

Near midnight, Wormy had been smoking a *frio*, telling about the time, in jail, that he was stabbed in the head. After that, he began talking about his father, a white guy who is doing time in prison. When the *frio* was finished, he got quiet.

Then he went off. He smashed a bottle on the sidewalk, uttered incantations to the devil, danced around in the grass. Then he focused on the white guy who was with them. He stood over the guy and shook his fists and bellowed, "Prejudice!" over and over and over again. Then he got quiet.

All of a sudden, an old two-toned Chevy rattled out of the darkness toward the park. Shots. Six, seven, eight, nine, ten. Quick, loud pops from a .22-caliber semi. Bullets whizzed overhead. Yogi rolled on top of Linda. Tequila gasped and rolled on top of Lil' Gato. Everyone else hit the dirt.

Five seconds later it was over. They watched a single taillight recede from their territory.

"There go those motherfuckers from Culver City again!" said Wormy.

"Cheese eaters!" said Yogi.

"Uh-oh!" exclaimed Tequila, pointing across the field.

Big Gato. Approaching at a dead run. Gato is twenty-seven, an older homeboy, a leader. He's got a thick scar across his cheek, two bullet holes in his side, another in his shoulder. To this day, he carries a shotgun pellet in his penis. He calls it his Mexican Tickler. At the moment he's pissed.

"What the fuck was that, homes?" screamed Big Gato.

"Just some of those cheese eaters from Culver City," said Yogi.

"Those motherfuckers again?" screamed Big Gato. "They drivin' by your ass again? Why don't you do something? They disrespecting you, homes!"

Nobody said a word.

Gato shook his head, clenched his fists at his sides. Lately, he thinks, everything is fucked up in Venice, everything is changed. These younger homeboys know as well as he does that if someone disrespects you—if he calls you a name, if he mad-dogs you, if he owes you money, if he shoots at you, if he talks shit about your old lady, if he makes you angry about anything at all—there is only one thing you're supposed to do. You get your gun, you hunt him down, you cap him. Or, if you can't find him, you cap one of his homeboys. You don't drive by. That's for cheese eaters. That's something new. For years Venice and Culver City have been shooting each other, but it was always done face to face. Those have always been the rules: never do you shoot from a car, never do you shoot at a house, never do you jeopardize children, moms or dads. A few years ago, one of the Venice homeboys shot into a church and killed a mom and a child from Culver City. As soon as they heard, the Venice homeboys beat up the *vato*, banished him from the neighborhood.

Now Big Gato surveyed the youngsters before him. He spit on the ground. "Somebody better do something soon."

Since 1900, when "Venice of America" was built, complete with canals, as a sort of residential theme park by the beach, the Oakwood section has been poor and predominantly nonwhite, one of the few ghettos of its kind along the pricey Southern California coast.

By 1970, according to U.S.-census figures, Oakwood's population of 8,000 was forty-three percent black, thirty-three percent Latin and twenty-four percent white. By 1975, Latins were up to forty-six percent as workers from Mexico, both documented and illegal, began to swell across the border and into Venice, drawn north by the promise of good pay and plentiful jobs in restaurants and light industry. Today the population is about 9,000. Almost fifty percent is Chicano.

The neighborhood claimed by V-13 is a ramshackle collection of bungalows with front and back yards, most with several big American cars, in various states of repair, in the driveway, and maybe an old stove dumped around the side, and walls covered with graffiti, the stylized markings of the gang and the male occupants of the house.

The insides of the houses are tidy, the furnishings cheap but clean. The TV is always on. Horror, action, gang movies play on the VCR. Usually a house has a big living room with lots of sofas and chairs, and a kitchen near that, and an iron skillet of beans on the stove, some tortillas on the table. Every other room, including the back porch, is used as a bedroom. Typically, four or five generations of relatives live in one house. Great-grandma's daughter and her daughter will share one bedroom. Grandma and an orphan great-niece will share another. A high-ranking daughter—the one with the best job—will have a room to herself. A young couple will also have a room. If they have a small child, the child will sleep with the ranking female, usually his grandma, who is usually a woman of about thirty-four. The females of the clan share an elaborate network of responsibilities. Everyone cooks, cleans, takes care of the kids. Young couples have the fewest responsibilities. They are encouraged to sleep alone, to sleep late, to make more kids.

Inside the house the women run things. Grandma or Great-grandma holds the lease and heads the house, and all the women work, many off the books so they can still collect from the government. Because the homeboys live at the pleasure of their wife or girlfriend's mother or grandmother and because many have no job and no intention of getting one, they are, in the sense of family ranking, pretty low in the pecking order. They do as they're told and are treated not so differently from the children.

Maybe this is why honor, their own particular brand of honor, has always been so important to the homeboys of Venice, and maybe this is why Big Gato is so upset about the lack of action on the part of the youngsters. Until recently, the homeboys never considered themselves a gang. Gang was something the police called them, something the newspapers called them. To themselves, they were, have always been, just a neighborhood: people who live in a place where they've lived all their lives, where a lot of their parents have lived all their lives. It doesn't matter that they own not an acre or a brick or a stucco wall. To some 4,100 Chicanos in Oakwood, this one square mile is their village, their home, their world, a society within society.

Here in the barrio, most everyone knows everyone, and they have known one another from the time they were born. So when somebody disrespects the neighborhood, when somebody from Culver City hits Lutie's mom on the head with a bumper jack or takes a knife to Beaver, or a bat to Tavo, or shoots Sleeper in the back, well, then the neighborhood is supposed to make sure that somebody from Culver City is bumper jacked or knifed or clubbed or shot. It is the job of the men to protect the honor of the neighborhood; they have to be, as they say, down for the 'hood.

Lately, the youngsters like Yogi and Lil' Gato have been forgetting this. Culver City—a longtime rival gang of Chicanos who live in the government projects nearby—has taken potshots at Venice two or three times in the last ten days. The youngsters have done nothing to pay them back.

If young homies like Yogi and Lil' Gato are going to claim the neighborhood, call themselves members, they must, as Big Gato says, be willing to bust a grape. That is the tradition. Back in the Seventies, there were no questions about what should be done.

"I remember the Venice from when I was gang banging," says Marianne Diaz, 29, an outreach worker with Community Youth Gang Services Project, a county- and city-funded program that works to defuse gang tensions and rehabilitate members. Diaz is a former member of Compadres, another Chicano gang in Los Angeles.

"Venice is such a big, old gang," she says. "Even back then they had, like, maybe a thousand homeboys. They were down. People respected them. Venice, Lennox, South Los and Eighteenth Street. Those were your four big gangs. Everyone has heard of Venice. I mean, if you got busted, you were gonna see twenty or thirty of them down in the pen, and they were the ones running things. Just about every older Venice homeboy I meet is a *veterano.*"

In Venice, just about every homeboy over fifteen has been to jail, which is why, perhaps, the chance for anything resembling a better life pretty much evaporates while he's still young. He figures the system is against him, and no one wants to give him a chance, and anyway, he might die tomorrow. Lil' Gato has done a total of four years so far; Yogi is about to go off and serve one. Oddly, many *veteranos* went to jail for crimes they didn't commit. As one has said, "I figured I'd already done about thirty or forty burglaries, so they had to get me for one of them, even if I didn't do it."

Being respected for going to jail is only one aspect of a curious system of beliefs in Venice. It seems as if the social stigma that most of America attaches to things like killing, going to jail and being addicted to drugs is not attached to such things here.

Take the Gonzales family. A Saturday night in the living room with popcorn and a video, the adults, the kids. Three people in the room are nodding out from heroin, somebody is smoking *yeska*, and the daughter's boyfriend and his friends are running in and out from the back yard, doing crack. Nobody pays much attention. Great-grandma looks up from the video. She laughs. "Oh, Thumper, I know you are doing that shit again," she says. "You are sprunger than a motherfucker! Oh, ho, ho, ho, ho!"

Of course, the homeboys' parents disapprove—they wring their hands, they wonder what they can do about their wayward kids. But in the end it seems their actions speak more of loyalty than of disapproval. Over the years, one twenty-seven-year-old homeboy's father, a $22,000-a-year city employee, has borrowed $40,000 to bail out and defend his son for various crimes. Another's father took a week off from work to help his son kick his heroin habit.

As a homeboy gets older, however, chances are he learns to like being out of jail. By the time he's twenty-five, if he lives that long, he's slowed down considerably. Some homeboys get jobs—in city sanitation, city maintenance, city deliveries, the best shots for ex-cons. Almost all have children, and they value the lives they've created, so they're not going to go shoot anyone unless they really get mad.

So now it's up to the younger homeboys. Times being what they are—with gang membership in L.A. County estimated at 70,000, with gangs of Samoans and Asians and blacks and whites and peewees and wanna-bes and never-bes running around the streets packing semiautomatic weapons—the younger homeboys have a big load on their shoulders. They haven't been carrying it.

As Diaz says, "The older homeboys are saying that the younger homeboys, all they care about is getting high. They're telling them, 'You like to wear Venice on your hat, you like to write your name on the walls and throw up a hand sign and get tattoos all over your body, but you won't bust a grape for nobody.'"

In the Forties and Fifties, says Diaz, the Chicano gangs that emerged in Southern California were "more or less derived from the Hispanic culture." Descendants of the Mexican *banditos*, and later of the zoot suiters, they inherited a macho culture dedicated to the preservation of territory and respect.

"Now," says Diaz, "things are changing. The rock cocaine has come in, and the blacks have taken over the gang thing. My partner—and he's black—says, 'My people took your idea and totally bent it and turned it around and took away any of the pride or the respect that was in a gang.' That's what he says. It's like before, in the old days, the leader of a gang was the homeboy who was downest. Now it's the homeboy who is richest. Other things are more important now than the 'hood. Getting high. Staying high. Getting that rock. That rock."

"Pssssst. Psssssst!"

Yogi starts. His eyes go wide. "What was that?" he whispers.

"What?" asks Lil' Gato.

"That noise," says Yogi. He eases off the narrow bed, stands, turns down the radio, switches off the fan, cocks an ear.

"What noise?" asks Lil' Gato.

"Pssssst! Hey! Yogi! Yogi! Let me in."

Yogi looks up, pulls back the curtain on the window over his bed. Outside there is daylight. The palms rustle in the breeze, and into the room come the scents of blue sea and pink hydrangeas, of refried beans and the exhaust from old Chevys. Panther is outside. He holds up a twenty-dollar rock the size of a marble.

Homeboys are all the time trooping into Yogi's, especially members of the Little Banditos, a twelve-member *cliqua* within the V-13 gang, which numbers roughly 300. A *cliqua* is an age-affinity group of homies who were all jumped into the larger gang at the same time. Currently in the 'hood, there are *cliquas*—of homeboys from their early teens to their late twenties—called the Banditos, the Little Banditos, the Tiny Banditos and the Midget Banditos. Likewise there are *cliquas* of Locos, Winos, Chucos and Dukes, all of them with subgroups ranging from Midgets to Bigs.

At any rate, when the Little Banditos come by, they check first with Yogi at the window, then go around the front and knock politely at the door, enter, exchange pleasantries with Yogi's mom and grandfather and little sister in the front room, then head down the hallway to the back room, where Yogi spends all his time. Yogi's mom thinks they're watching television back there, at least that's what Yogi says. In the last month, since he got his tax-refund check (he did some gardening for his uncle's company last summer), Yogi has not been away from his room for longer than an hour. That's what happens when you do crack, and at the moment, that is what Yogi and Panther and Lil' Gato are getting ready to do.

"I get first hit!" calls Yogi.

"No, I do!" says Panther. "It's my rock."

"Yeah," says Yogi, "but it's my room."

Panther hands over the rock, and Yogi breaks it with a razor blade, then puts a piece the size of a small aquarium stone into a tinfoil tube. He melts it a little with a Bic lighter, and then he blows out the air in his lungs and takes a blast. He inhales, holds, exhales. It is light clean smoke that smells like ether.

Yogi sits back, closes his eyes. Lil' Gato takes the pipe from his hand, then he and Panther begin to argue over who's next. Meanwhile, Yogi hears nothing. As soon as he exhales, there is an instant explosion of

pleasure inside his head, a rush, he says, that drills a hole from the top
of his scalp down to his groin and another between his ears, a kind of
ecstatic, physical, electric sign of the cross. He hears a buzz in his brain,
his sight blurs, he smiles.

Then, after a minute or so, the smile recedes, the feeling goes. He
begins thinking about the next hit.

The next hit. One more hit. That's all he can think about, all he
cares about. His teeth clench, his jaw muscles stand, his throat
tightens. Everything inside tightens. His dick shrivels, his veins con-
strict, his heart pounds. He chain-smokes cigarettes.

The problem is that with each subsequent hit the rush is less intense
but the desire is more intense. It's like a heroin habit, except you
acquire it instantly instead of over weeks or months. Heroin is a twice-
a-day obligation. You fix morning and night and forget about it. Crack,
though, is moment to moment. You hit it, rush, think about getting
more. It doesn't last that long. If you could wait thirty minutes and
forget about it, it could be all over; you'd be straight again. But you
can't not think about it. Your every thought is focused on the next hit,
and the next hit is never very good, but you don't care. You get, as they
say around here, *sprung*.

"So what are we gonna do?" asks Yogi, sitting on the bed in his narrow
room. It is just about noon, and the drugs are gone, again. Panther has
left to try and get some money some *vato* owes him.

"Let's go get a rock," says Lil' Gato.

"You got any money?"

"No."

"You do so."

"I do not."

"You do so."

The way you get a rock in the neighborhood is you walk out of your
house, turn left or right. Day or night, you can buy rock cocaine from
men or women, boys or girls, on the corners, in the alleys, in windows
of houses, in apartment buildings, in classic cars, in sports cars, in

Cadillacs, on bicycles, on front porches. The dealers don't use cute little glassine packages here. They sell the *pedasos*, the rocks, loose. They stash them in their socks, in their hands, in bags and beneath their tongues, a place the cops haven't learned yet to look.

There is constant commerce, and the curbside dealers range from businesslike slickers with theme songs ("I'm Billy D.!/ You stick with me!") to skinny, skinny rockheads, who by six in the morning are walking around like extras from *Night of the Living Dead*, trying to sell another rock to go score more. Drive into Venice to buy at this time of day, a time that the neighborhood is usually crowded with *gavachos*, white people, in their nice rides, and the rock creatures come staggering and rushing out from the curbs, sticking their hands inside the car, jockeying and fending for position, vibrating, clenching, exhorting, "Take mine!" "Me!" "I got you!"

Most of the dealers are *miatas*, blacks, members of the Shoreline Crip gang. The Shorelines coexist in the one square mile of turf that is claimed by the Chicanos of V-13.

There is a truce here now, but Big Gato remembers the days when things were different. He moved here with his parents from Arizona when he was a baby, and he doesn't remember a time when there weren't *cholos*, gang members, in the neighborhood. But, he says, things really began heating up in the Seventies, when he was in his prime.

"Nineteen seventy-seven was the first I remember somebody getting killed that I knew," he says. "And then soon there were, like, ten, twelve shootings a week. I mean, when we walked down the street, we carried a gun. We wore the whole outfit, the khakis and the Pendletons, the hairnets, the bandannas, the hats, the overcoats, the whole bit. We was clean, five creases in every shirt, and we ironed them ourselves. Between me, my brother and my father, we used to go through two cans of spray starch a week.

"I sometimes carried a twelve-gauge under my overcoat. And when we saw a car come with an open window, we automatically ducked. It was like the wild, wild West, man. You'd have homeboys on the roof, homeboys behind the trees, guns everywhere. For a while, the National

Guard had the streets barricaded. You couldn't get in except by police escort. The fire department, if a house got burned, they wouldn't go in until sunrise. It was up to you to put it out. That was a bad time, homeboy. A hell of a war. We was little, but we was down, homeboy, wasn't nobody meaner."

And so it went in Venice, and by 1979 the media figured out that there was a gang problem by the sea, and in March the *Los Angeles Times* did its special report. There were stories of stray bullets, innocent victims, grieving mothers, shattered lives and midnight death.

THE TROUBLE IN OAKWOOD, read a subhead on the front page, followed by this summation: "Swept by smog-free ocean breezes, bordered on the south by the affluent playground called Marina del Rey . . . Oakwood is a strangely incongruous center of poverty and tragedy. While crime and gang violence tear at the community from within, mounting coastal real-estate values threaten to crush it from without."

If this all sounds familiar, sounds like newspaper articles being written today, nine years later, it is because, to an outside eye at least, things are pretty much the same. But if you listen to Big Gato and the older homeboys, if you look around, you see that things have changed as the drugs have changed.

In the old days, *chiva* and PCP were the drugs of choice in the neighborhood. *Chiva* is slang for "goat" in Spanish. In Venice, *chiva* is heroin. Black, gummy Mexican tar. When *chiva* was the thing, a lot of the Chicanos were doing business, and not just the homeboys, either. One woman, the head of a household who works as a secretary for a Century City law firm, used to bankroll a small-time heroin operation that was run by her daughter and her son-in-law. In those days, it was the Chicanos with the cars and the money and the guns.

In the last few years, however, since crack came to the 'hood, the *miatas* have been in control. If you forget about Rock, a greedy, small-time dealer who's currently in jail, you find that unlike the Chicano homeboys in Culver City and Lennox, Venice homeboys don't sell crack. Many, however, smoke it, and homeboys like Yogi and Lil' Gato and dozens of others do it every day.

Because they don't work and don't have any money, every day is the same. In the morning, grown men go beg their mothers or their old ladies for five or ten dollars. They say they have to get a new driver's license or use some other official-sounding excuse. Or they say they need a new asthma inhaler or some other small, expensive thing that they can rip off and produce later to back up their story. Scam done, they buy two hits. They do those two hits, then immediately start scamming to get more. Sometimes they can get a *miata* to kick them down to a free rock.

If they can't get any love, the homeboys look around for something to sell. Many have sold their tools and their father's tools. There are great deals floating around Venice at three in the morning. Whole automotive tuneup kits for under fifty dollars. VCRs for twenty-five dollars. Many in Venice have even sold their guns, which is probably another reason that the Venice homeboys have been doing less capping lately. You can get a 22-caliber semiautomatic Ruger rifle for the price of a dove, which is what they call a twenty-dollar rock.

If they can't find something of value to sell, homeboys may go do a crime, perhaps a burglary or a robbery, but for the most part crimes take too long, and when you're sprung, as they say, any time is too long. Faster to scam ten dollars from your old lady. This is what crack does to you, and this, more than anything else, is the reason for change in the neighborhood. Proud Venice is slipping. Other neighborhoods are dis-respecting, and no one can bring himself to do anything about it.

Today, thanks to crack, the homeboys have nothing left. In the old days, no matter how bad all the killing was, at least the homeboys had self-respect; that, any social worker will agree, is something to work from. Today the young homeboys are down for nothing. Nothing, that is, besides rock.

"The worst thing about it," says Joe Alarcon, a former Lennox gang member who now works for Youth Gang Services, "is that at this point we don't have much to offer Venice. The real problems are in South Central. Down there we're getting, like, five homicides a week. The black areas are really bad. On a daily basis, something like eighty-five to ninety percent of all crimes are being committed by Bloods and

Crips. Those guys are crazy; they don't care. As far as everybody sees things right now, the Hispanic gangs like Venice are not a big problem. Because our resources are limited, we have to concentrate on the areas that are the worst. We kind of have to let Venice fall through the cracks."

"Really, now," says Lil' Gato, "how much *fedia* you got!"

"Two dollars."

"I got two, too," says Lil' Gato. Really, he has five. "You got any *fedia*?" Lil' Gato asks Tequila.

Tequila leans back and works three crumpled dollar bills out of the front pocket of her mini. She holds them up.

"Well, we got six," says Lil' Gato.

"Seven." says Yogi.

"What?"

"Seven. We got seven. Two, two and three. Seven."

Just now they hear footsteps coming down the hall, down the steps. A hard knock.

Yogi rockets to the door. He leans his sweaty nose to the crack, then asks, sweetly, "Who's there!"

"Me, motherfucker!"

Big Gato!

Yogi and Tequila trade looks. Lil' Gato's eyes bulge. The time has come. He has to answer to Big Gato. Five years ago, when Lil' Gato was still known as David, he went one day to Big Gato and asked if he could have his name. Gato was honored. Gato was willing. But there was a problem. Another homeboy was already calling himself Lil' Gato, though as it turned out, he was a cheese eater. If David wanted the handle for himself, Gato told him, he would have to earn it. David beat up the guy and took his name. Thereafter, he was known as Lil' Gato. And thereafter he owed allegiance to Big.

Yesterday, the day after the drive-by at the park, Big Gato called his namesake out of Yogi's. This is what he told him:

"Look, homeboy, I been thinkin'. We can't have Culver City dis-respecting us. We can't have that, *ese*. No, you do something, or I'm gonna have to. And if I have to, you're fucked, homeboy. You hear me, homeboy? You're fucked."

Now Big Gato is here to get the report, and Lil' Gato has nothing to say. He chews his thumb. He looks at Yogi. "Open the door," Lil' Gato says.

"So what have you got to tell me?" asks Big Gato.

"What?" says Lil' Gato.

"What you mean, 'What?' You done anything yet?"

"I ain't gonna do nothing," says Lil' Gato.

"We ain't gonna do nothing," repeats Yogi.

Tequila shrugs.

Big Gato looks at them in disbelief. He stares for a minute. A full minute. Then he explodes. "You got shot at the other day, homeboy! You got shot at three times in the last week. Do I have to go mess with those motherfuckers myself? Is there something wrong with you? Are you peeing in your pants? Are you fucked up or what?"

"Why should I do anything?" asks Lil' Gato. He shrugs.

Yogi shrugs.

Tequila shrugs.

A few moments pass. Big Gato stares. His mouth is pulled back in a tight grimace, and above his lip are little drops of sweat. His teeth are clenched, and you can see the strain in the muscles of his jaw. Then his eyes drift to the carpet. There are lots of little white pieces of paper and lint and cloth and cigarette ash down there. To him, each piece looks like a rock. Could be a rock.

"Gimme a blast," says Big Gato.

"We was just going to get a ten from Binky," says Yogi.

"A ten?" says Big Gato. He chews his thumb. He thinks. "A ten?"

"Yeah," says Yogi, warming. "We were gonna go get a ten."

"Well, go get it," says Big Gato.

"What about Culver City?" asks Tequila.

"Culver City?" asks Big Gato. "Oh. We'll get them later."

from Monster: The Autobiography
of an L.A. Gang Member
by Sanyika Shakur

Kody Scott (born 1963) joined the Crips at age 11, and by age 17 was among the most feared gangsters in L.A. His crimes landed him in some of California's toughest prisons, where he eventually embraced education and radical politics, changing his name to Sanyika Shakur. He wrote Monster in part to counter romanticized and reactionary views of gang life.

Trying hard not to come across too thuggish in front of China's grandparents, I sat stiff-backed, pretending to be interested in what Ben, China's ostensibly aristocratic grandfather, who drove an RTD bus, was saying.

"You youngsters don't have any incentive, no drive. You are always looking for someone to put something in your hands."

China, sighing loudly, nudged my leg and shot me a stare of "I've heard this a million times." She was eager to get back outside. We had only come indoors to retrieve China's coat but had gotten caught in one of Dot—China's liberal grandmother—and Ben's discussions on youth. Now night had fallen.

China's well-kept house sat smack in the middle of the block on Eightieth Street, our newest possession in our latest recruitment drive. I would imagine that our aggressive conquering of territory in those days, and still today, resembled Hitler's sweep through Europe.

The apartment complex on the left end of the block off of Normandie Avenue became our base for this block. We have since referred to it as the "blue apartments." We had "lost" the "white apartments" on Sixty-fifth Street to Bloods while I was a prisoner in youth camp. The battle, I'm told, was fierce, but not worth the price. Although we suffered no fatalities, our wounded and MIA list grew steadily. Besides this, the Brims, whom the battle was with, had called in reinforcements from the Rollin' Twenties Bloods. The white apartments thus passed to the Reds and new ground was sought.

Eightieth Street was just one street out of many that fell under our jurisdiction. The mechanics involved in taking a street, or territory, is not unlike any attempt, I would assume, on behalf of early Euro American settlers. Send in a scout, have him meet the "natives," test their hostility level, military capabilities, needs, likes, and dislikes. Once a military presence is established, in come the "citizens"—in this case, gang members. Those who are not persuaded by our lofty presence *will* be persuaded by our military might. All who are of fighting age become conscripts. The set expands, and so does our territory. Sometimes there is resistance, but most of the time our efforts are successful. China's younger brother was one of our first recruits from Eightieth. Recommended by China and sponsored by me, he became Li'l G.C.

"Listen now, Kody," Ben continued in a deep baritone, pronouncing every syllable of every word. "You have got to stop pussyfooting around with your life. We are quickly becoming a technological country, and computers are going to overtake manual labor. What that means is—"

A shot rang out, cutting Ben's monologue short. For an instant I thought he himself had been hit; he was belly down on the floor. Another shot resounded, this time a shotgun blast.

Jumping to my feet I headed to the front door, opened it, and ran out onto the porch. My heart was pumping, but my adrenaline was urging me on. Looking first to the right, toward the blue apartments, and then to the left, in the direction of Halldale, I spotted a burgundy

Cutlass creeping down the street, a shotgun barrel in the passenger's hand barely visible through the open window.

Jumping the Creeping Charlie plants on the porch, which grew in huge flower pots, I darted into the street. Pulling out my chrome .25 automatic, recently put on the set by a new recruit, I began firing at the car. The car sped away. I kept firing at its rear as it turned left on Normandie Avenue.

I turned and bolted toward Halldale to assess the damage of their ride-by. Once I reached that corner I heard Dee Dee, Butchy's sister, hollering. At first I couldn't make out just what she was saying in the midst of the escalating confusion. Civilians had come out of their homes, and homeboys were starting to gather in front of China's house. Then it dawned on me.

"Monster, here they come, they comin' back . . ."

Damn, I was out of shells! No sooner had I turned to run and take cover, thinking I'd be shot in the back, then a black-and-white police car hit the corner and all but ran into the shooters' car. The police pulled their weapons and ordered the occupants out of the car and face down in the street. We all gathered to identify our enemies—not to help the police, but for our own intelligence.

There were three occupants, a .38 service revolver, and pump shotgun, sawed off at the barrel for a spraying effect and sawed off at the stock for stealth and close combat. One shooter we knew—Bank Robber; the other two were obviously new recruits, probably putting in work for the first time. They were members of the Rollin' Sixties. My response went virtually unnoticed by the police, though I saw two holes in the passenger door. No one inside was hit. The shooters were taken away amid death threats and shouts of revenge. In the absence of the police, the car was promptly torn up and set ablaze. Ten minutes later the impound came and scooped up the remains.

On my trek by China's house on my way to the blue apartments I encountered Dot and Ben on their front lawn.

"Kody." Dot started in on me first. "You don't be runnin' *toward* no gunfire, you run *from* it. You could have been killed!"

"Yes, ma'am," I replied, grateful that they hadn't seen me firing on the car. Apparently Dot had dived for cover as well, joining Ben on the floor. "I just thought that one of my friends had been hurt."

"Well, goddammit, you are not Superman, boy," Ben said. "You could not have possibly helped anyone in such a crisis." He pronounced crisis like Nixon speaking on the energy crisis.

"You're right, Ben, I lost my head," I replied and put one foot in front of the other, trying to exit the conversation and get to the blue apartments to mount a retaliation.

"Where you going now?" Dot retorted with genuine concern. "Ain't nothin' but police out here."

"To the apartments to check on my little brother," I lied and kept on stepping.

At the apartments I was congratulated by the homies for a proper response, but I shook their flattery off. Shit, I wanted to know how, after I had alerted everyone to enemy presence, the shooters were still able to make it off the block and come back around to shoot again? Heads dropped and gestures of dismay abounded. I looked on in disgust, thinking then that I was the only serious one in this.

For the past five years I had gotten up every morning and ironed my gear with thoughts of nothing else but doing propaganda for the set. I did this with all the zeal of a religious fanatic.

Until I was nine years old we had lived on Hillcrest Drive in the Crenshaw district. This is a moderate middle-class neighborhood of block after block of sparse lawns, well-paved streets and shady trees. My mother and stepfather had lived there since 1965. This neighborhood is now Rollin' Sixties 'hood. Up until 1980 my mother still shopped at Buddah Market on Slauson Avenue, owned and operated by Orientals.

In the summer of 1980 my mother asked me to accompany her to Buddah Market to shop. I refused with vigor, but my resistance was in vain. Mom didn't understand the complexity of our conflicts with other gangs. We are trying to kill each other. Up till then she always took my spiel about our seriousness as melodramatic exaggeration.

I went to Buddah Market with her that day—and I weighed two pounds extra. I had a Browning 9 millimeter with fourteen shots. It was an unusually bright afternoon, and I recall feeling light and almost happy, content actually. Riding up Slauson past Crenshaw I remember tensing and cringing as I read line after line of their graffiti on walls and buildings. Amusing myself, I jokingly asked Mom to pull over so I could cross them out. In return I got a "you damn fool" look. Then I noticed Mom's face cloud over with what I took to be utter helplessness. Ironically, I never gave stopping an inkling of a thought. This was my career, my "calling," as church folks say when someone does one thing real well.

We traveled further west past West Boulevard, passing our old street. We both looked to the right briefly. Turning into Buddah Market's parking lot, I tightened my belt and gave my appearance the once-over. G-down (short for "gangster down," or dressed in gang attire) in my gear, I had on blue khaki pants, white canvas All-Stars, and a blue sweatshirt, with my hair in braids. Brownies—brown garden gloves worn by gang members for fighting and shooting—hung halfway out of my right back pocket, and a blue flag hung out my left. Crips wear their left ear pierced and their flag in the left back pocket. Bloods are on the right.

"Why don't you tuck in that old rag," Mom blurted out while she gave herself the once-over.

"It's not a rag, Mom, it's a *flag*," I said, wishing she would for once see my seriousness here.

This was not some awkward stage of my life. This was a job to me, and I was employed full-time, putting in as much overtime as possible. Life from that vantage point seemed to be one big test of show and prove, pick and stick.

Mom went through her usual greetings with the Orientals. They had known each other for years.

I was on point. Not only was *I* in jeopardy, but with me I had Mom, who I was sure would try to talk an enemy into doing an about-face. Fat fucking chance of that happening, I remember thinking.

"You remember my son Kody, don't you?"

"Yes, yes," I heard the Oriental woman saying amid other comments such as "he's so big, so strong looking." After a few other exchanges we started down an aisle. Canned goods, no interest here.

"Mom, I'm going over to the cereal section," I said and stepped quickly so she couldn't call me back.

Turning the corner at the end of the aisle, I felt relieved to be alone, both for my safety and Mom's. I had every intention of going to the cereal section when I was distracted by a nice-looking young lady in produce. I made a beeline for the vegetables, and that's when I saw him. Damn! Enemy! Enemy! My adrenaline alarm was going off. Sonic booms of heartbeat filled my ears. My throat got tight and my movements became automatic. We both reached for our waistbands simultaneously. The young lady had still not looked up from her inspection of the vegetables, yet the tranquil surroundings of an otherwise routine shopping trip were about to explode around her.

I managed the drop and drew first. He was still drawing his weapon. Shit, had this been "Baretta," or "Barnaby Jones," he would have thrown his hands up and surrendered. Not bothering to aim, I fired.

BOOM!

Confusion and chaos swept the aisle like buckshot, screams following in quick succession. Damn, I'd missed!

I fired again and hit him in the torso. The bullet knocked him back, and his weapon discharged into the air. He had what sounded like a .22, a small-caliber weapon. Folks now knew that two weapons were involved—one loud, my 9 millimeter, and one not, his .22. I shot at him three more times to create an atmosphere of intensity, then turned and went in search of my mother. Since my last encounter with the ride-by shooters, where I had emptied my clip and was left vulnerable, I had learned to keep "exit" or "safety" shells.

Running aimlessly about, frantically looking for Mom, I totally forgot I had the gun in my hand. I tucked it while jogging down the household appliance aisle. Not finding her there, I panicked, remembering how I had been locked in the surplus store. I made my way then to the door and there, among the other scared-to-death shoppers, I found Mom. She was grief stricken and with her nerves in shambles; I grabbed her arm and ushered her away from the crowd.

"Boy, was that you?" she said, hoping against hope that it wasn't. "Kody, *what* happened?"

I made no attempt to explain. My sole intent was a timely escape. We drove in silence, block after block. We never even looked at each other.

Back across Western Avenue I began to breathe better as I finally reflected on what I had done. Fuck him, he was going to shoot me. I justified my shooting of him with self-defense. This thing was very dangerous; we all knew one another. It's like the CIA and the FBI going to war. There's no escaping once sighted.

I thought for sure I'd be captured for this one. After all, the Oriental knew me, and folks had seen me with the strap (gun). However, my arrest was not forthcoming.

After getting out of camp in 1979, I met Tamu through my brother Kerwin and sister Kendis, who all worked together at the Thirty-second Street Market. Tamu was a looker, tall and graceful with a smile that shouted for attention; I was naturally attracted. However, she was older than I. In fact, we had nothing in common. She was tall, I was short. She had a job, I was an armed robber. She liked jazz, I liked funk. She had a car, I had a bicycle. She was drug and alcohol free, I smoked pot and PCP and drank beer. We clicked immediately.

Today she'll say she didn't chase me, but in actuality she did. Once she and I began to go steady, she'd let me drop her off at work and keep the car until she got off. Her shift was from 3:00 p.m. till 11:00 p.m. My attraction was not just physical, but to the fact that she was not of my world. She was a civilian. To me, that was most appealing. She was not with me because of my reputation or clout, but for me as an individual. So when I went around her I would present myself as Kody, without the Monster persona. I'd take my shades off, tuck my flag, and not let her know when I was strapped. I also would douse myself with some of the expensive cologne Mom had bought me. Later, Tamu told me that I had been using too much but that at the time she didn't want to embarrass me, for she saw that I was trying to impress her.

I would take Tamu up to the market and kiss her goodbye, drive to the corner, make sure she was inside the store and out of view, then reach for the glove compartment. I'd open it, pull out my flag, put on my murder-ones (dark shades, also called Locs or Locos), button the top button on my shirt, put my strap in my lap, and drive on to the 'hood. I did so many ride-bys, drive-ups, drive-throughs, and chase-aways in her car that it's a wonder she didn't either go to jail or get shot. I guess everyone assumed the car was stolen. Then, too, we left few witnesses.

Tamu and I continued to date up until the time she told me she was pregnant.

"Pregnant?" I asked in disbelief.

"Yes, pregnant," she replied matter-of-factly.

I felt so young at that moment, just a baby myself. I panicked. Anything but a child. Things had gotten too serious, out of hand. I began to dodge Tamu.

"Tell her I ain't here," I would tell family members when she called or came by.

Mom, however, adored her, and they would sit for hours and talk. Often I'd come in from a hard day of campaigning, shotgun slung over my shoulder, and Tamu and Mom would be in the front room talking. I'd acknowledge them with a nod, then head on down the hall to my room and fall out in a dead sleep. I began not to care if she saw me as Monster or not. I tried to push her away with the raw reality of who I was. She wasn't budging. Besides, Mom hated China for reasons I never knew—perhaps because she saw that she and I were on the same path, whereas Tamu could be a positive influence in my life.

I wasn't by any means ready to have a child, though. To me that meant settling down, another obligation. I already had pledged my allegiance to the set, so I was in a rough spot. I had to pick either Tamu and my unborn child or my career in the set. This ate away at me for several months. Sure I liked Tamu, but not enough to forfeit my stature in the set. All I had worked so hard to build would be left to dangle in the wind, unfinished. Enemies, I thought, would overrun the 'hood if no one rallied the troops. Then, too, I felt an obligation to Tamu. She hadn't got pregnant alone. Besides, the child would be a totally innocent party in this matter and deserved a fair chance.

In those months of consternation I shot more than a few civilians as my concentration was continually broken with zig-zag thoughts of my future. On July 28, 1980, I got a call from the hospital.

"I'm in labor," I heard Tamu's voice squeak over the phone. "Are you coming here?"

"Yeah, yeah, sure I'm comin'," I responded as all my confusion and indecisiveness boiled up and over the brink of comprehension.

I got my coat out of the closet in a complete daze, not knowing exactly what to do. I reached under my pillow and took hold of my 9 millimeter, checking the clip—fourteen shots. I was past the days of half-loaded weapons. Shit had escalated to the point where individuals were being sought for extermination. I, of course, was on at least three sets' "most wanted" lists. Walls told the story. In fact, enemies spray-painted my name on walls in death threats more often than I did to advertise.

Wearing my fresh Pendleton shirt, beige khakis, and biscuits (old-men comfort shoes, the first shoe officially dubbed a "Crip shoe"), I threw on my black bomber jacket and stepped out into the warm summer night. I walked up Sixty-ninth Street to Western Avenue and took a car at gunpoint. Still in a state of indecision, I drove toward the hospital.

I intentionally drove through Sixties 'hood. Actually, I was hoping to see one of them before I had made it through, and what luck did I have. There was Bank Robber, slippin' (not paying attention, not being vigilant) hard on a side street. I continued past him and turned at the next corner, parked, and waited. He would walk right to me.

Sitting in the car alone, waiting to push yet another enemy out of this existence, I reflected deeply about my place in this world, about things that were totally outside the grasp of my comprehension. Thoughts abounded I never knew I could conjure up. In retrospect, I can honestly say that in those moments before Bank Robber got to the car, I felt free. Free, I guess, because I had made a decision about my future.

"Hey," I called out to Robber, leaning over to the passenger side, "got a light?"

"Yeah," he replied, reaching into his pants pocket for a match or lighter. I never found out which.

I guess he felt insecure, because he dipped his head down to window level to see who was asking for a light.

"Say your prayers, muthafucka."

Before he could mount a response I blasted him thrice in the chest, started the car, and drove home to watch "Benny Hill." Bangin' was my life. That was my decision.

The next day I woke up feeling good. I got a call from China and we talked briefly about my decision. She had been totally bent out of shape by the fact that I had gotten a civilian pregnant. She felt disrespected, as she thought she was all I needed in a woman—lover, comrade, shooter, driver, etc. She didn't overstand.

I have always been intensely private, or at least I've always wanted a side of me to remain private. Being with Tamu in her world afforded me this opportunity. It was an escape to a peaceful enclave for a couple of hours. The places she took me, bangers didn't frequent.

This was before the influx of narcotics, primarily crack. We were all of the same economic status—broke. Now, with so many "ghetto rich" homeboys from every set, no place is beyond the grasp of bangers. I needed those escapes to maintain sanity. Often I felt that I was carrying the weight of the whole set on my shoulders.

On a chilly October night in 1980, about twenty homeboys were assembled in front of the blue apartments on Eightieth Street when a

'64 Chevy came barreling down the street with its occupants hanging out holding guns—long-barreled shotguns. Instinctively, we took cover. Instead of shooting, they just hollered their set—Sixties—disrespected ours, and kept on going.

Though I didn't know it at the time, simultaneously, four blocks away on Eighty-fourth Street, Twinky and his girlfriend were arguing. April wanted to go home that night instead of spending the night again. Twinky had no problem with that, but it was almost midnight. April insisted on being walked to the bus stop. Twinky gave in. Taking his .25 automatic along, they made their way to the nearest bus stop, at Eighty-third and Western. April lived on Sixty-second and Harvard in Blood 'hood. Once at the bus stop, they stood and talked about different things concerning the set. April was China's road dog, and a homegirl, too.

Suddenly Twinky spotted the Chevy, which we had identified as Pretty Boy's car. He pulled out his weapon to fire on the car, but April grabbed his hand, saying he should let them go on, they weren't bothering anybody, and that they probably hadn't even seen them. Twinky put away his strap.

Not three minutes later, the Sixties crept up from behind and fired one round from the long-barreled shotgun, striking Twinky in his upper left side below the armpit—basically a heart shot. Twinky, in shock, ran across the street and collapsed. The shooters sped away. Twinky's mother and younger brother, Jr. Ball—also a homeboy—were retrieved. It's been reported that in his last moments Twinky said repeatedly, "Mama, I'm gonna be good, I ain't gonna bang no more Mama, I'm gonna be good."

He died soon after with buckshot in his heart. Twinky was fourteen years old. At approximately 3:00 the next morning I was awakened by a call from Twinky's mother. I still did not know of his death.

"Kody," she said in an icy voice unfamiliar to me, "they killed my baby last night, they killed my James last night."

Then she started screaming frantically. "Who?" I managed to say through her screams.

"The motherfuckin' Sixties! Come over here *right* now, Kody, *right* now!"

I dressed quickly, strapped down, and rode my bicycle the twenty-four blocks to her house without so much as a care about security or the wind-chill factor. I had not put Twinky on the set, but I dug him. He was a stalwart soldier and would have been a Ghetto Star.

On Thanksgiving, 1979, he, another homie—Li'l Doc—and I were walking down the street. I was strapped with a .22 revolver and Li'l Doc had a .44. No sooner had I handed the gun to Twinky than the police rolled up on us. Twinky was captured with the strap; Doc and I ran. He had just gotten out of camp, and now he'd been murdered.

Grieving, I made my way up their drive and knocked at the door. It was opened by Jr. Ball with a fixed expression of grief and anxiety on his face. Stepping inside, I could feel the tension. In the living room I saw four guns on the coffee table—two shotguns and two revolvers. I looked from the guns to Twinky's mother, her face a mask of steel, eyes burning like hellfire. Doc came in after me. Once both of us were seated, Twinky's mother got to her feet and walked around to us.

"Those guns belonged to James," she said, picking up one revolver and then another. "He would want you to have them. He would also want you to use them. You were his homeboys, his friends, and because of this I have called you two over here to tell you personally . . . I don't want to ever see you again if you can't kill them motherfuckers that killed my boy! You bring me newspapers, you make the news, but you better do something to avenge my son's death!"

I just sat and looked up at her with total admiration. Damn, she was down.

"But first," she continued, "I want you two to come to April's house with me."

She grabbed her car keys and we both followed her out to her car. Once inside the car she explained that Jr. Ball had been unnerved by Twinky's death and had, that night, abdicated his oath to the 'hood. He could not be relied on for a retaliatory strike.

In front of April's house we sat momentarily, then Twinky's mother got out . . . with a revolver. Standing wide-legged on April's grass, she opened fire, emptying six rounds into her house. I thought about doing likewise, but I felt she needed to do that alone.

Back in the car she said she honestly felt that April had set Twinky up to be ambushed and that, she added, we should kick April off the set. I told her I'd talk to China about it.

Rumors about April's survival and Twinky's death spread. "Why hadn't April been shot?" and "Why did she instruct him not to shoot?" Rumors and ill feelings intensified when April went into hiding. Not long after that she was specifically targeted and a hit was put on her.

We made the 5:00 p.m. news that day and the day after. On our third night we found the Sixties 'hood empty. Weaving our way through the streets we found it hard to believe that they had knuckled under. Not a soul was in sight. We drove down Third Avenue by the Fifty-ninth Street school, where they hung, circled the school once, then pulled to a stop and sat idle, peering into the darkness of the school yard. The Sixties had yet to procure a park and were using the Fifty-ninth Street school as a meeting place.

"Hit the corner once more," Frogg said from the passenger seat, a .357 magnum sitting firmly in his lap. Li'l G.C. sat on edge behind me. He had a .22 Remington rifle with eighteen shots.

Starting off around Third Avenue again we picked up a tail. Keeping my head straight, so as not to seem panicky in case it was the police, I surveyed the front grille and lights. No, it wasn't a police car. The police, at least the Seventy-seventh Street Division in our 'hood, were driving Furys. This car behind us was a Chevy, a '66 Impala.

Keeping my head straight I spoke softly to Frogg. "Cuz, you know why we can't find these fools?"

"Why?" Frogg answered.

" 'Cause these muthafuckas is behind us!"

"Don't look back," Frogg mumbled and adjusted his rearview mirror. "Just keep straight, keep straight. Now speed up a little and turn left on Fifth Avenue." Frogg was instructing me like a driving instructor. "At the first driveway, bust a U-turn."

Speeding up to Fifth Avenue past Fourth, I thought about the danger of clocking (continuously, nonstop, as in time) these cats three days in a row. Perhaps we had put too much on it. No doubt, they were out on patrol and were possibly heavily armed in hopes of finding some intruders, just our fuckin' luck. Frogg was fresh out of prison and already on the campaign trail. He loved the set intensely.

Turning left on Fifth Avenue I made another hard left into the first driveway. No sooner had I backed out and come to a rolling stop at the corner of Fifty-ninth and Fifth, than the other car slowly bent the corner in front of us. Had they been good military tacticians they would have stopped in front of us and prevented our forward motion, while simultaneously having their shooters try to take out the driver to leave the occupants stranded and on foot to be hunted and killed. But no, this was not their tactic. They drove slowly around, coming along-side us, but facing the opposite direction.

As they inched closer and closer I said to Frogg, "Shoot, shoot these muthafuckas, man!"

"Hold on, hold on," he said. Both of us were sitting still in the front seats like we didn't have a care in the world. "A little more, a little . . ."

BOOM, BOOM!

Frogg was leaning right over me, shooting into their faces. Powder and cordite flew into my face from the gun's cylinders.

Pac, pac, pac, pac I heard from behind my head. Li'l G.C. was shooting with the .22.

Caught by surprise, their driver panicked, punched the accelerator, and hit a light pole, which fell across the hood and roof of the car. We sped away down Fifth Avenue to Slauson and made a right. When we got to Second Avenue we turned back into their 'hood, heading toward our set. I saw two of their little homies on bicycles and ran one over. Well, actually not *over*, but I hit him and he flew a few yards—about twenty. He didn't get up before we had gotten off the block.

I felt nothing but a sense of duty. I had been to five funerals in the pre-vious two years and had been steeled by seeing people whom I had laughed and joked with, played and eaten with, dead in a casket. Revenge was my every thought. Only when I had put work in could I feel good that day; otherwise I couldn't sleep. Work does not always constitute shooting someone, though this is the ultimate. Anything from wallbangin' (writing your set name on a wall, advertising) to spitting on someone to fighting—it's all work. And I was a hard worker.

Gangsta Life, Gangster Death
by Ivan Solotaroff

The distinction between life and art is often hazy in the world of gangsta rap. Ivan Solotaroff's account of rapper Tupac Shakur's murder offers a case in point.

Las Vegas Boulevard, Sept. 7, 1996, 11:10 p.m.

It's a prizefight Saturday night, hot and mobbed. A black BMW 750 inches down the Strip, followed by a half dozen other black luxury cars. Tupac Amaru Shakur, twenty-five, stands up through the open sunroof, which is probably not too wise. Not if you live in the crosshairs you've spent your life creating—making yourself into Public Enemy Number One with the incendiary gangsta raps you write, the cops you might have shot in the back in Atlanta, the child you might have shot four years ago, the woman you sexually assaulted in New York, the rappers you assault with bats and fists and guns or with the words of every other song. Not if you've been in two fights yourself these last three hours—both with Crips gang bangers. Not if the self-styled Blood driving the Beamer, Marion "Suge" Knight, the chief of Death Row Records, says he's got three contracts on his own head.

But this is life imitating art—players, riders, cops and robbers, OGs (Original Gangstas), bitches and ho's—the stuff that Tupac draws his own life and art from. High rollers, in town for the Mike Tyson–Bruce Seldon fight at the MGM, are shopping the casino sports books for spreads on tomorrow's football games. Biker gangs are revving up at red lights next to the bicycle-patrol cops who cover the Strip. Pasty-white bridesmaids in pink-and-blue chiffon waft out of the MGM past crack-addict hookers on the corner of Tropicana Road. And the drag is filled with both gangstas and gangsters—both rappers and the real ones—traveling with requisite entourages.

Even in the teem of the Strip, it's the MOB crew (people say it stands for "Member of Bloods"), Suge's crew, that's turning heads. Suge is out in front, looking pensive at the wheel, a BMW wagon behind them, then the Lexus, the Benz, the Miata. Music is blasting from the huge speakers in the trunks; a neon gleam—every color in the rainbow—is flashing off the expensive silver rims.

A strobe from a paparazzo's camera catches Tupac, now sitting in the passenger seat as they cross Harmon Avenue. This is party time. Shakur's buddy Iron Mike has put prison and the rape conviction in the past, just as he has, and tonight they're both champs, headed for the same party. Everyone from the West Side of L.A. is in town, and Tupac tells them all to get in the line down to "Suge's place," Club 662 on Flamingo Road. Everyone's "throwin' up Wesside"—a hand sign forming a W: Compton, Watts, Inglewood. For Tupac, it also means West Coast. It means him: He's not only put the Bronx childhood, the Baltimore art school, the black-radical background of his family behind him, he's also taken on the East Coast rap scene single-handedly and beat them all. Suge makes a right on Flamingo, guns it, and everyone does the same. After the congestion of Las Vegas Boulevard, the three lanes curving up- and downhill past Bally's are an invitation to floor it, fan out, and drag the three miles to 662.

Flamingo was the original crossroads of the Strip; but it's been in a slump for a decade, a lull between the huge new family-oriented casinos like the MGM and the Mirage, half a mile to the north and south, where land can fetch more than $2 million an acre. Here, one long avenue block east takes them down the price scale—very quickly. By the time they hit the next intersection, Koval Lane, the glitter's gone. To the left is a Comfort Inn, a parking garage, a small power station; across the long avenue are the dim lights of a twenty-four-hour gas station and convenience store. A massive semi is turning left at Koval, and the BMW wagon, now in front of Suge's sedan in the right lane, has to stop.

Just beyond the right-turn lane is a high chain-link fence. The lot behind is the size of six football fields, empty but for a few slag heaps, a piece of earth-moving machinery, and garbage perpetually blown in the southerly wind that comes out of the desert. Not much to look at, especially when there's an Olds with two beautiful, real friendly women in the left lane checking out Suge and Tupac.

No one sees the white Cadillac with California plates that pulls out of traffic into the right-turn lane and noses up to Suge's idling 750.

Las Vegas Boulevard, the MGM, Sept. 7, 1996, 7:55 p.m.
The wall of televisions in the hotel's mammoth lobby is showing fights: a promo loop hyping Seldon and Tyson, who are fighting in the Grand Garden tonight. No one's expecting much from Seldon, but this is Mike, fighting for the WBA crown he lost to Buster Douglas, and for an hour or two this is the amoral center of the world. Hip-hop is here—Too Short, Run-DMC, and New Edition, Roseanne's been spotted; ballplayers such as Gary Payton and Vegas's own Stacey Augmon; the famous OGs. It's Crip-heavy tonight: Rolling through in his wheelchair is Mike Concepcion, an original Crip who got shot down, then, like so many gangsters, went into the recording business and helped negotiate the Crips-Bloods truce four years ago.

No truces for Tupac tonight, though. He's come to kick ass and take names, even though his own road entourage and bodyguards, the Outlaw Immortalz, haven't made it here as they were supposed to.

He's already acting as if he owned the place before the MOB crew gets through the lobby, talking loud and turning heads.

The MGM is a Death Row kind of place: larger-than-life, self-mythologizing, glittering, money-hungry. Inside, everything is Hollywood—every store, arcade, and restaurant recessed into the walls to resemble a movie set—and designed to keep people moving along into the enormous casinos. This is most obvious on the way into the Grand Garden on fight nights. Squeezed past the baccarat pit, next to Wolfgang Puck's, you walk shoulder-to-shoulder with ten thousand people through at least two casino areas, through increasingly narrow halls, to a red-carpeted bridge—the Studio Walk—into the arena. Suge hates the crowds and as always has managed to arrive late, just a minute or two before Tyson's own entrance.

Flanked by the crew, Suge and Tupac cut a straight line down the two dozen steps to the VIP seats. As always, some bums are sitting in their seats in the fourth row. As always, Suge is pissed, the look on his face usually enough to send them scurrying. These bums, however, happen to be Crips—it's not known if they're local or from L.A. or a little of both—and they don't want to move, or maybe they just don't like the attitude they're getting from the MOB crew and from Tupac. The sudden confluence of big black bodies squaring off can be seen from fifty rows away, then some brief but intimidating and very disrespectful shoving. No punches are thrown, and none are needed. Neither, for that matter, is the "Fuck out my face, nigga" that someone—probably Tupac—is screaming as the Crips leave and the arena darkens for Tyson's entrance.

One hundred and nine seconds, two knockdowns, and some innocuous-looking punches later, it's all over but the shouting. There's a lot of that going on: obscenities about Seldon's manhood; "fix"; "bullshit." Before the emcee can hold up Tyson's glove and declare him the new WBA champion, people are streaming out, tramping over the Studio Walk, past the Grand Ballroom. At the narrowest passage back toward the casinos, in front of the boarded facade windows of a

Marshall Rousso's boutique that's been remodeled, the crew runs into the Crips from the fourth row, and this time fists start flying.

The music being piped through the cavernous building is Bruce Springsteen's "My Home Town," which may or may not go a long way toward explaining the animus. Among the five thousand card-carrying gangsters that Metro Police estimate now live in Vegas, a good number are relocated from L.A. The cops even have a joke about it: They migrate here for the dry heat to spell the rheumatism that comes from having bullets lodged in your spine or skull. But their sense of territory is dead serious and testy—what with other guys always coming over from L.A.

The fighting starts in earnest. One of the Crips is down, and Tupac and the MOB crew are on him. "Nigga got an old-fashioned stomping," says an MGM employee who witnessed the latter stages of the fight—six or seven men "just kicking and kicking at him like a dog, total disrespect." The Crip getting stomped is the one who gets detained by MGM security, while Tupac, Suge, and the MOB crew walk. Fuel to the fire.

In the lobby, still pumped with adrenaline, with that strange mixture of rage and bonhomie that fuels him, Tupac runs into a camera crew and for the last time in his life addresses the media that for the five wild years of his career he's baited, used to hype himself, and used as a sounding board to predict his own violent death. "Did you all see that?" Shakur asks the camera, referring to the Tyson fight. "Fifty punches. I counted fifty punches. I knew he was gonna take him out. We bad like that—come out of prison and now we running shit."

Las Vegas suburbs, Sept. 7, 1996, 10:00–10:30 p.m.

Suge Knight's gated redbrick mansion sits beside a luxury golf course in the horn of a cul-de-sac in the valley's most exclusive development. Across the street is Wayne Newton's big corner house; next door is Mike Tyson's estate. The proximity to Tyson helped induce Suge to buy it in May as a party house. This morning, even though it was a fight day, Mike was hanging outside the house, real relaxed, signing autographs for fans and well-wishers from his green Mercedes.

Like many L.A. honchos, Suge heads east with the MOB crew to Vegas on free weekends, covering the three hundred miles across the desert in three hours in one of his—at last count—thirty-four cars. Suge's crew is always around if there's a hot fight, and if it's Mike in the ring, testosterone levels run high, which is how Suge likes it. Even though the Seldon fight was bullshit, tonight was still hot. Tupac just couldn't kick enough ass at the MGM. Gangsta ass.

The mansion came Suge's way with some of its own gangster history: art imitating art. It was the set for the estate of "Ace" Rothstein, the casino boss played by Robert De Niro in *Casino*. And it's red, with a redwood deck wrapped around the swimming pool. Suge likes red things: red satin sheets, the red wall-to-wall carpeting he put down in the master-bedroom suite. He even had the swimming pool painted bloodred. (Unfortunately, chlorine and the desert sunshine turned it an ugly shade of orange, and the filled pool looks like a huge glass of Tang.)

Red, as in Bloods. You can see that in the diamond-and-ruby ring Suge wears everywhere he goes. It spells MOB. The whole crew wears MOB rings.

It could mean "Member of Bloods" or, maybe, "Money over Bitches," which is Death Row's version of corporate culture. When you sign on with Suge, you enter a man's world, and your signature is your male bond. Never more so than with Tupac, because the two ride as one: Everything Suge doesn't have, Tupac does, and vice versa. Suge, they've agreed, is the don, Tupac the capo-de-regime. It doesn't matter that Tupac's fiancée, Quincy Jones's daughter Kidada, is in town tonight. (Tupac's got her name tattooed on his right arm; she's got his on her back.) Tonight is party time, MOB-style, and Tupac's told her to go back to the Luxor and wait for him.

MOB: On the telephone keypad, that's 662, the club where tonight they'll be holding a benefit for a retired fighter and Las Vegas cop who has a program to keep kids off the streets by teaching them how to box. Tupac loves benefits for kids and is looking forward to the party. THUG LIFE: The jailhouse tattoo across Tupac's gut is another acronym—The Hate U Give Little Infants Fucks Everybody. The I in LIFE is a bullet.

After taking calls, Suge changes out of the formal banded-neck shirt-waist he wore to the fight to casual slacks and a multicolored Cosby-like Coogi sweater. Tupac has dropped the blue jeans and flowing orange-gold silk shirt he wore and is ready to party. Now it's sneakers, blue-green sweatpants, a gray-black basketball jersey, and his favorite neckwear—a nugget-thick gold-link chain with a huge medallion, a nasty, ruby-studded paperweight that's pure Tupac: a huge, ripped, winged black man wrestling with a serpent, holding a pistol so big it looks like a hair dryer. The man has a halo.

He wore it to the fight, rather than his Death Row medallion—a solid-gold hooded man in an electric chair—which Suge presented to him when Tupac came out of Clinton Correctional Facility in Dannemora, New York in October of 1995. He stepped onto Suge's private plane and stepped off in L.A. to start cutting records for Death Row. In ten months, he recorded a career's worth: not just *All Eyez on Me*, the double album that debuted in February at number one, but two, three other albums' worth, plus another, to be released under the name Makaveli. The alias fits: Tupac never stops manipulating for power, proudly, out in the open. Suge used to have a capo named Dr. Dre, the genius who created the Death Row gangsta sound, who basically invented the genre, who brought in a South-Central kid named Snoop to get the label off the ground, who produced and cowrote one of the hit singles from *All Eyez*. Tupac says he's the one who got Dre off the label two months ago. Money is power; power is everything. Just look at his angel medallion: two ounces of gold.

What Tupac decides not to wear is his bulletproof vest, though he's taken it everywhere since he got shot in New York. "It's just too hot," he says.

Corner of Flamingo and Koval, Sept. 7, 1996, 11:15 p.m.
Perhaps because of the flirting women in the Olds to the left of Suge's
BMW, no one has noticed the white Cadillac that stops on the right.
Or the Caddy's rear left window, which is down, or the tall black man
who gets out of the back. No one but Tupac: He's already scrambling,
trying to get out of his deep bucket seat through the well between him
and Suge, into the back before the shooting starts.

In the dark intersection, two guns flash as they discharge—loud
semiautomatic pistols. The one in the Caddy is blasting, tommy-
gun-style, in a straight line through Tupac's open window. The man
standing outside the Caddy tracks Tupac with his gun through the
windshield and the window—boom-boom-boom-boom, through
Shakur's hand and leg. Follow: boom-boom-boom, into his chest and
gut, as the whole entourage in the other cars, armed bodyguards
included, slumps reflexively into their seats.

The firing stops, and in the smoky silence comes a tinny sound, perhaps of new clips being slapped home, because the flashes and the
boom-boom-boom come again, both guns now firing point-blank at
Tupac. He's been hit with a fusillade like this before, three years ago,
in the lobby of a recording studio in Times Square. He not only lived
but went upstairs in the elevator, like James Cagney, bullet wounds in
his skull, to accuse some rappers and record executives of setting him
up. Those were .22 slugs, though. These are heavier and faster, ripping
through his lung and pinning him down in the seat, and Shakur's
starting to pass out.

The tall man runs around the back of the Caddy and gets in the rear
passenger seat. It takes a hard right on Koval, never to be seen again.
Suge is bleeding, grazed on the forehead by a bullet fragment. He pulls
the BMW 750 into a wide, screeching U, whipping Tupac's head into
the soft black leather as they race back up the hill toward the safety and
bright lights of the Strip. Tupac is talking. "Gotta keep your eyes open,"
he says.

Someone from the entourage, who got out of the Lexus during the shooting, starts screaming at everyone to follow Suge, and a massive U-turn exodus begins. Even in their panicked state, first the driver of the BMW wagon then the others slow almost to a halt as they hit the high median between the east- and westbound lanes, making sure they don't dent their rims.

Not Suge. Fifty yards up ahead, he's already snarled in traffic. Careening into the left-turn lane and flooring it, he hits a red light at Las Vegas Boulevard at full throttle, then drives his right hand up the wheel, taking the car into a wild left that gets his right wheels and rims caught up on the curb, instantly flattening the tires. He straightens out and keeps control somehow, screaming in and out of lanes for a quarter mile down the Strip, running another red as police sirens fill the night and bicycle-patrol cops converge from all sides. There's a wall of cars up on Harmon, and Suge throws the Beamer into another left, this time taking it sharper, so sharp he gets caught up on the median and grinds to a halt.

When the entourage catches up with the 750 at the corner, Suge is out of the driver's seat and flat on the pavement, bleeding heavily now from the head, his arms clutched over his chest, his eyes wide. Cops are everywhere, screaming at everyone to get their faces on the ground; shotguns are shucking, and pistols are up against people's heads when they make the slightest move.

EMS arrives from the University Medical Center, and the police start letting traffic through, stopping only black folks in black cars. The bodyguards who'd been packing apparently went the other way, and with no guns to fear, officers finally let people get their faces off the street. Tupac's getting carried off, fully conscious, but his shirt is covered with blood, too much blood. So are the two front seats of the 750. Blood is everywhere. To the people who know him, the look on Tupac's face suggests he's going to survive—again. It's that wide-eyed, knowing appraisal that's never a smile, never a glare, just somewhere in between: the Rasputin of rap whom bullets, jail time, lawsuits, and felony charges can't keep down.

"I need a hospital?" he reportedly said to Suge. "You're the one shot in the head."

Fighting for breath in the back of the EMS van as it heads across town, though, Tupac seems to know better. "I'm dying," he says.

Shakur lost a testicle in the New York shooting; he'll lose a lung in Las Vegas as the doctors try in vain to save him. On September 13, at 4:03 p.m., he finally succumbs. After suffering "respiratory failure and cardiopulmonary arrest," Tupac Amaru Shakur is pronounced dead. Shortly after, he'll be cremated in a private ceremony.

The Hotel Nikko, Beverly Hills, Sept. 28, 1996, 10:00 a.m.
Five lethal-looking kids—Crips, if the freshly laundered blue bandanna do-rags are any indication—are splayed languorously on cement benches by the valet parking desk outside the front door of this $200-a-night hotel. One is packing what looks like a .45-caliber pistol inside his denim jacket. I stare at them from the lobby through the big glass door, they stare back, and I decide to look for a side door.

I'm headed down to Compton to talk about Tupac with a former Crip, an OG I'll call Steel. I'm not looking for clues, just some understanding of the shooting, which, three weeks later, is looking more and more like a West Side street crime, only one that happened in Las Vegas. Like everyone I've spoken to—MGM employees, fans at the fight, members of the entourage, even the Vegas cop who convinced me it was an L.A.-based hit—Steel, whom I've talked to on the phone, is too nervous to go on record, which is saying a lot. This is a guy who graduated to lethal violence at twelve, killing a kid in juvenile hall who helped stomp Steel just because he was from Compton, who by twenty-five was "running things" at Folsom State Prison, where he spent a decade of his life. New York tabloids are publishing stories about a renewed Crips-Bloods war, with twelve retaliatory shootings logged so far. These kids outside are making me sweat.

The south exit, through the pool, is no good: There are a half dozen gangsters chatting on chaise lounges. I follow yet another gang, coming off the elevators out the front door, where a limousine and a convoy of luxury rental cars await them. The wagon backs are stacked with cameras, lights, sound equipment. "Fuck you doing?" the gun-packing kid asks one of the Crips in a Volvo sedan. "You had the Volvo last shoot. That's mine." Welcome to gangsta L.A.—Hollywood.

Steel, tucking into lunch in a Compton restaurant off Wilmington Boulevard half an hour later, couldn't agree more. "Tupac was a media myth, just like his whole gang-banging, stupid negativity stereotype," he says. "This is a man who leeched off the community, gave nothing back. This is a man who owed people, just like Suge does. This is a man who was gunned down because he owed. Fuck Tupac Shakur."

I ask Steel if there was a Vegas connection or if it was all L.A., and he shrugs off the question with a look that says: Is there any difference? Did the famous East Coast–West Coast war have any connection? He looks disgusted, then describes what gang-banging is really like. He makes the "rap wars" sound like World Wrestling Federation stuff, which has a ring of truth. "Tupac owed people," he repeats.

Steel won't get into whom Tupac owed—and there's no pressing him—but this, too, has a ring of truth. A cursory look into Tupac's and Suge's finances shows that some commonly reported "facts" are probably nothing of the kind. First, that Suge bailed Tupac out of jail for $1.4 million. A Reuters report from Tupac's release day has Atlantic records, his distributor before he joined Death Row, putting up $850,000, the remainder being split by two other parties, neither of whom appears to be Suge. Second, that Club 662 is "Suge's place." His financial ties to the club appear to be tertiary at best. Third, that Death Row has sold six million units of *All Eyez on Me*. Though the album reentered the Top Ten after Tupac's death, the last total was less than half that. With Dr. Dre gone and Snoop still facing gun charges and going on three years since his last album, Death Row is in serious trouble. There are people out here now who say Suge isn't even a Blood, just a kid who grew up on the same block.

"No," Steel says, "Suge's connected—believe me." Steel riffs out a long digression about the drug money that funded the gangsta industry: "Suge came up when all that money was going into the business. That money still comes back through here, and it's still dirty. The stuff they portray in those videos hasn't been real for years, but it became real for Tupac. It's like me. I mean, I wasn't born to be a killer; it was a mask I put on to stay alive in juvenile hall, but it became me. Tupac wore a mask but he was older and smarter, and he knew what he was doing, riding with someone like Suge."

I'm not so sure of that. Tupac's whole rap was that he was more "real" than any other artist. Toward the end, however—East Coast/West Coast, players/gangsters—the line between art and life was erased in his mind.

Look at the art: Much was made of what amounts to Tupac's last testament, the video for "I Ain't Mad at Cha." Released a week after his death, it shows Tupac in a baggy white Italian suit, looking far more like Groucho Marx than he might have imagined, going to a klieg-lit heaven after he's gunned down. Greeted by Redd Foxx, he's backed by Miles Davis, Jimi Hendrix, and Dizzy Gillespie, then comes back from time to time to console a grieving friend.

Look at the reality: Twenty-four hours after his death, I visited a very empty Club 662. Aerosoled in red and blue on the side wall was the title of a Tupac song, "Shed So Many Tears," with an R.I.P. written backward. The paint was still wet, and there was an overpowering smell of cheap beer on the ground below it: This was a traditional ghetto memorial, pouring out tribute to a dead brother. There was amazingly little glamour here, just a sad, ugly feeling, very creepy, very hollow. No art, no life, just ashes.

La Post-Guerra: War Without End
in the New El Salvador
by Scott Wallace

*Reporter Scott Wallace spent the 1980s cov-
ering civil wars in Central America. He returned
to El Salvador in the late 1990s to report this
Harper's article, which describes the United
States' contribution to one of the region's new
problems: gangs.*

One day in late September 1983, I stood in the blinding white light of midmorning on the ravaged town square of Tenancingo in central El Salvador, gagging on the stench of rotting corpses. Three nights earlier, hundreds of rebels from the Farabundo Marti National Liberation Front, who were fighting the U.S.-supported government for a share of their country's political power, swept down from the nearby Guazapa volcano to overwhelm the army garrison in Tenancingo. Barricaded inside the colonial church on the square, the army's desperate commander ordered an air strike on the town in a futile attempt to stave off the rebels. As the FMLN guerrillas captured the captain and seventy other soldiers and fled into the mountains, U.S.-supplied aircraft laid waste to entire blocks of the town, killing scores of villagers and leaving survivors staggering through the wreckage with dazed, vacant stares.

After the army retook Tenancingo, soldiers in surgical masks picked their way through dust and rubble, aided in their search for bodies by emaciated mongrels scrounging for a meal. The warplanes had vanished, ceding the pale-blue sky to squadrons of circling vultures. Despite the humiliation government forces had suffered, an army colonel convoked the townsfolk with a victorious flourish after his troops unearthed a bloated rebel carcass from a heap of adobe. Holding aloft a shattered M-16 stripped from the dead guerrilla, the colonel cried, "This is proof the terrorists are getting their weapons from Nicaragua." His claim was lifted straight out of the script written by the Reagan Administration to justify U.S. intervention in El Salvador and Nicaragua. As I jotted down the colonel's comments, I wondered if he—and American officials, for that matter—really believed in the lines they were parroting. After all, the United States was furnishing the Salvadoran army with tens of thousands of M-16s, which the rebels were seizing in routine skirmishes and coordinated assaults on government garrisons and armories. In the attack on Tenancingo alone, the rebels were said to have captured ninety-seven rifles.

Standing amid shattered buildings, hastily dug mass graves, scorched family portraits framed in shards of broken glass, the villagers listened to the colonel's words in silence. But his speech was really for a distant, far more influential audience, whom he would reach through us, the foreign journalists, there to record the spectacle with our notepads, microphones, and cameras. We knew, of course, that the United States was, in effect, the single largest supplier of lethal materiel to both sides of the Salvadoran civil war, but few reporters dared to deviate too far from the official line; our credibility would have been called into question. So the colonel's statements—and a cascade of similar claims emanating from Washington—went largely unchallenged, and the American public was cushioned from some of the more uncomfortable truths about El Salvador.

Some sixteen years after the rebel attack on Tenancingo and seven years after peace treaties ending the war were signed, I'm sitting in the back of a police pickup as we hurtle past the outskirts of the town and wind our way up a dirt track toward the mossy green peaks of Guazapa. The rebels have long since departed, and the land mines that once blocked access to their mountain base have been removed. Gone, too, are the legions of foreign journalists who documented the carnage of the 1980s in meticulous detail. But the events set in motion years ago have not yet run their course, and America has exported a new form of violence to El Salvador. The police agents aboard the Toyota 4 × 4 chamber a round and train their rifles on the dense underbrush on our flanks as we rush to re-supply beleaguered government patrols with warm bottled water and tin cans of chicken fricassee.

El Salvador's troops are on the move again. In cities and towns across the country, the police are battling two L.A.-imported gangs whose members fled to the United States in the 1980s as children only to be deported back to El Salvador in the 1990s as full-fledged gang-bangers. Here in the Guazapa area, police are pursuing one of a dozen criminal bands made up of ex-soldiers and former guerrillas who now use the volcanic massif as a base to wage a campaign of terror and banditry across central El Salvador.

In the 1980s the fugitives roving Guazapa were Marxist rebels fighting for social change, and the names, like the Revolutionary Army of the People and the Popular Liberation Front, succinctly captured their ideals. [*] But the triumph of Capital has spawned a breed of out-laws who have more immediate imperatives and a whole new nomen-clature more befitting their current sources of inspiration: Los Millionarios, The Fat Ones, Los Power Ranger, and Hatchet Face. Only a few days before, a small army of masked gunmen calling themselves the Armed Social Group forced a farmer to flee his property on the vol-cano's northern slopes. They shot up his home, wounding a laborer, and delivered a note directing the owner to hand over his twelve-year-old daughter—evidently she was to serve as collateral against a yet to be articulated demand for ransom. Scrawled in a pathetic chicken scratch and laced with misspelled words, the letter warned the landowner that his entire family faced a "massacre" if he refused to give up the girl.

---

[*] During the civil war, five rebel armies espousing a range of leftist philoso-phies and distinct military doctrines joined under the umbrella of the FMLN.

Such threats are not to be taken lightly. On the other side of the volcano, another group of bandits recently executed a nineteen-year-old university student they had kidnapped from the town of Aguilares when his mother failed to come up with the 5 million *colones*—about $600,000—they demanded for his release. Even after they murdered the student, the kidnappers continued to torment his mother, calling her several times a day to deliver new threats. The mayor of Aguilares also received death threats, and extortionists were driving farmers from the slopes of Guazapa with promises to put their crops to the torch if they refused to pay for protection.

A cluster of six separate peaks, Guazapa was created thousands of years ago when a powerful eruption blew the entire top off the massive volcano. That distant geological event left behind an intricate labyrinth of jagged ridgelines and densely vegetated hollows that radiate outward for miles. Nahuatl warriors took to these hills to wage a hit-and-run war against Spanish conquistadores, and in the 1980s, Guazapa's rugged folds afforded FMLN guerrillas a virtually impenetrable fortress only fifteen miles north of the capital of San Salvador. Back then, when I used to lie in bed at night and listen to the bombing of Guazapa roll in like thunder on the wind, Salvadoran officers and their U.S. advisers jokingly referred to Guazapa as Asshole Hill, because they were always trying to "wipe it clean." U.S.-supplied Dragonfly jets and hovering gunships that flew round-the-clock sorties made Guazapa the most heavily bombed piece of real estate in the history of the Western Hemisphere. The gullies of Guazapa fell within the confines of the FMLN's "liberated zone," where peasants collectively cultivated corn and beans, elected their own leaders, and organized their self-defense. Surrounding towns and hamlets, in turn, were ruled by national guardsmen in Prussian jackboots and steely-eyed paramilitaries who saw the Communist virus lurking inside anyone who wasn't one of their own. Death-squad killings were more highly concentrated around Guazapa than anywhere else in the country. It is probably no accident that today the same area hosts the largest collection of kidnapping rings in El Salvador.

At the crest of a steep incline, where spectacular sugarcane fields sprawl below us to the horizon, we come upon an exhausted eight-man patrol. It is a strange sort of déjà vu, seeing soldiers once again combing Guazapa in search of an elusive enemy. "It's difficult to track them down," says police agent Jose Rigoberto Ramirez, as he wipes his sweat-drenched face with a sleeve. "They know the terrain, and they know how to operate. They all have *armas de guerra* and military knowledge. These are people who participated directly in the war."

Lasting a dozen years, the Salvadoran civil war left some 75,000 dead—most killed by right-wing death squads or their allies in the military and police—and forced more than 20 percent of El Salvador's 5 million people to flee the country or seek shelter in USAID-funded resettlement centers. For all its Cold War trappings, the Salvadoran conflict was essentially a textbook case of class warfare—pitting the interests of the U.S.-supported business elite against those of the poor. Armed opposition grew out of a broad-based struggle for social reform that was greeted with bullets and a succession of stolen elections throughout the better part of the twentieth century. By 1980, the year the conflict boiled over into full-scale civil war, government troops were slaughtering street demonstrators by the hundreds; anyone who opposed the regime became a potential target for abduction and assassination. The Sandinistas had just toppled the Somoza family dynasty (a longtime U.S. ally) in nearby Nicaragua, and American hawks saw El Salvador as the next "domino" poised to fall to Marxist revolutionaries. When Ronald Reagan assumed office in January 1981, he immediately proclaimed he was "drawing the line" in El Salvador against "Communist expansion" in the hemisphere.

By the mid-1980s, El Salvador had become the third-largest recipient of U.S. foreign aid, after Egypt and Israel, with economic aid alone topping $430 million in 1985. Armed and advised by the Pentagon, the Salvadoran army racked up a growing list of battlefield atrocities, but no massacre or abuse of human rights proved sufficient to derail America's commitment to bring "democracy" to El Salvador. Aided in turn by Cuba and Nicaragua, the rebels proved a resilient foe, enduring each escalation with new tactics of their own. As the civilian body count mounted, combatants on both sides became increasingly adept in the dark arts of espionage, abduction, extortion, and murder.

Then the Soviet Union fell, and, with support from their respective Cold War allies drying up, the antagonists signed peace accords in 1992. In exchange for laying down their arms, the guerrillas managed to wring some concessions from the government: commanders suspected of links with the death squads were dismissed, the army's ranks were dramatically scaled back, and the FMLN emerged as a political party that is a true rival to the conservative Nationalist Republican Alliance, a crucial development for a country in which the democratic aspirations of the populace had been thwarted for decades. But those responsible for atrocities on both sides were never brought to trial, and the big questions—like how to overhaul El Salvador's highly skewed distribution of wealth— were left largely unresolved. Now the violence has taken on a distinctly commercial character, and the range of potential victims has expanded to include just about anyone. "It's like it was at the beginning of the war," Officer Ramirez said, as he pointed to a palm-shaded adobe house recently vacated by its owners at the base of Guazapa. "They're pulling people from their beds at night. Only now it's a business."

The war may have ended eight years ago, but permutations of it continue to surface every day in the "New El Salvador," the preferred term among government officials eager to attract new investors and tourists. El Salvador remains the most violent country in the hemisphere, with a murder rate 40 percent higher than that of Colombia. The World Bank now ranks San Salvador as Latin America's most crime-ridden city; one of every three of its citizens has been a victim of crime. El Salvador's 6,000-plus homicides in 1998 matched the country's annual body count at the height of the war in 1983, the year I arrived in El Salvador fresh out of journalism school to cover what appeared to be America's inexorable slide toward our "next Vietnam."

I left Central America in 1990 something of a war junkie, but while my colleagues pushed off for new conflicts in Somalia, Iraq, and Bosnia, I found myself drawn toward the reporting of crime. I covered Mafia stories in the former Soviet Union, land theft in the Amazon, arson for profit schemes in Upstate New York, home-invasion robberies in Arizona. But late at night, with my wife and kids fast asleep, I would open my journal and find myself invariably wandering back to the dusty, blood-drenched streets of El Salvador. And somewhere along the way, I came to realize that my Salvadoran experience lay at the root of my subsequent fascination with crime and its variable responses from law enforcement. We may not have understood it at the time, but the journalists who covered El Salvador in the 1980s were as much crime reporters as war correspondents. On any given day, we looked at death and contemplated its authorship, often showing up on the scene of a killing, or multiple killings, before the authorities did, if they came at all. We were like criminal investigators in a place where official inquests were a pro forma undertaking, designed to cover up rather than reveal. So I went back to El Salvador last year a seasoned police reporter returning to the scene—of both the crime and the war. I would come to find that *la post-guerra*, the term first coined at the end of the war to define the period of anticipated reconstruction, has come to signify the new, more bewildering, and seemingly more intractable turmoil that has unfolded instead.

At first glance, El Salvador's postwar mayhem seems similar to that of other countries emerging from years of conflict, such as South Africa, where unemployment, family disintegration, the dismantling of repressive security forces, and the ready availability of combat weapons have conspired to fuel astronomical crime rates. But another unforeseen factor has entered into the Salvadoran equation: the rise and proliferation of *las maras*—street gangs. Shortly after the civil war ended, our Immigration and Naturalization Service ended the special refugee status for Salvadorans who had come to America seeking asylum from the violence. So began the mass deportation of undocumented Salvadorans from the United States, thousands of whom returned to implant gang rule, block by block, throughout every city and town of their home country.

Officials estimate that there are more than 20,000 full-fledged gang members in San Salvador alone—four times the number of guerrillas that three successive Republican administrations spent hundreds of millions of dollars trying to vanquish. Washington force-fed El Salvador with a steady diet of infantry weapons: tens of thousands of automatic rifles, bazookas, land mines, hand grenades. And then, just as U.S. aid began to slow to a trickle, we began to export hardened veterans of our inner cities and federal pens. In 1998, INS deportations to El Salvador topped 5,300, and Salvadoran church officials estimate that 16 percent of the *deportados* arrive with what they call "grave antecedents" for criminal behavior—the rough equivalent of dumping 1,300 violent felons onto the streets of Chicago each year.[*]

"*Maras* control the entire city," San Salvador's police chief, Eduardo Linares, said when I dropped by his office. "They come with specialized knowledge from the States. They've brought with them new types of crime that didn't exist here before." Linares—a former FMLN commander with a drooping mustache and unruly brown hair—steered me to a large wall map of the city. During the war, police forces used the same map to plot assaults on suspected rebel safe houses and infiltration routes. Now the multicolored grease-pencil smears on Linares's map indicate zones of prostitution, drug trafficking, and black-market activity.

"I apply the theory of the broken window," Linares said, referring to the doctrine of former New York City police commissioner William Bratton in the early 1990s, which targets building-code violations and other petty offenses as a strategy to preempt more serious crime. "We close down the brothels, round up the dope dealers. It helps prevent delinquency."

It was curious to hear Linares—who spent twenty-one of his forty-eight years as a guerrilla in the FMLN, including nine as an urban commando in San Salvador's underground—extol the virtues of New York's Finest. But even during the war, Linares earned a reputation as a

---

[*] Recent revelations in the unfolding LAPD scandal indicate that officers in the Rampart Division may have planted evidence on Salvadoran gang members to bring about their deportation. Rampart officers are also under investigation for improperly turning over suspects to the INS in order to remove them as possible witnesses to police wrongdoing.

free-thinking strategist, granting spontaneous interviews at the front, speaking his mind, and not merely repeating the orthodoxies laid down by the supreme comandantes. True to his old self, Linares now acknowledges that neither his 500-man municipal force nor the 20,000 national police officers can combat what he calls the "deeper causes" fueling El Salvador's surging crime. "At the bottom, it's a problem of structural poverty," he said. "The neoliberal economic model is too exclusive. The same problems that gave rise to the war have not been addressed."

Now, Linares said, on top of the explosive conditions of gross social inequity, abusive authority, and widespread corruption that predated the civil war, El Salvador has become a refuge for powerful criminal syndicates who use the *maras* as a convenient smoke screen to deflect attention from their activities. "Organized crime enjoys almost total impunity," he lamented, while street gangs offer the criminal syndicates, largely composed of former death-squad members and military officers, a vast market for illegal narcotics and weapons as well as a recruiting base for mid-level pushers and cheap triggermen.

The old lines of conflict have blurred almost beyond recognition, but their vestiges can be vaguely discerned in the criminal elements each of the warring parties has spawned in *la post-guerra*. Urban slums, where the rebels once held sway, are now home to a tribal culture of violent gangs, while former army officers have vanished into shadowy quasi-legitimate enterprises in which the old military chain of command is faithfully replicated as the corporate hierarchy. One private security agency alone employs 6,000 laid-off soldiers and cops—including specialists in electronic surveillance, abduction, interrogation, and summary execution. And in places like Guazapa, ex-combatants from both sides have banded together to form a hybrid collection of social misfits ready to prey on any target, large or small.

The one bright spot in an otherwise dismal picture, Linares allowed, was the peace accords' provision that created the new civilian police authority—the Policía Nacional Civil—its ranks filled with former guerrillas like himself, many of whom are now trying to build a professional, competent force without the ideological baggage that made El Salvador's old security forces the backbone of political repression.[*] Unfortunately, PNC officers are poorly trained, underfunded, and lacking in the most rudimentary investigative know-how. "They solve one case out of every thousand," he said as he shrugged. And it's unclear whether the PNC has the will to pursue El Salvador's organized crime groups. While former guerrillas now account for 20 percent of the PNC's officer corps, the detective division is riddled with fascistic elements, thus ensuring both an enduring cover-up of atrocities and a whole new genre of collaboration between state intelligence and the criminal underworld. And inadequate screening of recruits allowed dozens—if not hundreds—of delinquents to penetrate the new force, undermining efforts to win the public's trust. "Criminality springs from the very same police force," Linares said. "They take off their uniforms and stage assaults with the same weapons they're issued to enforce the law."

During the war, foreign reporters would pile in our vehicles, the letters "TV" taped to our windshields, and head off to the front in search of the "Boys" or the "G's"—code words we favored, since the word "guerrillas" could be too easily recognized by eavesdroppers lurking in San Salvador's restaurants and hotel lobbies. As far as the army was concerned, journalists talking to rebels were often considered collaborators and subject to ambush. On the other hand, the highly disciplined, media-savvy rebels were almost always non-threatening. If you were really lucky, you'd run across a straight talker like Linares in the plaza of some abandoned town, where red revolutionary graffiti exhorted government soldiers to desert the "army of the rich." It was getting there—and getting out—that presented the greatest challenge.

But a whole new dynamic exists in the New El Salvador, and I wasn't

---

[*] In March 2000, the FMLN won a congressional plurality, but only 38 percent of the public bothered to vote. Such a low turnout indicates a widespread lack of faith in any party's ability to break the country's vicious cycle of poverty and rising crime.

sure what to expect as I rode out to the colonial city of Quetzaltepeque, just west of Guazapa, to look for the *maras*. Once a frequent dumping ground for the death squads, the city remains one of El Salvador's most dangerous, the scene of ongoing turf battles between local *clickas*, or cliques, of Mara Salvatrucha and Calle 18, gangs born on the streets of L.A.'s MacArthur Park area in the 1980s. The walls along Calle Urrutia, the city's main drag, are smothered in gang graffiti, which include several memorials to slain homies. I directed my driver to follow the rutted back streets along the city's eastern edge, 18th Street territory, but drug dealers greeted us with icy stares at every corner, and it looked too dicey to attempt a conversation.

So we headed instead to the Las Palmas neighborhood, a stronghold of the Mara Salvatrucha on the south side of town, where the paved streets turned to dirt and single-story homes abutted a coffee grove. There, we came upon a thin man with a goatee in his mid-twenties dressed in a sleeveless white T-shirt, his black hair slicked back to a ducktail. To my surprise, he introduced himself in perfect L.A. Spanglish. "Hey man, soy Giovanni Castro," he said, extending a hand attached to a sinewy, tattooed arm. "But you can call me Wito. That's what the homies call me here."

Wito fled the country at the age of twelve, he said, after death squads dragged his mother from a local movie theater and murdered her. "They cut her hands and arms off," he said. Wito eventually found his way to Los Angeles, traveling alone by freight train through Tapachula, Mexico, and on to the border town of Nogales. Once in L.A., Wito hooked up with a Latin *pandilla*—or gang—called White Fence and made a living selling drugs on the corners of West Hollywood. He was arrested for shooting a rival dealer who had shaken him down, stripping him of twenty-six hits of angel dust. "The guy put a gun to my head and took my drugs. So I went around the corner, got my piece, and shot him." I listened with studied nonchalance, as though Wito were telling me about a movie he'd just seen. Wito was deported after serving five years in prison, including a stint at Folsom. With seven siblings and two daughters still living in the L.A. area, Wito hoped to find his way back there. "I just need 400 bucks to get to T.J.," he said with an expectant air, as if I might be willing—or able—to help him out. "I got friends there who can get me across."

Wito's story is typical of the thousands of Salvadoran gang members who learned the ropes on American city streets. They were refugees who fled right-wing violence in the 1980s or children of those refugees. While the wealthy packed their kids off to condos and private schools in Miami or San Francisco to wait out the war, children of the poor who stole across the border were often left with a single working parent or sometimes no parent at all, largely abandoned to the streets once they reached the States. They learned gang rites at a young age, inhabiting a world within our borders that is almost completely hidden from our view. As anti-immigrant sentiments reached a fever pitch in the mid-1990s, Congress broadened the range of criminal acts that could result in expulsion, producing a surge in deportations to El Salvador. Salvadoran jails are overflowing, and local authorities have no choice but to give the *deportados* a fresh chance once they return home, since they have no criminal record in El Salvador. Often speaking little Spanish and with few hopes of finding gainful employment, the deportees quickly find themselves immersed in a culture of drugs and gangs remarkably similar to the one they left behind in the States.

Wito had hoped to leave gang life when he returned to El Salvador in 1997, but he was forced to join forces with the Mara Salvatrucha—or M.S.—after local 18th Street cliques decided his L.A. affiliation with White Fence made him a de facto enemy. "They'll kill me if they find me in 18th territory," he said. As we spoke, a number of young M.S.'ers gathered round to take in the curious spectacle of Wito speaking broken English to a gringo reporter. Carlos Alejandro, a husky eighteen-year-old wearing a White Sox cap and baggy, calf-length jeans, pulled down his sweat sock to reveal a nasty, purplish welt above his right ankle—a gunshot wound inflicted by 18th Street *maras* two weeks earlier. "They ambushed us from behind that tree," Carlos said, pointing to a tall locust just over Wito's shoulder. "They infiltrate through the *cafetal* [coffee grove] and attack us."

Tit-for-tat warfare among the *maras* undoubtedly accounts for the preponderance of gang casualties. But resurgent death squads—with names like the Voice of the People and the New White Hand—have claimed credit for a number of executions of gang leaders in the past few years. The anonymous communiqués issued by the *grupos de exterminio*, as the new "social cleansing" squadrons have come to be called, bear a remarkable resemblance in their patriotic discourse to those that followed right-wing death-squad slayings during the war. Then, victims were dragged from their homes in the dead of night by hooded gunmen, their disfigured bodies reappearing days later bearing unmistakable signs of cruel interrogations. Today's groups have little use for intelligence gathering; they forgo the torture sessions and proceed directly to the *tiro de gracia*—a clean shot delivered to the back of the head. Some of the most recent victims had been spearheading efforts to steer their cliques away from drugs and violence, suggesting that organized crime may be attempting to keep the gangs isolated and dependent on their profitable network for weapons and narcotics.

Even when no communiqués follow the mysterious shootings, the careful selection of targets—and the efficiency with which the victims are dispatched—have fueled fears that criminal elements within the police or private security companies may be moonlighting as contract killers. "You live with the fear that *la Sombra Negra* [death squads; literally, the Black Shadow] can come to get you at any moment," Wito said. "The police put the hoods on and come out to kill. It's the police who enter here; they are the death squads."

It's not only the *pandilleros* who fear the reactivation of the death squads. Progressive priests and other intellectuals who were targeted in the 1980s worry that the organized killing could once again be turned in their direction. "Now they are latent," one Jesuit activist told me, referring to politically motivated death squads. "But that which is latent could become active."

Street gangs were a feature of El Salvador's urban landscape for some years prior to the war's end. But armed only with knives and machetes, and with little access to illegal drugs, these gangs were scattered, small-time outfits with limited appeal and less power. During the FMLN's offensive on San Salvador in 1989, gangs in the tough working-class slums of the capital got their first taste of full-fledged combat when they joined the rebels' ill-fated call for a broad insurrection. "The *maras* saw the Front as a rebel group that stood up against the repression," said Rocko, a soft-spoken former gang member and ex-guerrilla with a wispy mustache and emaciated frame. Now thirty years old, Rocko has set up a small foundation to channel funds from foreign NGOs into work programs for gang members seeking to escape the violence. I spent an afternoon talking with him in an overgrown garden behind the temporary quarters of his organization. Already a gang veteran back in the mid-1980s, Rocko was tapped by the FMLN to identify and recruit potential guerrillas from among the capital's street toughs. "We knew the territory and could serve as guides at any given moment. We identified with the rebellion. After all, we were all rebels."

That sense of identification may help account for the vast proliferation of gangs in *la post-guerra*. Just about everything having to do with Salvadoran gang culture—from the graffiti *maras* scrawl on city walls and tattoo on their faces to the guns and violence that underlie their rituals—suggests the lurking presence of sublimated revolution. But when the guerrilla leaders laid down their weapons and joined the political process, their new role as loyal opposition obliged them to forsake the country's youth—one of their core constituencies and nearly 50 percent of El Salvador's population. Under the free-market policies urged by international lending agencies and adopted by the Nationalist Republican Alliance, plans to create ample educational, recreational, and employment opportunities for teens have largely evaporated. Youngsters have been left to fend for themselves in a new world without signposts, where local traditions are rapidly succumbing to an entire zeitgeist of imported food, music, and fashion.

More and more, Salvadorans are finding their daily nourishment at gleaming new convenience stores that appear to have been uprooted from Anywhere, U.S.A., and magically plunked down amid the wild elephant grass of El Salvador's tropical squalor. The shops come replete with piped-in hip-hop, Bunn-omatic serve-yourself coffee, and Subway sandwich counters (with step-by-step hints to help bewildered first-timers select their combination of meat, cheese, bread, and garnishes). The bustling Esso Tiger-marts do offer features that distinguish them from their North American cousins: prominent displays of vodka, *aguardiente*, and rum, and shotgun-toting security guards, who are often called upon to engage bandits and gangs in pitched parking-lot battles.

The guerrillas' goal of recarving El Salvador's pie to include a greater cut for the masses now seems like a distant, naive dream. The old landed oligarchy has mutated into a new cabal of wealthy bankers and industrialists, with the usual suspects jumping on the country's highly profitable postwar wave of privatization. Meanwhile, 30 percent of the country's workforce is underemployed, and nearly 25 percent of the population live in "absolute" poverty. Young Salvadorans who find themselves on the outside looking in have been primed by MTV culture to embrace that other big U.S. export: street gangs. "The majority of those deported were *maras* who had been hardened in American jails," Rocko said. "Those who came from the States brought with them their organization—and the same dress and manner of speaking that kids here had seen in the movies. They attracted the attention of kids who were hanging out, looking for someone they could look up to."

As the Mara Salvatrucha and the Calle 18 came to El Salvador, they quickly grew into national organizations, with "branch offices" across the country. Since many of the deportees returned to the same remote war zones their parents had fled in the 1980s, they spread U.S. urban gang culture deep into rural communities, creating satellite cells dependent on the larger city-based outfits for drugs, weapons, and directives. Like a series of corporate mergers, the old homegrown neighborhood gangs—with names like The Roosters, Mao Mao, and Baby Gang—were forced into *clickas* affiliated with either the M.S. or the 18th Street. Today, nearly every city and town in El Salvador is carved up into an intricate patchwork of rival cliques, nearly all pertaining to, or otherwise dependent on, the two archrivals from L.A.

"What has us really worried now is the flood of drugs flowing into the country," said Rocko. "Since 1995, the country's been awash in crack." That year, according to police sources, the Colombian cartels began to insist on paying "in trade" rather than with cash for rights to refuel their northbound aircraft on the dirt strips that service large plantations strung out along Central America's highlands and coastal plains. To convert the drugs to cash, hacienda owners, corrupt customs agents, and others linked to the Colombian trade were obliged to increase sharply local demand for cocaine. "*El crack* has accelerated the violence among the *maras* tremendously," said Rocko. "But on the national level, no one seems to care. Drug trafficking is not on the agenda."

Along with scattered private efforts like Rocko's, progressive elements within the Catholic Church have been spearheading efforts to channel the gangs' raw energy in a more positive direction. To diffuse tensions, clergy and lay workers have brought leaders from rival cliques together, offering workshops in car mechanics, furniture making, and word processing.

One night in San Salvador's working-class district of Ilopango, parish lay workers arranged for me to meet with an articulate gang leader named Murra. At twenty-two, Murra was already a nine-year veteran of the hundred-strong Trident clique—an 18th Street ally that controls a square mile of urban turf surrounded by hostile chapters of the Mara Salvatrucha. Murra sported none of the wild graffiti usually tattooed across the foreheads, chins, and forearms of Salvadoran gang-bangers. Such tattoos serve to bind gang members together and distinguish them from rivals, creating a kind of artificial tribalism in the absence of the ethnic differences that have fueled conflicts in places like the Balkans or Central Africa. Evidently, Murra had staked out a more thoughtful position than most of his peers on the use of tattoos. "It's an immediate giveaway to los perros [the dogs]," he said, referring to the police. Murra pointed to his single tattoo: a small, three-dotted triangular formation etched just above the knuckle on one finger. "It's the Trident—drugs, sex, and rock and roll," he clarified. "Only now it's hip-hop. You know, *la vida loca*."

We sat on a bench in the pale glow of a barren light bulb under the tin-roof eaves of the parish house. The sky thundered and a torrential rain broke loose, soaking our boots while puddles the size of small lakes spread across the dirt courtyard. Murra's darting eyes kept a close watch on the street from beneath the visor of a Philadelphia Eagles cap. "We're in enemy territory here," he explained. The last time Murra came to the church, about a month earlier, his presence was detected by M.S. lookouts. They closed off the quadrant of single-story cement-block houses and fired shots into the church grounds. Murra scrambled into the parish office and phoned his comrades, who arrived within fifteen minutes in two separate caravans to extricate him.

The enforcement of gang turf in San Salvador is ferocious, leaving the *maras* virtual prisoners within their own neighborhoods. To move beyond his own clique's zone of control, which lay twenty blocks away, Murra said he had to either hop a bus or assemble a posse of at least two dozen armed comrades, deployed military-style along both sides of the street. Even taking the bus presupposed a certain risk. I met several *pandilleros* who had been seriously wounded—or who themselves had inflicted serious wounds—in the kind of shoot-outs that erupt weekly aboard city buses. In fact, Murra committed his first murder at the age of thirteen while riding a bus, when he knifed a *huanaco*—a member of the Mara Salvatrucha.

"I felt joy and sadness," Murra told me. "I had killed my first. But then I knew I was no longer safe walking on the street. You live with the fear they're going to do the same thing to you." I casually asked how many he had killed in his nine years with Trident. "Probably ten," he said, between gang rivals and local street dealers who failed to pay their "taxes." Murra paused for a moment, then added: "That's not counting the ones I left agonizing on the ground." Murra's stature in the clique grew with each murder, until he emerged a few years ago as its undisputed leader.

Trident members pooled their money, gradually acquiring an arsenal of increasingly potent weapons: pistols, hand grenades, shotguns, Uzi submachine guns. "In this country, it's easy to buy guns," he said. "You see the news every night—the deaths inflicted each day by heavy-caliber weapons. These are the guns that remained here after the war. First we had *la guerra*. Now it's *la post-guerra*."

Lately, as the father of two young children, Murra had begun to wish for a chance to start over. "If someone had been there when I was younger to offer advice, I wouldn't have gotten involved," he sighed. After he began meeting with Ilopango's evangelizing laity, he had tried to keep a low profile with the gang, counseling his underlings to forswear violence. He was waking up early to get to his minimum-wage job on the assembly line of a foreign-run *máquila*. But Murra knew he had traveled too far down a certain road to be able to retrace his steps; like the Mafia and the CIA, gang life is forever. "If someone wants to leave and he knows too much about the gang, we kill him." Murra shrugged, implicitly acknowledging his own predicament. "When he leaves he'll start to talk. We can't let him out alive."

When the time came to evacuate Murra from the barrio, a lay worker in his early twenties named Noe went out into the rain to look for a taxi. The cab's windshield wipers slapped back and forth as we drove through the damp, deserted streets, past high cement walls topped with razor wire and shards of broken glass. Someone had painted an enormous English slogan—WELCOME HOMEBOY—which ran along one wall for nearly an entire block. "It's only because of guys like Murra that we can walk the streets here," said Noe smiling and giving Murra an affectionate pat on the knee. "They provide protection for us." We left Murra under a street lamp at a corner where a dirt road lined by walled-in houses branched off and receded into deep shadows thrown by swaying palms and locust trees. Before he got out of the car, Murra asked if I might send him a Spanish-language copy of *Bound by Honor*, a Mobster testimonial he had heard about, when I got back to the States. I told him I would do my best. "Good luck," he said, offering a firm handshake. He turned and vanished into the night.

"He's got to be careful," Noe whispered. "He's a marked man." The body of another Ilopango gang leader who was working to diffuse street violence had recently turned up one morning with his thumbs bound behind his back and a single bullet delivered to the head—an execution that bore all the hallmarks of the death squads that operated during the war with the connivance of government security forces. "The squads investigate their targets thoroughly," Noe said. I was surprised he even called them by the same name—*los escuadrones.* "You see them cruise the streets in new cars with polarized windows. They're from the private security companies. They know where they're going to find their *cliente.*" The same people—"high-ranking officers," Noe called them—had also taken a dim view of Noe's work evangelizing among the gangs. Anonymous death threats had been mailed to the parish, and on a recent night Noe was intercepted on a dark street by a surly man with a baseball cap pulled low over his eyes. "You dogs better watch out," the man snarled. "We know who you are. We're keeping tabs on you." Such encounters had convinced Noe that elements of the old guard were operating to keep El Salvador's youth steeped in gang violence. "They don't want the gangs to disappear," Noe said. "It's a distraction, a big screen to hide the huge theft they're committing from the eyes of the people."

It stands to reason that reactionary forces might see the perpetuation of gang warfare as a useful mechanism for blunting whatever danger of revolution might remain. In a single generation, El Salvador's urban youth, who formed the backbone of one of the most powerful revolutionary movements in the history of Latin America, have lowered their sights from molding a socialist utopia to enforcing gang rule within the circumscribed perimeters of their respective barrios. The far right, in contrast, has remained largely intact, using both legal and extralegal means to pound fresh nails into the coffin of reform. [*]

Although it was only nine o'clock, Noe deemed my own exit from Ilopango too risky. After sunset, *bandas* of former rebels and soldiers

---

[*] In fact, the FMLN—disillusioned with the slow pace of reform and the ongoing right wing violence—is rumored to have counseled the Irish Republican Army to hold on to its weapons for as long as possible, lest its adversaries renege on peace-deal promises, as has happened in El Salvador.

emerge to kidnap and loot along the lonely two-lane highway that sep-
arates the barrio from the center of San Salvador; it was best to stay put
until morning. Through the course of a sweaty, sleepless night, I lay in
bed with my ears straining at every creaking branch and passing foot-
step, cursing myself for letting the cab driver know exactly where I
would be staying. In the new El Salvador, you never know who might
be willing to trade such information for a few extra pesos.

Perhaps no single person better embodies El Salvador's long slide into
twilight than a seventeen-year-old gang leader and hired assassin named
Gustavo Adolfo, better known by his suggestive gang name, El Directo—
"The Direct One." Since his arrest in January 1999, El Directo has
emerged as a dark celebrity, the subject of lurid hip-hop verse and sensa-
tional tabloid headlines. According to court officials, El Directo was the
prime orchestrator of a two-year wave of terror that swept across the
overgrown lots and graffiti-smothered blocks of the eastern city of San
Miguel. He is said to have hacked apart street urchins with machetes and
pickaxes, disposing of their bodies in a communal well. And he allegedly
lured a series of schoolgirls behind a gleaming new Miami-style shopping mall, where he led his Mara Salvatrucha comrades in ceremonial
gang rapes that ended with the execution of the victims.

El Directo's penchant for murder put him out on that murky, ill-
defined frontier of Salvadoran crime where gang violence intersects
with the more calculated business of terror for profit and *pandilleros*
graduate from street toughs to foot soldiers for organized crime. El
Directo was getting money from somewhere; neighborhood kids said
he never lacked for drugs or weapons. And police say that on a number
of occasions, Gustavo served as a *sicario*—a hired gun—for an unidentified clientele. Authorities suspect El Directo of at least seventeen
grisly murders—one for each year of his short life.

While covering the war back in the 1980s, I met plenty of reputed
killers who justified con gusto the wholesale ideological cleansing
then under way in El Salvador, even if they disavowed any direct par-
ticipation in it. But when my eyes met the flat lifeless ones of Gustavo

Adolfo, I sensed I was in the presence of a new sort of animal, for whom killing was a matter of simple expedience, with no more need for explanation than the imperative of eating breakfast in the morning.

"I don't mess with anyone who doesn't mess with me," El Directo said in a bored monotone barely audible over the raucous banter of other juvenile offenders wrestling outside in the prison courtyard. "Because, quite simply, those that did . . . I made them disappear."

Gustavo came to gang life the way many kids do in El Salvador. Raised by a stepfather who sexually abused him and a suspicious mother who kept him in isolation from the rest of the household, Gustavo finally found a family when he joined the local clique of the Mara Salvatrucha at the age of eleven. He became an eager student of weapons of every sort—from assault rifles to homemade bombs—and displayed a startling disposition to put them to use, rising higher in the ranks with each successive rubout. "The weapon I used depended on where I happened to be," he said matter-of-factly, when I asked about his firearm of choice. "We stashed guns in different parts of the neighborhood." Gustavo displayed an encyclopedic knowledge of the various infantry weapons left behind from the war and the price each could fetch on the black market. "We'd buy our guns from a police agent," he said, declining to be more specific. "He would take the guns off other *maras* in San Miguel and sell them to us."

I was grateful to be meeting El Directo in circumstances that stripped him of the kind of power he exercised over his quarry on the streets of San Miguel. I studied the bewildering array of spiderwebs, clown faces, and gang symbols tattooed on his face, neck, and arms. A cellmate had just added a fresh addition to El Directo's body art, etching an M and an S in large Gothic letters on the back of each hand. The raw and pussy grooves hurt just to look at, and I redirected my gaze toward a distant point on the puke-green prison wall.

Attempting to explain Gustavo's ferocious behavior, a court psychologist told me this story: When his mother went to the hospital in an advanced state of labor seventeen years earlier, she rode in an ambulance bay filled with the disfigured victims of a suicidal soldier who had just pulled the pin on a grenade inside a crowded saloon. Curiously, when police arrested El Directo at his home last year, he lunged for a similar fragmentation grenade he kept on a shelf in his room, perhaps intending to depart this world the same way he had entered it. "This is the fruit of a generation who grew up with the war," the psychologist said.

That war is in the past, and the United States has taken a considerably lower profile than back in the 1980s, when we were pumping $1 million a day into El Salvador, when every utterance of our ambassador was quoted prominently in the local press and the State Department drew up plans to move the old earthquake-damaged embassy to a vastly expanded new facility on San Salvador's western outskirts. The U.S. mission occupied the sprawling new compound in 1992, just as the war was ending. Built to wartime specifications and intended to house a legion of bureaucrats, spooks, and military advisers, much of the complex would now sit empty were it not for USAID's decision to warehouse many of its regional functionaries in the new *embajada*.

I passed through a series of security checks and air-locked doors into the silent, climate-controlled sterility of the embassy. On the fifth floor I met with Marjorie Coffin, a cheery State Department spokeswoman, who gushed over San Salvador's prodigious road and building construction projects and the wonderful changes under way in postwar El Salvador. To get a look at the new face of American aid to El Salvador, Coffin urged me to check out "New Horizons '99"—the ongoing civic action exercises out east in Chilanguera, where two-week rotations from the U.S. Army Reserves were putting up a new school and rechanneling the river in the town hardest hit by Hurricane Mitch in 1998. I decided to follow up on Coffin's suggestion.

With the Chaparrastique volcano looming in the distance in a perfect Fujiesque cone, giant earthmovers painted in green-and-black camouflage lumbered across the mudflats, scooping monstrous rocks from the bed of the Chilanguera River. A cluster of African-American engineers in yellow hard hats and olive fatigues—"Bravo Company, sir.

467th Engineering Battalion, Greenville, Mississippi. What can we do for you?"—huddled around a topographical map, trying to square its obsolete representation of the meandering river with the hilly terrain of scrub and blooming jacarandas that Mitch had rearranged around them. Everything was going fine; no incidents to report, and the locals were friendly. "Wish we could understand them though," said one as he pointed over his shoulder at a group of women standing knee-deep in the river, scrubbing away at laundry on the rocks. The soldiers' de facto translator, a reservist from Puerto Rico, had gone home with the last rotation, leaving the Americans clueless as they went about their good works. "We wave and smile, and they wave and smile."

I waded across the waterway to a mud-and-stick hut perched on the opposite bank. Barefoot children chased baby chicks around the clearing amid peals of laughter. An emaciated man dressed in rags put down a bucket of water he had just hauled up from the well and sauntered over to introduce himself. "It's good, what they're doing," said Perfecto Ramos, nodding across the way at the Mississippians. "Only thing, they don't understand anything we say. Maybe you could ask if they'd push the bank up a little more on this side? I'm afraid the ground is too low here and it will flood again."

Ramos said he and his family had survived Mitch by climbing to higher ground as the Chilanguera overflowed its banks and swept over the town. But he wasn't so lucky fourteen years before, when a U.S.-supplied Cessna spotter plane rocketed his single-room dwelling. "We lived up on that hill over there." Ramos pointed to a distant ridgeline. Five members of his family were killed that day, including a daughter and three nephews. The date rolled straight off his tongue: April 18, 1985.

"We thank God things have changed," Ramos said. Then his face darkened. "But now we have a new problem—los *delincuentes*." Armed cattle rustlers roam the hills now, hauling away farm animals with impunity. "We don't know who they are, because the police never come here to investigate." Ramos said he had begun tethering his goats and pigs at night to the poles on his open-air porch, hoping to save his animals from the bandits.

On Guazapa three weeks before, I had heard similar tales of *cuatreros* rounding up animals from pastures at night, loading them on large flatbeds, taking them off to black-market buyers and clandestine slaughterhouses. It seemed cattle rustling was rapidly developing into a national industry. Fearing the rustlers would kidnap their animals in the dead of night, farmers were beginning to share their living quarters with chickens, pigs, and cows. But even then, masked gunmen were kicking in doors, using the occasion to take away not only the animals but their owners as well. "No one opposes them," one peasant had told me, "because they have the guns."

I slogged back over the river and communicated Ramos's message to the Greenville engineers. They cheerfully agreed to rework the bank. "So that's what he was trying to tell us." I chose not to mention the bandits lurking in the hills around them; I didn't want to give them any thoughts about oiling up their M-16s. But despite the indubitable service the reservists were performing for the people of Chilanguera, I found something vaguely disturbing about their presence. Or perhaps what bothered me more was the *timing* of their presence. I had the feeling the C-5 Galaxy time machines that dropped them from the sky had overshot by twenty years. I wondered what might have been if we had come here with the tractors and backhoes two decades back, when it really could have counted. And if we had left the guns at home. Maybe then there could have been a New El Salvador after all.

Bo Ying

by Fredric Dannen

Frederic Dannen's (born 1955) 1992 article about gangs in New York City's Chinatown is a story about victims—innocent and otherwise.

Around seven o'clock on the night of July 16, 1989, Anthony Gallivan went out drinking with his wife, Christine, and another couple. The Gallivans, who were both in their early thirties, were born in Ireland, but at present they lived in Jackson Heights, Queens. It was wet and windy, so the two couples took a cab to the Liffey Pub, an Irish bar in Elmhurst. They laughed and talked and drank Guinnesses until after nine, and then decided they were hungry for Chinese food.

This was a commodity not hard to come by in Elmhurst. In two decades, Elmhurst, Flushing, and other sections of Queens within a two-mile radius of Shea Stadium had become a second Chinatown, cleaner and more prosperous than the one in lower Manhattan. (The No. 7 subway train to Flushing was dubbed the Orient Express.) The Gallivans and their friends ducked into the Tien Chau, a Taiwanese restaurant just a short jog from the Liffey Pub. They had planned to order takeout, but now it was raining heavily, so they sat down at a table for four.

The Tien Chau was a small restaurant, with only about a dozen tables, and at nine-thirty on a wet night it was almost empty. Seated near the cash register, Gregory Hyde and his Chinese-American wife, Carol Huang, were getting ready to leave. When they got up to pay the check, two well-dressed Chinese boys were arguing with the manager, a thirty-five-year-old Taiwanese named Mon Hsiung Ting. Well, Greg figured, we might as well sit down and let them finish their discussion. Moments later, Greg heard what sounded like firecrackers. When he turned around, one of the boys was crouching, his feet spread apart. He was firing a pistol.

"Carol, duck!" Greg yelled. Carol dived under the table, her eyes on the shooter. The boy caught her looking at him. She later estimated that they made eye contact for two or three seconds—long enough for her to fix an image in her mind of a handsome young man with spiky hair, huge eyes, and, for an Asian, very fair skin. He wore a black suit and a white shirt with black pinstripes. He appeared quite calm. Then he fired in Carol's direction, and she instinctively covered her face with her hands.

Greg Hyde was struggling to get under the table as well. His back was to the shooter. He tried to slide out of his chair, but it was stuck, and when he pushed back hard he was forced upright. Suddenly, his legs gave way under him, and he knew that he had been shot. Hyde fell to the floor, face forward, on his arm. He tried to move, but his legs were paralyzed. He could feel his body going into shock.

At her table toward the rear of the restaurant, Christine Gallivan looked over to her left and saw her dish fall. Her husband clutched his chest and said, "Christine, I think I've been hit!" She glanced up and saw a young man with a small, "James Bond–type" gun, his arms bouncing in recoil after each shot. Blue smoke rose in the background. Tony Gallivan was sliding off his chair. One of his friends grabbed him and laid him on the ground on his back. There was blood on his

T-shirt in the middle of his chest, a dot the size of a pen top. It was an exit wound; the bullet had entered his back on the right side and passed through his heart. Christine was screaming. She later recalled, "I held him in my arms, and his eyes rolled and his color changed. And I figured he died then."

The restaurant manager, Mon Hsiung Ting, staggered out from behind the cash register and collapsed, dead, in the middle of the floor. His blood was splattered on the wall mirrors, and gushed out of holes in his body. He had been shot nine times, by both boys.

The second boy grabbed his companion in the black suit and pulled him out the door. Carol got up from under the table and screamed at a waitress to open the cash register for a quarter to phone 911. She returned to her husband's side, and Greg said an Act of Contrition. He believed he was dying. He would live, though, crippled for life; a bullet had entered his shoulder and damaged his spine. Carol had escaped unharmed, and she had seen so much that in time the boy in the black suit would regret not having killed her.

The boys drove to an apartment on Eighty-seventh Road in Woodhaven, Queens, about ten miles south of the Tien Chau restaurant, where the boss who had ordered the shooting awaited their return. His name was Chen I. Chung, and he was the *dai lo*, or big brother, of a Chinese gang called the Green Dragons. *Dai lo* is a term of respect accorded to one's elders, or to a boss, in a gang, and Chen I. Chung was both a boss and an older gang member. He was twenty.

The Green Dragons were based in Elmhurst, and their principal competition in the borough of Queens was a Flushing gang known as the White Tigers. The Dragons and the Tigers maintained an uneasy truce, and on occasion ranking members of the two gangs would sit down in a restaurant or a nightclub and attempt to resolve territorial disputes. Besides mutual animosity, the Green Dragons and the White Tigers had something else in common: both were patterned after established gangs in Manhattan's Chinatown. Youth gangs started to emerge in Chinatown in the sixties and seventies, and they have a distinctive culture—a bizarre mixture of traits borrowed from the

Hong Kong triads (secret criminal societies) and the clichés of American and Chinese gangster movies. Gang members dress all in black and have their chests and arms tattooed with dragons, serpents, tigers, and sharp-taloned eagles. They can be as young as thirteen. Once enlisted, a gang member loses contact with family and school; the gang becomes both. Members live in safe-house apartments, often several to a room. Gangs have territories—certain streets, certain hangouts—and the appearance of a rival gangster in the wrong place can lead to bloodshed.

It would be simplistic to compare gangs such as the Green Dragons and the White Tigers, as some have tried, to the Jets and the Sharks of "West Side Story," or even to the color gangs of Los Angeles. They are not youth gangs in the usual sense but, rather, a young form of organized crime. They have a clearly defined hierarchy, and junior members will obey the instructions from the *dai lo* or someone else of high rank even if the order is to kill for reasons not explained. Asian gangs engage in a recognizable pattern of racketeering, the bedrock crime being extortion. It is difficult to find a restaurant in Chinatown that was not at one time or another shaken down for protection money by a youth gang.

The Green Dragons and the White Tigers imported this tradition into Queens. Sometimes the restaurants would put up a fight. This was not something that Chen I. Chung could allow. If word were to get around that a restaurant had successfully refused to pay the Green Dragons, no one would take the gang seriously. According to the testimony of former gang members (a prime source of information for this account), Chen I. Chung repeatedly complained that the manager of the Tien Chau, Mon Hsiung Ting, was "hardheaded." Finally, he decided to send a pair of Dragons to kill Ting. One of the boys he selected was Alex Wong, who had been the good-looking boy in the black suit. The other killer was Joseph Wang. Both boys were sixteen.

Now Alex and Joe were reporting back to Chen I. Chung after the shooting, and the *dai lo* was satisfied, with one reservation. Alex said that the customers had ducked when the shooting started—all except one man. He had stood up, so Alex had fired at him. (That was Gregory Hyde.) Alex perhaps did not realize that he had shot and killed Anthony Gallivan, but he knew that the man he had hit was Caucasian. Chen I. Chung did not like that part of the story. Victimizing a non-Asian might bring heat from law enforcement. Gangs did not think American justice cared much about Asians, and the Asian community seemed to agree, for most extortions and many armed robberies went unreported.

Chen I. Chung was Taiwanese. He was familiarly called I. Chung (with "I" pronounced like "E"). I. Chung had immigrated to Waco, Texas, in 1981, at thirteen, along with two older sisters and an older brother, and had moved to Chicago before settling in Queens. His parents opened a Chinese restaurant in Buffalo. He was about five foot seven and skinny, with a tattoo of a tiger on his left shoulder and a gold ring in his left ear. His face was catlike. On Christmas Eve, 1987, two Asian youths opened fire on I. Chung as he sat in his car, at a red light. He managed to drive to the hospital with a bullet lodged in his skull. Since then, I. Chung had experienced severe headaches at times of stress. After eight years in America, he spoke almost no English. He had been with the Green Dragons from its inception, in 1985, and had moved steadily up the ladder. As *dai lo*, he had his own apartment and a platinum American Express card. It is commonly thought that gang members kill mostly one another. The Green Dragons dispelled that myth: they preyed on the innocent.

With two dozen active members at most, the Green Dragons was a relatively small gang compared with Chinatown gangs such as the Ghost Shadows and the Flying Dragons. It was also more autonomous, since the Chinatown gangs had to answer to a more senior criminal hierarchy. Chinatown, which was established in the eighteen-hundreds, operated on a system of tongs, or fraternal societies, which constituted, quite literally, the local government. (The Hip Sing, with headquarters on Pell Street, was the largest and most powerful tong; next in line was the On Leong, on Mott Street; and then the Tung On, on Division Street. The tongs controlled Chinatown's commerce, and allegedly profited from drug trafficking, gambling, and prostitution. Each tong enjoyed the allegiance of a youth gang. The fear that gangs inspired in merchants was enormously useful to the tongs, which governed the community through intimidation.

The tongs and the gangs were often equated with Mafia enterprises, but a far better analogy was to the Black Hand, the precursor of the American Mafia which in the early part of the twentieth century also preyed on its own ethnic group—first-generation Italian immigrants who spoke little English and did not trust American law enforcement to protect them. Most of Chinatown's population was also foreign-born, and regarded police and prosecutors with the same skepticism.

Throughout the eighties, the government did seem more intent on fighting "traditional" organized crime—the Mafia—than Asian crime, which had existed in America just as long. There were exceptions. In 1985, Nancy Ryan, of the Manhattan District Attorney's Jade Squad, convicted twenty-five members of the Ghost Shadows of numerous acts of racketeering, including thirteen murders. The Ghost Shadows served the On Leong tong. A few years later, the Flying Dragons, the gang overseen by the Hip Sing tong, was infiltrated by a police officer, David Chong. He fooled the Flying Dragons so thoroughly that he rose to the status of *dai lo* and became a street lieutenant, with a crew of twelve soldiers. Chong long remembered one of his most deplorable jobs as a *dai lo*, recruiting new gang members. This was typically done at school.

"I drove a Corvette, I had handfuls of money, the prettiest girls, the best jewelry, so you know what I would do?" Chong said. "I would have my kids go to a high school in Chinatown and look for the turkey right off the boat. You want him in ninth or tenth grade, he can't speak English, he's got a stupid haircut. And when you find this kid, you go beat the shit out of him. Tease him, beat him up, knock him around. We isolate this kid; he's our *target*. What will happen, one day I'll make sure

I'm around when this kid is getting beaten up, and I'll stop it with the snap of my finger. He'll look at me—he'll see that I have a fancy car, girls, I'm wearing a beeper—and I'll turn around and say, 'Hey kid, how come these people are beating on you?' I'm gonna be this kid's hero, this kid's guru—I'm gonna be his *dai lo.* I'll take the kid for a drive, take him to a restaurant, order him the biggest lobster, the biggest steak. Eventually, I'll take him to the safe house where I keep kids and guns. Then I slowly break him in."

Part of the allure of joining a gang is that it attracts a certain type of girl. Gang girls are not actual members, though they do sometimes hide guns or abet crimes in other ways. One girl involved with the Green Dragons, Tina Sham, was atypical. She was extremely shy and frightened by violence. Her grandfather was a prominent, upper-middle-class Hong Kong shipping executive, and a devout Buddhist. Her father, Robert, the ninth of ten children, was a rock musician. As a teenager, he heard the Beatles and discovered his destiny. By 1967, at the age of twenty, he had formed a Hong Kong rock group called Jade. Robert played drums. "We were very popular," he said. "We got four LP. I am quite famous." He smiled.

At twenty, Robert was already married; his wife, Rita, was half Chinese and half English. They had a daughter, Tina, in 1968; a son, Alfie, in 1969; and another son, Trini, in 1970. That year, they were divorced. Tina moved in with her cousins Beatrice and Dorothy Chan, the daughters of Robert's oldest sister.

In 1983, Robert relocated to Queens, taking Tina and Trini with him. (Alfie remained with his grandmother in Hong Kong.) He had long contemplated the move: "America, you have one big song, you win a fortune. When you hit"—he snapped his fingers—"that's *it!*" Rita had arrived in America a year earlier, remarried, and settled in Brooklyn. The Chan cousins moved to Queens soon after Robert did. Tina and Trini bounced from home to home, in Brooklyn and Queens. Robert's big plans did not seem to include child rearing. He wanted to make enough money to build his own recording studio.

The fame Robert had won so early in Hong Kong eluded him in America. By 1985, he was beginning to feel desperate. At a nightclub, Robert met a heroin trafficker named Henry Chan. Henry needed another courier to smuggle his contraband from Hong Kong to New York, and he was willing to pay that person ten thousand dollars per pound. In May and June of 1985, Robert went to Hong Kong, loaded the false bottom of a steamer trunk with heroin, and mailed the trunk to himself with musical equipment inside. Both times, the trunk cleared customs undetected. At Christmas, Robert made a third trip for Henry, only this time he took the trunk on the plane. So far, Henry told him, that was twelve pounds of heroin—one hundred and twenty thousand dollars. Henry paid Robert in small bills, stuffed in restaurant take-out bags. On March 20, 1986, Robert arrived at John F. Kennedy International Airport with his fourth shipment—eight pounds, this time, according to Henry. He was called aside by a customs agent. When Robert did too much talking, the agent got suspicious, examined the trunk, and discovered the false bottom. Robert was arrested. He decided to cover for Henry Chan, but then, to his shock, customs weighed the heroin at more than sixteen pounds—twice what Henry had told him. Realizing he had been cheated, Robert turned state's evidence against Henry. Thanks in large measure to his testimony, which filled nearly three days of a one-week trial in early 1988, Henry Chan was convicted. He got twelve years and was fined two hundred and fifty thousand dollars.

Robert, as a reward for coöperating, was sentenced to the two years he had already served while awaiting Henry's trial. He returned in disgrace to his apartment in Rego Park. He had brought dishonor to his family, and his grief was compounded by an incident that had occurred only four months after he was stopped at Kennedy Airport. It concerned his son Trini, who had had the misfortune to fall in with the Green Dragons.

Trini was prime Green Dragons material. At fifteen, he was already five-eleven, and tough. Officially, he lived with his mother, Rita, in Brooklyn, but he did not get along with his stepfather. The Green Dragons provided him with a floor mattress at a safe house on 128th

Street in Queens. Soon he was given an assignment: to dispose of two guns used in a shooting—a .38-calibre pistol and a .357 magnum. At 4:30 a.m. on July 22, 1986, as Trini prepared to toss the weapons into Columbus Park, in Chinatown, he was stopped by a police officer—James Dora, of the Fifth Precinct. In a panic, Trini brandished the .38, which was loaded, fired, and hit Dora in the right hand and the neck. (Dora eventually recovered from his wounds, but not without considerable suffering.) Dora returned fire, wounding Trini. The boy dropped the guns and fled. For the next three days, he hid at the Queens gang apartment. On July 25th, police officers from the Fifth Precinct, acting on a tip, burst in and arrested him. On January 5, 1987, Trini pleaded guilty to attempted murder in the second degree, a Class B felony. He ended up serving five years as a juvenile offender.

For Tina Sham, seeing her father and brother go to prison as, respectively, a heroin smuggler and a would-be cop-killer was just the latest sad chapter in a difficult life. She had dropped out of school and tried to find work, but had few advantages, other than good looks. All her facial features were strong: large eyes set far apart, a shapely nose, a sensuous mouth. "She's too pretty," her cousin Beatrice Chan recalled thinking. "People will mess with her." Tina was a shy girl. "Tina never talked," Beatrice said. "She never even say one word back to you if you scold her. She just sit down and listen—sometimes she smile. And she never complain, whether she has enough money, food to eat, whether her rent could be paid."

Beatrice and her sister Dorothy had looked after Tina as a little girl in Hong Kong. At a house they shared in Woodside, and, later, in Elmhurst, they became, in effect, her foster family. Bea was married and had two small children; Dorothy was single; both worked at law offices in Chinatown.

"Tina don't really have a proper life," Beatrice said. "She's always with this relative, that relative. Relatives, if you don't have money to bring with you, they don't love you. You can't imagine how sad life she has. I get so mad with my Uncle Robert. Tina love her father very much, she want to stay with him, but the father don't know how to take care of her. He's a total lost person. He has a band in Hong Kong, very famous, and he come here and can't get fame. Then he goes into the wrong sides with doing the drugs, and got himself into a jail, and Tina got no place to stay, and jobs is hard to find. I have my own family, but still I try my very best. This is the only place she can stick around."

Tina seemed happy in the Chan household. "She loves my daughter Nicole, always she hugs her," Bea said. "She cooks for her. Tina even teach her how to eat French fries. And my son, Eugene, whenever his birthday, if her pocket has ten dollars, she buy the toys, she spend it all. She loves him."

Still, Tina could not seem to stay in one place. "She move around a *lot*," Bea said. "More than ten places. I help her move more than five places. I myself bring her food. And the apartment they live in is not good apartment."

One of Tina Sham's temporary addresses, an apartment on 164th Street and Parsons Boulevard, was a safe house for the Green Dragons. Tina lived there for a good part of 1986 with her boyfriend, a high-ranking Dragon named Johnny Tran, who was Vietnamese, which did not at all disqualify him for membership. Inside the gang, he was known by the nickname Johnny Walker.

Beatrice knew that Tina was dating a gang member but did not believe it was her place to object. "I'm very open, I take life easy," she said. "I know what they hang around with, I've been here since '83. Kids, you can't force them—they won't take anything from you. If I know my brother smoke, I don't object, but don't smoke it in the house."

She drew a similar line when it came to Johnny Walker. "He some-times drive Tina to my old house in Woodside, but I don't let him park in front, because they usually come with a whole bunch of gang kids in the car. I tell him, 'Dump her a block away.' I don't want my neighbor to see gang kids—what do you think about us? But Johnny can come over. I even ask him to stay for dinner. That kid never wants to stay. He was around nineteen, and I know he was in the gang with the Green Dragons. But he's not that bad, he's very polite. These are just kids, you know?"

The Golden Q, a pool hall on Queens Boulevard in Elmhurst, was a popular hangout for Chinese gangs. One day in October, 1986, Sonny Wong wandered in and met several members of the Green Dragons. Sonny Wong was sixteen. He worked at a Baskin-Robbins ice-cream parlor in Elmhurst and, a month earlier, had entered Newtown High School in the tenth grade. His English was not bad—he had come over from Hong Kong at age seven—but he was an indifferent student, with a truancy record.

Sonny's best friend at Newtown was a boy he had met in junior high, Steven Ng. At school, both boys were viewed as likely gang targets. They resisted joining the White Tigers and a Chinatown-based gang, the Tung On Boys, and were roughed up as a result. But when Sonny Wong encountered the Green Dragons at the pool hall, Steven Ng was among them.

Sonny had not seen Steven for a week, and Ng explained that his father had kicked him out of the house, and that he'd had nowhere to go, so he had moved into a Green Dragons apartment at Jamaica Avenue and Seventy-sixth Street. Johnny Walker, who was at the Golden Q that day with his girlfriend, Tina Sham, asked Sonny if he was living at home. Sonny said he was, and Johnny explained that if he, too, wanted to join the gang he would have to leave his parents and move into a safe house. Sonny looked around the poolroom at the Green Dragons and sized them up: they had fancy clothes, and money, and beepers, and did not go to school. They had cars. On the spot, he decided to become a member.

That was it. There were no initiation rites. It was considered proper to get a tattoo, though, and Sonny soon had three tattoos on his chest and arms—green dragons and an eagle. He began to dress like his gang brothers, in a black jacket, a black turtleneck, tight black jeans, and black canvas slippers, leaving his ankles bare, even in the dead of winter. Another gang affectation was to have one's hair permed, and streaked with red, yellow, or green dye; some members went every day to Linda's Beauty Salon, in Elmhurst.

The gang apartment at Jamaica and Seventy-sixth was on the top floor, with one private bedroom, belonging to the *dai lo*. He went by the name of E.T. Two other bedrooms were chockablock with floor mattresses, for five other gangsters, and Sonny would make six. Sonny got an allowance of forty dollars a week, and after Christmas the amount was doubled.

Gradually, Sonny came to understand that there was an even bigger boss than E.T. His name was Paul Wong, and he had founded the gang, a year earlier. Wong was considerably older than the other gang members; he was born on December 14, 1955, in China's Fukien Province—hence his nickname, Foochow Paul. He had a mustache (a Fukienese trait). Paul Wong had been a *dai lo* in the Fuk Ching gang, on East Broadway in Chinatown, which was affiliated with the Fukien American Association tong, and, thanks to his rank, he had become a millionaire in the heroin business. Except for one weapons bust, which had cost him a seven-hundred-and-fifty-dollar fine in 1984, he had stayed out of the clutches of the law. But because of the huge sums generated by drugs, and by another illegal business, the smuggling of aliens, the Fuk Ching was full of internal strife and killing, and Foochow Paul finally found it prudent to drop out and form a gang of his own. He apparently chose the Elmhurst section of Queens because it was virgin territory; the White Tigers already had a strong foothold in Flushing. Foochow Paul had no interest in giving his gang kids entrée into the drug business, but he was beneficent, providing money for rent and cars and guns, and also high-priced criminal lawyers when they got arrested. A big man in China-town, he was, in effect, the Green Dragons' tong. It gave the Green Dragons "face" to say they were "Paul's kids," and the gang enhanced his status and provided him with bodyguards. Foochow Paul maintained residences in Hong Kong and on the mainland, but for the moment he was living in a private house in Forest Hills.

Sonny didn't get to meet the big boss right away. First, two seventeen-year-old flat-mates broke him in. One of them was Chen I. Chung, and the other went by his nickname, Chicken Wing. As with all new members, I. Chung gave Sonny instructions on how to perform a "clean" kill. These were the essentials: shoot multiple times, to make sure the victim is dead; see that there are no witnesses; and, because murder weapons have to be discarded after a killing, always use the least expensive gun.

Chen I. Chung and Chicken Wing were considered brothers, as the result of a special ceremony, in which they cut their fingers and drank each other's blood. But privately Chicken had his doubts about I. Chung's leadership skills. "He looks dumbfounded sometimes," Chicken told Sonny. "It's not that he's not smart, the shit-face—he just doesn't bother to *think*, you know?" But Chen I. Chung was on an upwardly mobile track, because those more qualified to lead than he was would soon be dead or in jail.

On November 8, 1986, Chen I. Chung turned eighteen, and that evening his birthday was celebrated at the Foliage Restaurant, in Elmhurst. Everyone from the Jamaica Avenue and Parsons Boulevard apartments was present, including Tina Sham. About the only person absent was the boss, Foochow Paul himself. The Foliage was a large restaurant and bar, and the Dragons had rented the upper level in the back, which looked down on a dance floor. At some point in the evening, four Tung On Boys walked into the restaurant and sat down at a table on the lower level, directly below the party. The T.O.s proceeded to get drunk and twirl their guns on the table. At around two in the morning, E.T. got up to pay the manager for the party. He, too, was drunk, and I. Chung told Sonny Wong and Steven Ng to watch over him. They stood with E.T. by the cashier's table, but it was taking a long time for the manager to calculate the bill, so Sonny went off to get a soda. As he returned to the cashier, he saw E.T. arguing with one of the Tung Ons. Then E.T. smacked the Tung On in the face, and the T.O.s started shooting. Sonny ducked behind the bar. When he got up, E.T. and another Green Dragon were dead, and Steven Ng had been shot eight times in the chest. (Ng survived and returned to the gang, but never chose to get a tattoo, perhaps reasoning that eight bullet holes were adequate.)

On New Year's Day, 1987, Sonny Wong got an urgent phone call from a friend named Cindy Pak. She said she was being harassed by two Fuk Ching boys at a roller rink on Roosevelt Avenue in Jackson Heights. Sonny went to the rink to investigate, identified himself as a Green Dragon to the two boys, William Mei and Jinbo Zhao, and asked why they were bothering his friend. The boys told Sonny to back off—it was just a misunderstanding. Sonny left the rink and returned with six Green Dragons, in three cars. The Dragons escorted the two Fuk Ching boys out the door, and Johnny Walker threw them against a wall and began punching them in the face. Then they were forced into the Dragons' blue Pontiac, and driven off.

They were brought to the Parsons Boulevard apartment, where Tina Sham was living with Johnny Walker. She was in the bedroom, getting dressed, when the captives were hustled in. Tina looked through the narrow slats in the bedroom door, and saw the two boys on the floor, being interrogated and struck by one of the Green Dragons. Sonny was punching them as well, saying, "You wanted to hit me before. Why don't you hit me now?" Then Johnny Walker entered the bedroom and led Tina and another gang girlfriend out of the apartment. Frightened, Tina walked quickly to the front door with her head down, but looked up long enough to recognize several of the Green Dragons.

After the two girls left with Johnny, the Fuk Ching boys were strung up by their fingers against the living-room wall. For two hours, they were interrogated. Then Sonny was told to get take-out from downstairs. He returned with the food, and, with the gang's permission, untied the Fuk Ching boys and gave them some mushrooms and rice. Sonny later claimed that he left the apartment soon afterward, and never again saw William Mei and Jinbo Zhao. Three months later, their badly decomposed bodies were found floating in a marsh off the Saw Mill River Parkway in Westchester County, in the village of Ardsley. Each had been shot once in the head.

• • •

A few days after the roller-rink incident, on Chinese New Year, Sonny Wong at last got to meet Foochow Paul. The boss dropped by the Parsons Boulevard apartment, handed out around two hundred dollars to each of the gang members, wished them Happy New Year, and left. A week or so later, Sonny met Paul Wong again, at the Silver Pond Restaurant in Flushing, at a dinner to introduce the boss to some of the newer members. Paul asked Sonny his name and where he was from. They seemed to hit it off, which pleased Sonny tremendously.

Lately, Sonny had had reason to fear that he was losing the respect of his gang brothers. They had made fun of him for ducking behind the bar during the shootout at the Foliage Restaurant, and for giving food to the Fuk Ching boys. On February 13th, Sonny was offered an opportunity to prove his manhood: he was selected, with three others, to murder a *dai lo* in the Tung On gang in retaliation for the death of E.T. The youngest member of the shooting party, Billy Kim, was fourteen. Chen I. Chung kept a statue of the warrior god Gung Gong by the door, and he asked the four boys to pray before heading out. So they knelt down and burned three sticks of incense to Gung Gong, and then went off to kill the Tung On boss.

Johnny Walker drove the four boys to the Taiwan Center in Flushing, a meeting place for Cantonese people, where the Tung Ons had been partying earlier that evening. When the Green Dragons arrived, the party was over and the Taiwan Center was closed. So Johnny suggested that they try the 888 Restaurant in Jackson Heights, a popular T.O. hangout. Johnny parked the car in front, and the four Green Dragons went inside. There were T.O.s in the restaurant, all right, but far more than the Dragons had bargained for—maybe thirty of them, at four tables in the back, including a few that Sonny recognized as his tormentors at Newtown High School. Sonny and his gang brothers took seats up front and weighed their options. They agreed they could not back out. Sonny, armed with a .357, and Billy, carrying a .38, would hit the boss, and the two other boys would stand guard up front to cover them if the Tung Ons gave chase. The main dining room at the 888 was elevated, so Sonny and Billy were gazing down at the T.O. boss, at a distance of about forty feet, when they opened fire. Each got off six rounds, then fled, uncertain of who, if anyone, had been hit. (Five people were wounded, none seriously.) Johnny Walker sped off with the four Dragons and returned them to the safe house.

Though the mission was not a success, Chen I. Chung was satisfied that at least the Tung Ons had been put on warning. In any case, Sonny Wong's status rose dramatically after the shooting, because Foochow Paul took him under his wing. During the next three months, Sonny was Paul's personal bodyguard, at the boss's house in Forest Hills and on two trips to Hong Kong. Sonny also smuggled one hundred thousand dollars of Paul's drug profits through Hong Kong customs.

Meanwhile, Paul conceived of another role for Sonny. Because he spoke good English, Sonny would be the liaison between him and the attorney who appeared to be the Green Dragons' house counsel. That man was Arthur Mass, a criminal lawyer who defended a lot of drug dealers and mafiosi. (Mass vehemently denied that he was the gang's house counsel: "All I am is a defense lawyer who works for anybody who's busted, and because I'm good at my job the Green Dragons called me. That doesn't mean I work for the Green Dragons. I work for individuals.") In April of 1987, according to trial testimony, Paul Wong introduced Sonny to Arthur Mass at a Japanese restaurant in Manhattan. The three of them met once a week after that, at the same restaurant; sometimes Mass brought his girlfriend.

Mass's services were soon needed, for on June 27th, while Sonny and two other Green Dragons were driving on Queens Boulevard, their car was stopped by the police. They were told to get out and lie on the ground. The gang members were then handcuffed and driven to a police station in Westchester. Sonny was separated from the others, taken to an interview room, read his rights, and shown photographs of William Mei and Jinbo Zhao, the Fuk Ching boys who had been abducted from the roller rink and murdered. As Detective Thomas Dixon later told it, Sonny began to cry, and then said, "I didn't kill them both." A Green Dragon named Hock Jai had murdered Zhao, he said. Sonny never signed a statement, and his gang brothers refused to believe that he had cracked, which was fortunate. Coöperating with police was a violation of gang rules, punishable by death.

Tina Sham was terrified. She was only nineteen, both her father and her brother were in jail, and now she was being threatened with arrest as an accessory to murder. On the day Sonny was arrested, Tina was hanging out with Johnny Walker in a safe-house apartment in Brooklyn. The police burst in and led Johnny out, then escorted her into the hallway for questioning. When she refused to speak, she was handcuffed, taken to police headquarters in Westchester, and interrogated for two or three hours by a detective. Finally, Tina described all she had seen and heard through the bedroom-door slats on New Year's Day, and whom she recognized as she was leaving the apartment. Two days later, she was held at a Westchester motel as a material witness.

In Westchester County, before a secret grand jury is convened defendants may request a so-called felony hearing, which is held in open court. A judge determines whether there is enough evidence to warrant sending the case to a grand jury. The felony hearing in the case of People of the State of New York v. Siu Man (Sonny) Wong et al. began on July 2, 1987, before a local judge at a small courthouse in the village of Ardsley, where the bodies of the Fuk Ching boys had been found. Each of the nine defendants was represented by an experienced New York criminal-defense lawyer; Hock Jai's attorney was Arthur Mass. Bruce Bendish, the Westchester assistant D.A. prosecuting the case, was impressed. "It was obvious to me that money was not an issue," he said.

On the first day of the hearing, which lasted two days, Bendish called to the stand his most important witness, Tina Sham. She was led in before the eyes of the defendants, including her boyfriend, Johnny Walker. As Bendish took Tina's testimony, her voice was barely audible, because her head was down. Judge Walter Schwartz remarked that he was within five feet of her and had to lean forward to hear. "I remember her," Pat Basini, the Ardsley Village court clerk, said. "Pretty little thing. She was so scared—never raised her eyes." Nevertheless, Bendish managed to elicit from Tina that the Fuk Ching boys had been beaten in the Green Dragons' apartment, and the names of those who had participated.

At the conclusion of the hearing, on July 3rd, Judge Schwartz ruled that there was indeed enough evidence to hold the defendants without bail pending a grand-jury investigation. Before that could occur, Bruce Bendish left the Westchester D.A.'s office, and his successor inherited the case. He did not inherit the star witness. Tina Sham, convinced that her life was in grave danger, disappeared. The grand jury failed to indict four of the defendants, including Chen I. Chung, who was released from the Westchester County Jail after about fifty days. Billy Kim pleaded guilty, apparently to take the heat off his gang brothers; because he was fourteen when the homicides took place, he could not be sentenced as an adult. After two years in prison awaiting trial, Sonny Wong was found not guilty; apparently, the jury, like the gang, did not believe he had confessed. The Westchester D.A.'s office plea-bargained relatively short jail terms on lesser charges for Johnny Walker, Chicken Wing, and Hock Jai.

The D.A. never had a chance to serve Tina Sham with a grand jury subpoena. Within days after the felony hearing, she had been hustled off to San Francisco with her cousin Dorothy Chan. The two remained there for four months.

"After they come back from San Francisco, I put them in an apartment in Woodside near my house," Tina's cousin Beatrice Chan said. "I tell Tina to stay with Dorothy. Don't go out anywhere, come up to my house for lunch. After six months, we thought it was safe for her. We said, 'Maybe it's time to find a part-time job around here—don't go to Chinatown.' So she applied for a job at the Key Food on Queens Boulevard. The wages is not good, but she works there. She goes to movies in Queens and midtown, but not Chinatown. So after a year two detectives go to Key Food. They know where she is. They tell me, it's all right now. The case is finished."

● ● ●

Chen I. Chung, unfortunately, held grudges. By mid-1989, with the Westchester case over, he was now the *dai lo*, answerable to no one but Foochow Paul himself. It was time to avenge an insult to the gang even more grievous than the one committed by Tina Sham.

A year and a half earlier, on January 3, 1988, the gang's shakedown tactics had met with unprecedented resistance. That afternoon, four Green Dragons—Chen I. Chung, Lung Gor, Danny Ngo, and Allen Wong—had lunch at the Broadway Noodle Shop, a restaurant in Elmhurst that had just opened. Sometime between two-thirty and three, they finished eating and got up to leave. The owner, a burly Taiwanese named Peter Chung, confronted them and demanded, "Why don't you pay?" Danny Ngo flung a lighted cigarette at him, and suddenly everyone was shouting. An employee came out of the kitchen with a gun and opened fire. Ngo was wounded slightly in the arm. Lung Gor was shot dead.

Now Chen I. Chung had just the hit man in mind to settle the score—a Vietnamese, recently arrived from San Francisco. His name was Tony Tran, but he was more commonly known as Dai Bay, or Big Nose. On the evening of May 2, 1989, I. Chung sent Big Nose to the Broadway Noodle with orders to kill the owner. He carried two guns, a .38 and a 9-mm. semi-automatic. The job was a cinch; Big Nose didn't even have to go inside. Peter Chung was standing by the front entrance, so Big Nose just walked up and shot him three times at close range. The gunshots shattered the restaurant's glass door. Leaving a trail of bloody footprints back into the restaurant, Chung collapsed into a chair, fatally wounded. The day after the shooting, Chen I. Chung appeared at one of the gang apartments with a copy of a Chinese newspaper carrying the story, and handed it over. The gesture was well understood: it was I. Chung's way of saying that whoever did it would get recognition. He made only one comment, *"Bo ying"*—a Cantonese expression meaning "What goes around comes around."

One day in June, 1989, as Foochow Paul walked out the door of a private house in Flushing, two or three young Asians hiding behind the bushes on his front lawn jumped out and opened fire. Paul was hit four times. He managed to get himself to Booth Memorial Medical Center. The Green Dragons' beepers began sounding, and word of the shooting spread rapidly throughout the gang. Several members caucused at the hospital, including Sonny Wong, just recently out of jail and now Chen I. Chung's underboss. The next day, Paul Wong came out of surgery, and I. Chung smuggled two handguns into his room, in the hollowed-out core of a Yellow Pages. On the pretext of being relatives, gang members remained in Paul's room around the clock, to make sure no one took another shot at him.

In a few days, Paul Wong recovered sufficiently from his wounds to be released from the hospital. He had an apartment at Broadway and Fifty-seventh Street, in Manhattan, and gang members took him there to recuperate. Paul said that when he was well enough to walk he would leave the country, and then he wanted the Green Dragons to avenge his shooting. Not many people knew the address of the house in Flushing, apart from Wong's partners in the drug business, and Paul's suspicions centered on one of them—Kin Tai Chan, better known as Ah Tai. Paul told the Dragons that if Ah Tai had formed an association with a fraternal society known as the Taiwanese Brothers it would be proof of his treachery. By early August, Paul was back on his feet and was in China. One afternoon, Chen I. Chung spotted Ah Tai leaving a condominium in Flushing with members of the Taiwanese Brothers. That evening, by telephone, Paul Wong ordered his death.

On the night of August 23rd, two Dragons in a gold Honda Accord spotted Ah Tai's girlfriend, and followed her to a house in Jamaica, Queens. Sometime after 10 p.m., Ah Tai left the house toting a shoulder bag full of laundry and strolled down the driveway. As he opened the door to his car, a white Jeep Cherokee, a member of the Green Dragons—it was later alleged to be Steven Ng—jumped out of the Honda and shot him once in the head and three times in the back with a .380 semi-automatic. Another bullet tore a gold Rolex off Ah Tai's left wrist; it landed near a sewer. Police searching Ah Tai's dead body ruled out robbery as a motive; he had on his person over eighteen hundred dollars in cash. It was alleged that while firing the fatal shots Steven Ng told him, "This is from Paul."

Although Paul Wong was nearly twice the average age of his gang kids, there was no evidence that he ever acted as a restraining influence. But his money did. Wong helped the gang defray its largest expenses—lawyers' fees, bail, firearms, rent—reducing the need for armed robbery. Once he left Queens for China, in August, 1989, that source of funds for the gang dried up. Chen I. Chung continued to take direction from him over the telephone, but now the young *dai lo* was in charge. And the Green Dragons were out of control.

By the winter of 1989-90, Chen I. Chung was having difficulty meeting expenses, even though he had stepped up the pace of extortions. From an operations standpoint, the Green Dragons were in the red. Finally, I. Chung asked a cousin of his named Allen Lin, who was not in the gang, to scout out sites for armed robberies. Lin heard of a private apartment in Elmhurst where medium-stakes mah-jongg games were held. He went there one night and found two game tables, at which perhaps one or two thousand dollars changed hands. A middle-aged couple was in charge of the action, and the wife served soft drinks.

The apartment was occupied by a Taiwanese man, who will be referred to here as Charlie Lo, and his wife, his mother, and the wife's cousin. Lo was twenty-seven and worked in a restaurant from ten in the morning until ten at night. His wife, Susan, put in similar hours at a different restaurant. She was twenty-four and was born in Malaysia. On January 23, 1990, Susan Lo returned home at about eleven and found her mother-in-law and her cousin on the living-room sofa watching television. It had been a long, hard day, and Susan changed into a robe and prepared to take a hot bath.

Charlie Lo, arriving home a few minutes later, encountered a young man in a black jacket loitering in the lobby. He was a Green Dragon named Jay Cheng. As Lo climbed five steps to the door of his apartment, another youth passed him, on the way down. At his door, Charlie looked around nervously, then turned his key in one of two locks. The second lock jammed, and as he struggled with it five Green Dragons surrounded him and pulled him over to the mailboxes facing the door. Four of them had guns, and the fifth brandished what the gang called its Rambo knife.

"Open the door. Please don't fuss," Lo recalled being told. He protested that the lock was broken, and offered the key. Again, he was ordered to open the door, and this time he succeeded. The gang members rushed in together, pushing Lo to the ground. After several minutes, he was taken into a bedroom and forced to strip to his underwear. Jay Cheng found a bank card in Charlie's wallet and demanded the code number. With two guns pressed into his back, Charlie gave it to him. "Is the number real or not?" Jay demanded. "It's real," Charlie said. "If you don't believe me, you can go and try it." Jay told him that if the number didn't work, or if he reported the robbery to the police, his entire family would be killed.

Susan Lo had finished taking her bath when she heard noises that sounded like furniture being moved. She opened the bathroom door a crack, saw a black-jacketed man with a small gun, and heard someone say, in Cantonese, "Where is your money?" She tried to climb out the bathroom window, but it was too small. For half an hour, she huddled in a corner, hoping not to be discovered. Then Brian Chan, an eighteen-year-old Green Dragon, kicked the door open. From the adjoining room, Charlie Lo could hear his wife screaming.

Pressing a small black gun against her shoulder, Brian Chan led Susan into her bedroom. Her husband, her mother-in-law, and her cousin were lying face down there, in their underwear. The room had been ransacked. One of the robbers was rummaging through a desk beside a large fish tank. Jay asked Susan where she had hidden the money. "There is no money," she said. If he found even one dollar in her room, Jay told Susan, he would kill her. She was made to take off her robe and lie face down next to her husband. The robbers tore through a closet and turned the bed upside down. After perhaps half an hour, Susan Lo and her cousin were led into the cousin's bedroom and raped.

By 1:15 a.m., the apartment was quiet. Charlie found his wife, naked and sobbing, under a blanket. In a little while, Susan got up and made a tour of the apartment. The sofa had been overturned. Videotapes were scattered on the floor. All the cabinet drawers were pulled out, and clothes and shoes were tossed in heaps. A table had been kicked over, and mah-jongg tiles were strewn about. All the telephone lines were slashed. Susan got dressed and called the police from a corner pay phone.

Back at one of the gang's apartments, the proceeds of the robbery—cash, jewelry, and pearls—were poured out on a coffee table. Chen I. Chung counted the money and gave most of it to Sonny Wong to be used for lawyers' fees. The rest was divided up. Jay Cheng went to a cash machine and tried Charlie Lo's bank card. He got five hundred dollars.

In 1989, Tina Sham turned twenty-one. She had not seen any of the Green Dragons for two years. Johnny Walker was still in jail. Tina had felt sufficiently safe from harm to commit another offense against the Dragons: she dated a boy nicknamed Mosquito Steve, who happened to be a member of the White Tigers. Meanwhile, she got a job as a cashier at a Chinatown beauty parlor. Around Christmas, she was formally introduced to a young man whose best friend's sister knew her cousin Dorothy. The young man wanted to date her, but Tina was not sure what she thought of him. He was different from the guys she was used to going out with—a hardworking ethnic Chinese from Vietnam who made his living repairing jet airplanes. His name was Tommy Mach.

Tommy's father had been a prosperous pork distributor in Saigon, but after the Communists took over he escaped with his wife and seven children, on October 2, 1977, in a small, crowded boat. The Machs almost died of thirst during the five days it took the boat to reach the

Philippines. After the family had spent ten months in a refugee camp in Manila, the United States Catholic Conference sponsored their passage to New York, first boarding them at an old hotel near Lincoln Center, and then renting a small apartment for them in Elmhurst. Tommy's father was very strict, and the entire Mach family was suffused with the Asian work ethic. The Mach children spent up to eight hours a night trying to do their homework in an unfamiliar language.

In 1981, Mr. Mach decided he could make a better living elsewhere, and moved out of the city with his wife and two youngest children, who were girls. The five oldest children, down to Tommy, now fourteen, remained at the apartment in Elmhurst. Mrs. Mach was worried that, with no parent around, her youngest son might fall in with a gang. In fact, Tommy was himself so fearful of gang kids that in junior high he avoided making friends with any Chinese at all. "Tom said, 'Mom, we've gone through a lot of difficulty to get to this country, and I'm not going to waste my life and be an idiot,' " his older brother Steven recalled. "I was very proud of him."

Far from wasting his life, Tommy had rapidly become proficient in English. He passed an entrance exam for Aviation High School, one of the best in New York City, and breezed through with good grades. After he graduated, he obtained F.A.A. certification to work on all aspects of aviation maintenance. He accepted a job at Butler Aviation. At the age of seventeen, not yet old enough to drive, Tommy Mach was repairing jet planes.

By 1986, it seemed that the long struggle was over for the Mach family, and that, as Steven put it, "God couldn't treat us better." The older children had graduated from college and gone into finance and other high-paying professions. Steven became a software engineer. The Machs bought their first home, in the suburbs. Steven lived there with his parents, and so, for a while, did Tommy, who happily contributed toward the mortgage.

In September of 1989, Tommy, bored with suburban life, decided that the time had come to move back to Queens. He took a job with USAir at LaGuardia Airport. At twenty-two, he was earning over fifty thousand a year. One weekend, Tommy came up to see his brother with news of a romantic interest.

Steven recalled, "He said, 'I met this girl and she looks really cute and all that, but I just don't know if she like me or not.' That girl is Tina. I said, 'Don't worry, just let it go easy, let it go natural. If she's yours, she's yours.' And then nothing work out, because he said that Tina, for some reason, is kind of hold back. I said, 'Did you talk to her?' 'Yeah, I talk to her a couple of times; she doesn't seem to show any interest.' I said, 'Hey, what's the big deal? If she doesn't respond, there's a lot of other girls out there. Maybe she's trying to play hard to get.' "

By February of 1990, Tommy had been back in Queens for six months, and city life was beginning to wear on him. His mother was begging him to return home. Finally, Tommy confided to a friend that he planned to ask Tina Sham out one last time, on Valentine's Day, and if she refused him he was going to pack up and move back in with his parents and Steven. Whether the threat was genuine will never be known, because Tina accepted.

After Valentine's Day, Tommy was a constant presence in the Chan household in Elmhurst. Some nights, he would pick up Tina in his car, a red Subaru, and take her dancing at a Manhattan club, the Limelight. Other nights, he would stay over for dinner and play mah-jongg with family members. "He's very sporty," Beatrice Chan recalled. "He never can sit still. But Tommy, he's not a bad kid, he earns his own way. I tell Tina he's quite good. I said, 'Go disco.' "

Within days of their first big date, Tommy was talking openly of marriage and children. Tina was clearly fond of him, but at the same time she seemed deeply troubled; apparently she had not yet found the nerve to tell Tommy about her past. Or perhaps she was worried about Johnny Walker, who would soon be getting out of prison and might still view her as his girlfriend. "Tina, she sits here sometimes by herself watching TV, but she's not watching TV," Beatrice said. "She's somewhere else. Maybe she don't want us to worry, but she don't tell us anything."

• • •

On Friday, February 23, 1990, Tommy Mach had the day off. He planned to take Tina and Beatrice for dim sum, but Beatrice bowed out at the last minute, because her husband was returning from a trip that day. Around three o'clock, Tommy arrived with Tina at the Crown Palace Restaurant, on the corner of Queens Boulevard and Van Loon. Tina was wearing jeans, cowboy boots, a sweater, a black silk blouse, and hoop earrings. Tommy was dressed in a white shirt with black polka dots, jeans, and a black leather jacket. Tina had been to the Crown Palace a few times before, and one of the waiters recognized her. Even more familiar to him were the Green Dragons who just then filed in, taking their usual table, by the back door. The gang collected two hundred and fifty dollars in extortion money every Sunday from the Crown Palace, and had dim sum at the restaurant two or three times a week.

Chen I. Chung, as befitted his rank as *dai lo*, took the corner position at the table. Big Nose sat next to him. There were some new faces in the gang. Aleck Yim was that rarity—an American-born Chinese gang member; he was seventeen, and had been recruited out of Forest Hills High School. Yim was called Moon Jian, which means Small Eyes.

Brian Chan was also at the table. One month earlier, he had found Susan Lo cowering in her bathroom and marched her out at gunpoint. Brian was born in Hong Kong in 1972 and baptized Roman Catholic. Ten years later, he had immigrated to America with his family, and was enrolled at St. Patrick's Semi-Military Academy, in Harriman, New York. He wore a full-dress uniform, maintained an A-minus average, and graduated in 1986. Brian spoke a number of Chinese dialects and fluent English. In the winter of 1986, Brian's father died. Both Brian and his older brother, Perry, dropped out of high school. By the summer of 1988, the two boys were in the care of an uncle: their mother had evidently abandoned them. Along the way, the brothers suffered another trauma: they were beaten by Chinese teen-agers, and Brian was stabbed. Close together in age, Perry and Brian moved in opposite directions. Perry obtained a high-school-equivalency diploma, worked his way up to contract administrator at a Manhattan financial company, and began studying for an M.B.A. By late 1989, Brian had joined the Green Dragons.

Roger Kwok was another relative newcomer to the gang. He was born to Chinese parents in Phnom Penh, Cambodia, the third of four children. In 1979, when Roger was six, he and his family were forced by the Khmer Rouge to walk two hundred miles to a detention camp in Thailand. From there, the Kwoks moved to New Jersey. Roger's father was a stonecutter, and his mother found a job at General Motors. Roger was a good student, but began running away from home at age fifteen and hanging out with the Green Dragons. Desperate to keep his youngest son from becoming a gangster, Mr. Kwok shipped Roger to California to live with his grandparents and attend a parochial school. This arrangement lasted one month. In August, 1989, Mr. Kwok tried another tack: he moved his entire family to Middletown, in upstate New York. Roger dropped out of Middletown High in January, 1990, and now, a month later, sat at a table with his gang brothers. After all the gang members had taken their places, the manager signalled for the waitress to serve them. They began to eat.

Sonny Wong arrived late. When he took his place at the table, Chen I. Chung gestured across the restaurant, toward the right-hand side. Is that Tina? Sonny believed it was. The boy was unfamiliar, but he had a black jacket and looked like a gang member; he must be the White Tiger that Tina supposedly went out with. I. Chung sent three Green Dragons to the table to verify the girl's identity and frisk the boy. They came back and reported that the girl was most definitely Tina Sham but the boy had neither a gun nor a tattoo. I. Chung asked Sonny what he should do. "You're the boss," Sonny reminded him. Throughout the summer of 1989, I. Chung had repeatedly insisted that Tina Sham must be killed for testifying in the Westchester case and for dating a White Tiger. "She's been around long enough to know the rules," he had said then, more than once. Now I. Chung had to make a decision quickly, because, unnerved, Tina and the boy were hastily paying their bill and preparing to leave. The back table fell silent, except for intense whispering between Chen I. Chung and Big Nose. All eyes were on the *dai lo*. As Tina and Tommy were walking out, I. Chung made a gesture with the back of his hand. The gang understood.

Someone tapped Aleck Yim on the shoulder, and he got up. He and Big Nose left through a side door, and Brian Chan and Roger Kwok went out the front. Tommy and Tina had reached the door of his red Subaru, in the parking lot across the street from the restaurant. Suddenly, they were surrounded by four Green Dragons with their guns drawn. "What do you want?" both of them asked. Aleck took Tina's bag. Big Nose swung around in the gang's car, a two-tone blue Mercury. Tommy and Tina were forced into the car, and it drove off. Big Nose was in the driver's seat, and Aleck was beside him, aiming at the captives. Tina and Tommy, in the back, were squeezed between Brian and Roger, who were also pointing guns at them.

En route, Big Nose explained to the other gang members what I. Chung had told him: this was for revenge. None of the four abductors had ever met Tina Sham, but they had heard about her. The boy was a mystery—apparently not a gang member. That was simply too bad— the killing must be clean, no witnesses. The restaurant staff, they were certain, would be too frightened ever to testify. Big Nose told Aleck that they had to find a quiet place with no one around, and asked for directions, because he was from San Francisco and was unfamiliar with the area. By now, they were on the Long Island Expressway. Tina was crying and begging; Tommy was very quiet. Meanwhile, Brian, Roger, and Aleck took their belongings. Tina, who was both Catholic and Buddhist, handed over her silver cross and a gold chain and a gold-plated Buddha inscribed "Chinese Happiness." Tommy surrendered a stainless-steel Charles Jourdan watch, a gift from his brother Steven, and a jade Buddha that Steven had brought him from Thailand after having a monk bless it to keep Tommy safe from harm.

The drive went on for more than forty-five minutes, and finally Big Nose left the L.I.E. and turned down a residential street. There were too many houses. They circled around for a while and came across a dirt road. The road ran along the bottom of a ravine and cut through dense woods—an ideal spot for an execution. Big Nose remained by the car, telling Aleck to make sure they went all the way down the path, and to bind the hands of both the boy and the girl. And he added, "Let the new kid do it."

Aleck understood. Brian Chan had an expensive automatic; Roger Kwok, the new kid, sixteen years old, was carrying a less expensive .38. The three abductors forced Tina and Tommy down into the ravine, which was slippery with dead leaves, and onto the road. They walked for about two hundred and fifty feet, and then, though Big Nose had told them to go farther, Aleck stopped, because he was scared. Roger got Tina to kneel, pulled back her sweater, and knotted it behind her; Aleck pushed Tommy to his knees and performed a similar maneuver with Tommy's leather jacket. Then Aleck gave the signal: ready, go. Roger killed Tommy first, with one shot to the back of the head, and then Tina. They both slumped forward from the impact and landed together on their right sides. As they lay there, probably already dead, Aleck took his gun and pumped bullets into Tommy's left armpit and abdomen and Tina's left abdomen and hip. Then the three boys ran.

Big Nose asked Aleck why he had fired his gun. Aleck said nothing, but then Big Nose reassured him: "It's O.K. You're getting good with this." Back in the car, they passed the guns forward to Big Nose. He put them in the usual hiding spot, the air-conditioning vent. The murder weapons would later be disposed of by Aleck in a lake in Flushing Meadows–Corona Park, off the Grand Central Parkway. They took the L.I.E. back to Queens, to an Asian-American garage where Chen I. Chung had gone to get his car fixed. The assassination team met I. Chung there, told him that the deed was done, and divided up the victims' money. Aleck showed I. Chung an expensive-looking cigarette lighter he had lifted from Tina, and asked for permission to keep it. I. Chung told him to go ahead. The *dai lo* was pleased. The only regrets were those expressed by Big Nose. On reflection, he said of Tina Sham, "We should have raped her first."

Ever since Tommy Mach moved back to Queens, he had called his mother every Friday night, without exception, but on the evening of February 23rd the phone never rang. Strange that he doesn't call, Mrs. Mach said. By Sunday, the entire Mach family was in a panic. Steven and an older brother arranged to take off two weeks from work and began driving aimlessly around New York, looking for Tommy's red Subaru.

As the days went by, Tina's cousins also grew increasingly afraid that something terrible had occurred. "The whole family of us can't sleep," Beatrice said. "Sometimes cry, all the aggravation, Tina's friends coming in, Tommy's friends coming in. Finally, I go to fortune-teller, and they tell me she's not dead. But signs are not good. Tommy's friends want to go to psychics, not fortune-teller, because they're more American kids. The first psychic is a very good one. He says, 'Bring her clothes and bring Tommy's clothes.' When we bring them and walk up the corridor to the psychic's house, he sees us and says, 'Go away! I don't want to see you guys now!' We're shocked. That was almost the first week. I keep praising the Buddha, but nothing happened."

Robert Sham took a different approach to trying to find his daughter. From his son Trini, who was still in state prison, he got a beeper number for Sonny Wong. Trini and Sonny had been good friends in junior high. Robert beeped Sonny and got a call back. Robert said his daughter was missing, and arranged to meet Sonny at a McDonald's on Queens Boulevard. Before the meeting, Chen I. Chung briefed Sonny on how to handle Robert Sham; Sonny denied any knowledge of what might have happened to Tina, and suggested that she might have run afoul of the White Tigers. He also attempted to learn from Robert what, if anything, the police knew.

In fact, the police knew nothing at all, because the bodies had not been discovered. That all changed on March 10th, sixteen days after the murders. The dirt road on which Tina and Tommy were killed was a service road for the Long Island Lighting Company, well hidden between two country estates in Sands Point. A caretaker eventually stumbled on the bodies and called the local police, who in turn notified the Nassau County Homicide Squad. Tommy Mach was identified from a pay stub found in his jacket pocket. Before sunup, police located Tommy's sister in New York and broke the news to her.

The next morning, members of both families were asked to identify the bodies at the morgue. Because it was winter and bitterly cold, the corpses were exceptionally well preserved. First, Tina's body was wheeled into a small room behind a glass partition, a sheet covering all but her face and shoes. "We go together, but they only allow the parents to go in, Robert and Rita," Beatrice Chan said. "When Rita start crying very loud, we heard that. All of us start crying very loud, we know that's her."

Then Tommy's body was wheeled in. "I was the first one that identified him," Steven said, struggling in vain to suppress tears at the memory. "The doors open, and the first thing I saw was his shoes—he bought a pair with me—and I just almost faint, because it finally hit me. Until that moment, I still have that dream, that hope, that Tommy is somewhere, that he just run away with Tina. I'd come up with a reason that is really outrageous. He just ran away to the Caribbean with Tina, to a little hideout, and have a sudden marriage, just to surprise us. I keep thinking, If I see him I'm gonna beat him up. But then when I see that pair of shoes my heart just fell, and it fell like to a bottomless cliff, or whatever you call that. I saw his face. He— he looks like he's asleep, but the expression on his face is very complex. It's a little anger, a little sorry—like sorry that he went down, sorry what had happened. But I know one thing. He is scared! Not only that he face what he has to face with guys surrounding him with guns and all that. But the biggest fear I think he has is that probably the family will never find him, because the place is very secluded. I want to talk to him, I keep asking him to wake up or something. I knock on the glass. But he just lie there. All of a sudden, I have a feeling like an invisible hand grab hold of my heart and just squeeze it and squeeze it, and it's so painful. That's when my sisters take me out the door. Even now, I still dream of that face."

As a reward for the double homicide, Chen I. Chung soon put Roger

Kwok in charge of a gang apartment on Ithaca Street. Roger had fired fatal bullets. Brian Chan still had not done so. But another opportunity arose only four days later.

The Green Dragons were bitter enemies of a Vietnamese gang called Born To Kill, headquartered at a shopping mall on Canal Street in Chinatown. A large gang, with more than a hundred members, Born To Kill took its name from a popular slogan on G.I.s' helmets in Vietnam. Many members were tattooed with the letters "B.T.K." and a coffin and three candles, signifying "no fear of death." Born To Kill was the only major Chinatown gang not affiliated with a tong. The gang took direction from a latter-day Fagin named David Thai, who ran a prosperous counterfeit-watch business and a couple of massage parlors. Born To Kill terrorized Vietnamese establishments on and around Canal Street, and also wormed its way into Queens.

On February 27, 1990, Brian Chan, Roger Kwok, and Big Nose were cruising in Brian's bullet-pocked car. Some time between 5:20 and 6 p.m., they spotted four young men walking toward Linda's Beauty Salon and believed them to be Born To Kill members. Brian made a sharp U-turn and chased them. At the corner of Britton Avenue and Ketcham Street, Brian stopped the car, jumped out, and shot one of the young men dead with a .380 semi-automatic. Police found the body face down on the sidewalk, legs crossed. The victim appeared to have fallen in mid-stride.

It turned out that the victim was not a member of Born To Kill. His name was Jin Lee Seok, and he belonged to a gang called Korean Power. This was a problem, because the Green Dragons and Korean Power had a peace agreement. Tony Kim, one of the bosses of Korean Power, got on the phone with Chen I. Chung and expressed his outrage. The two gangs quickly came to terms. No one in Korean Power would testify against Brian Chan, because of the unwritten rule that gangsters must never coöperate with the authorities. However, Korean Power had permission to settle the matter privately; that is, if the gang wished to kill Brian, that was all right with the Green Dragons.

• • •

The murder investigation of Tina Sham and Tommy Mach was turned over to a Nassau County homicide detective named Peter Blum. He had never worked on an Asian-crime case before. When he learned that Tina's father had been busted as a "mule"—federal prosecutors' slang for a low-level heroin smuggler—and had agreed to testify against his drug supplier, Blume initially thought that Tina might have been murdered in revenge. Robert Sham assured Blum that this was not possible. Then Blum learned that Tina Sham had also been a government witness in the Westchester case against the Green Dragons.

Blum needed to find the last people to see Tina Sham and Tommy Mach alive. Tommy's red Subaru was missing, so Blum ran the plate number through a computer and traced the car to the Ace Towing & Recovery Company, in Queens. The Subaru had been hauled away on February 28, 1990, from a parking lot across the street from the Crown Palace. Blum visited the restaurant with the only Chinese-speaking officer he could find in Nassau County. The eleven-member restaurant staff was extraordinarily unhelpful. (Chen I. Chung had come back after the murders and explicitly cautioned the staff against talking to the police.) When they were shown photographs of Tommy and Tina, they all drew a blank. The workers, mostly Cantonese, claimed not to understand the Chinese police officer, who spoke Mandarin. "Their attitude was 'I do not speak your language. Goodbye,' " Blum said.

The New York Police Department provided Blum with a Hong Kong native named Joemy Tam. He spoke Cantonese, and he was extremely persuasive. Tam lectured the restaurant staff on why the Asian community needed to band together and resist intimidation by thugs. Gradually, some of them bought what Tam was selling. One day, Tam and Blum picked up a Crown Palace waitress in front of her house and drove her down Queens Boulevard. It was raining, and they sat under the El. She looked over a police-photo spread, settled on a picture of Chen I. Chung, and said, "That's the *dai lo*." Tam was able to lure others to an interview room at Nassau County police headquarters. Yip Ming Lee, a waiter, identified seven Green Dragons, and remembered which of them had followed Tina and Tommy out of the restaurant.

The two police officers had identified the abductors in less than a month. Tina Sham's relatives believed they had assisted them by putting a red handkerchief in Tina's suit pocket at her cremation. According to Chinese custom, if a murder victim is given something red to wear, the color will "stick to" the killer and he will be caught. Peter Blum was not one to scoff at Chinese superstition, because of an incident that, he said, "still gives me chills." Tina's parents and her two cousins asked Blum to lead them to the ravine in Sands Point where she had been murdered. According to Buddhist lore, when a person dies violently the soul remains at the spot where death occurred. Tina's family wished to coax her soul into an incense stick and reunite it with her body at the funeral parlor. "The family is dressed all in black," Blum said. "They stack up oranges"—a traditional offering to the Buddha— "and put a big incense stick in the ground where Tina was murdered, and bow three times, and pray for Tina's soul to come. All of a sudden, a large brown butterfly appears—must have been two and a half inches in diameter. We had half a foot of snow five days earlier, and it's freezing out, and there is no reason for a butterfly to be coming around. It flies to the top of the knoll and sits on a branch. The family is crying and bowing and praying to this butterfly. They believe it's Tina. I'm standing twenty feet away with two other detectives. The butterfly does a complete circle around us, then circles the family, and is gone. Robert says, 'I told Tina that you were the detectives who were trying to solve her murder. When she flew overhead, she was thanking you.' "

After speaking with the Crown Palace workers, Blum had probable cause to arrest a number of Green Dragons for murder. But the federal government asked him to refrain. Not far into his investigation, he discovered that the United States Attorney's office in Brooklyn also had its eye on the Green Dragons. The office planned to use the Racketeer Influenced and Corrupt Organizations, or RICO, statute against the Dragons, after a decade of deploying it effectively against the Mafia. At the same time, the Brooklyn office was preparing a second RICO case—this one against Born To Kill.

The federal Green Dragons case had its origin in an investigation of a Queens drug lord named Lorenzo (Fat Cat) Nichols. Between March

and August of 1988, the F.B.I. had bugged the telephone of Fat Cat's
sister Viola, and two strange voices speaking Chinese piqued the
interest of Michael McGuinness, a New York City police sergeant. One
of the voices belonged to Foochow Paul Wong, who may have been sup-
plying heroin to Fat Cat. In November, 1989, the Justice Department
created C-6, a task force made up of a dozen New York City police detectives (including McGuinness) and an equal number of F.B.I. agents. By
December, C-6 had connected Paul Wong with the Green Dragons.

Mike McGuinness steered the Green Dragons case to an assistant
U.S. Attorney in Brooklyn named Catherine Palmer. Nicknamed the
Dragon Lady, because of her success in prosecuting Asian heroin cases,
Palmer was petite, athletic, perky, and quite fearless. She came close to
being the only federal prosecutor killed in the line of duty. On January
29, 1990, a package arrived at her office containing a briefcase, which
she had been expecting as a belated Christmas gift from her parents.
Palmer would have opened the case immediately except that the return
address was unfamiliar. A D.E.A. agent and a police detective slowly
lifted the lid, and inside they found a fully loaded sawed-off .22-cal-
ibre rifle with a string around the trigger. In July, 1992, David Kwong,
a D.E.A. informant who had previously lost his job because Palmer
had exposed him as a liar, was convicted of attempted murder. After
the attempt, Palmer complained loudly that United States marshals
assigned to guard her were getting in her way. The Green Dragons
could not have asked for a more stubborn prosecutor.

In five years of operation, the Green Dragons had become con-
temptuous of American law enforcement, and not without reason.
Throughout its spree of murder and racketeering, the gang had faced
only state cases, most of which had ended in acquittal or in relatively
light sentences. The federal government was far better equipped to
attack the structure of a criminal enterprise. The hallmark of an F.B.I.
investigation is electronic eavesdropping—a costly and labor-intensive
procedure, but very often a gangbuster. By August of 1990, C-6 had
court approval to listen in on four Green Dragon phones, including a
cellular model. Over the next four months, six Asian members of the

task force monitored hundreds of conversations, in Cantonese, Mandarin, Fukienese, Vietnamese, and, occasionally, English. Besides gathering evidence to be used one day in court, C-6 learned of crimes still in the planning stage. The trick now was to prevent them without prematurely exposing the investigation.

On September 7, 1990, the C-6 task force drew on a combination of wiretaps and physical surveillance to thwart the robbery of a private house in Yorktown Heights. The house belonged to Chen I. Chung's granduncle—a graphic illustration that gang loyalty came before family. Two police detectives, George Annarella and Richard Arbacas, tailed the robbers to the house. (This was a chore, Annarella said. "The Green Dragons drove with no regard to traffic laws. They would cut across three lanes at eighty miles per hour.") Alerted by C-6, Yorktown police set up a roadblock and stopped the gang's car as it left the crime scene. Police found two handguns in the car's air vent, a sock stuffed with ammunition, and a baseball bat on the floorboard. They also found a bag of jewelry and $25,554 in cash. Three Green Dragons were taken into custody.

The next day, C-6 agents listened with amusement to a conversation between Chen I. Chung and his cousin Allen Lin, who had tipped off the *dai lo* that their granduncle was sitting on a pile of money.

"Mother! Damn!" I. Chung said. "It was going all right. It was going fine, and all of a sudden the police showed up! . . . We were just waiting to split up the money. . . . Mother! Right now, I'm really having a headache."

Chen I. Chung had ordered the Yorktown robbery because of the need to replenish the Green Dragons' legal-defense fund. The gang was tens of thousands of dollars in debt to the law firm of Arthur Mass, and was too broke to hire a new attorney. A number of Green Dragons sat in jail awaiting trial for various state offenses, and none of them placed much faith in court-appointed lawyers. For the moment, I. Chung was particularly worried about Alex Wong, who had been arrested the previous year, at age seventeen, for gun possession, and incarcerated in the juvenile wing at Riker's Island. Alex not only had a hearing coming up on the gun charge but was now a suspect in the double murder he had committed—the shooting at the Tien Chau restaurant of Mon Hsiung Tang and Anthony Gallivan.

Carol Huang, the woman with whom Alex had made eye contact during the shootout, was proving to be a first-class nuisance. First, she described him in remarkably accurate detail to a police sketch artist. Then she identified his picture in a photo spread. Then she picked him out of a lineup at the Fifth Precinct, in Chinatown. Alex did not care for this at all. He could handle three years on the gun charge if need be, but not twenty-five-to-life in a state murder case. On a wiretap he was overheard to say, "The most important thing is, after getting out, I could be still in my twenties, or even my thirties would be fine. Motherfuck!—Just don't let me be in the *forties!*"

On August 18, 1990, it became clear to what lengths the Green Dragons would go to prevent Alex Wong from suffering this fate. Alex was speaking to Sonny Wong by prison phone.

"Everything, everything, is Carol this and Carol that," Alex said.

"Yeah, man," Sonny said. "Motherfuck the bitch!"

"The bitch!"

"I'll see how long she'll last right now. . . . Just let her talk. Talk, talk, talk, talk. . . . And then the next time our lawyer will go up, and if she says something different, then she'll *drop dead*—you know what I'm saying?"

Alex knew precisely what Sonny was saying, and if C-6 had any doubts, the doubts were dispelled in a conversation on August 29th, in which Chen I. Chung told Alex, "That girl, it would be fine if she just disappears." On September 9th, Alex called I. Chung excitedly to tell him he had found "that female's address," accidentally disclosed in some legal papers. According to trial testimony, I. Chung then instructed Sonny to buy a street map, find Carol Huang, and have the gang kill her and burn her body. Fortunately, by this time Carol Huang had been warned by the police and had gone into hiding.

By November 5th, Alex Wong was feeling desperate and disillusioned.

"Whether I am going to sit in jail or not, it all depends on you guys, man," he told Brian Chan.

"I know."

"You *know*. . . . Motherfuck, man! I might as well wash my ass to sit in jail."

"Fuck! Don't say that, man! Shit!"

"No, man. . . . Every time I talk to [Chen I. Chung], he says just wait a fucking while. Fuck his mother, I have waited for six months. No fucking thing has been done. . . . I'm going crazy, man! Freaking, man! . . . I don't even have a single fucking lawyer, you know? . . . It caused my father to have died already. . . . That's why I'm so incensed. . . . Lost a fucking father, man. For what, man! For nothing! . . . I have followed [I. Chung] for three years. . . . Loyalty, *fuck you*."

At this point, Chen I. Chung might have begun to question his own loyalty to Foochow Paul, who was sitting pretty in hideouts in Fukien and Canton. But bugged conversations between the two revealed I. Chung to be as obsequious as ever. Paul's mind appeared to be on matters other than the financial worries of his gang. He considered investing two hundred thousand dollars to become a silent partner in a new *karaoke* club in Queens, but airily suggested that a member of the Green Dragons try to borrow bail money from his father. By November of 1990, Paul had been gone for four months, and there was no evidence that he had donated a cent of his enormous drug profits to his young followers.

"When are you coming back, Big Brother?" I. Chung asked.

"I am planning to come back."

"You are?"

"I won't delay any more."

He never returned.

Arthur Mass, the Green Dragons' alleged house counsel, was getting impatient.

"If I have the motherfucking money, O.K., I'll then give it to you guys, O.K.?" Sonny Wong told him. "If I don't have the motherfucking money, what do you want me to do, man?"

It was September 12, 1990, five days after the failed robbery in Yorktown Heights.

"Business is business," Mass said. "You know I know the problems. But when you make a statement that you're going to deliver and you don't, it hurts. . . . All right, get the word to your Big Brother."

The pace of restaurant extortions stepped up as the gang's finances sank deeper into the red. A grand opening was a welcome event, because it was traditional at such times for gangs to collect "lucky money"—a large inaugural extortion payment. Often the required sum was a multiple of a hundred and eight—a thousand and eighty dollars was common for a restaurant—because that was the number of Buddhist monks who defended the Shaolin monastery in the seventeenth century. The wiretaps were full of references to "the red envelope," traditional for gift-giving among Chinese and for the payment of lucky money. In September, there was much discussion of moon cakes, because September is the month of the Chinese Moon Festival, and the Green Dragons forced restaurants to buy twenty-dollar boxes of cakes for up to five hundred dollars apiece.

In October, Chen I. Chung and Sonny Wong went to Fa Chung Fa, a new nightclub on Queens Boulevard in Elmhurst, to talk to the manager about lucky money and weekly protection payments. She informed them that the club already had an arrangement with a Chinatown gang, the Ghost Shadows. A week later, the Green Dragons and the Ghost Shadows held a summit meeting at the club and came to terms: the Dragons would get a thousand and eighty dollars in lucky money, and each gang would collect three hundred dollars in weekly protection.

October was a month of diplomacy for Chen I. Chung. On the twenty-eighth, he sat down with the White Tigers and forged a peace agreement. The gangs would not fight, provided everyone kept to his own turf—Elmhurst for the Dragons, Flushing for the Tigers. Privately,

I. Chung remained wary of the Tigers, having read in a Chinese language newspaper that the gang was encroaching upon Elmhurst. The next day, October 29th, I. Chung mentioned this story to Brother Lok of the Ghost Shadows.

"No, no such thing, silly!" he was assured.

"It was reported so big in the papers."

"The papers! They just say so, they don't know."

But on November 13th I. Chung's worst suspicions were confirmed. An underboss in the White Tigers, who was known as Lobster, had gone into the Fa Chung Fa and collected a red packet full of lucky money.

Over the next five days, Brian Chan, acting as I. Chung's spokesman, had several heated discussions about this breach of contract with Chris Chin, the *dai lo* of the White Tigers, and Chin's brother Ah Kin. Finally, Ah Kin admitted that Lobster had collected the red packet, but countered that the Green Dragons had broken the agreement first by allowing the Ghost Shadows to operate in Queens. "Queens is supposed to be split up between I. Chung and us," Ah Kin reminded Brian. "We said, 'Is this fucking for real?' How could Gum Pai"—a street boss in the Ghost Shadows—"extend his living from Chinatown to Queens?"

This was war. All that was needed was a formal declaration, and it came in the early morning hours of November 19, 1990, in a telephone call between Chen I. Chung and an unidentified street boss of the White Tigers. Suddenly, leaders of two feared criminal enterprises showed themselves for what they were—boys.

"I'll kill you!" said the White Tiger. "You think the Green Dragons are so swell?"

"Fuck you!" said I. Chung.

"I'm going to kill your entire family, O.K.? I know where you guys live. . . ."

"I fuck your asshole. . . . I fuck your mother's asshole. . . ."

"Green Dragons!"

"What about Green Dragons?"

"Green Dragons are useless!"

"Then you come out!"

"Come out!"

"Ha!"

It was agreed: the gangs would face off at 3 p.m. that day, at a record store on Northern Boulevard. The Green Dragons, however, never showed up, for as they set out to rumble the White Tigers Chen I. Chung and the top members of his gang were placed under arrest.

The government had not wanted to collar the gang suspects quite so soon. More than enough evidence had been gathered to dismantle the Green Dragons, but the big boss, Paul Wong, was still at large, and there was no extradition treaty between China and the United States. Chen I. Chung's explosive parley with the White Tiger boss left the Feds little choice. If the suspects were not apprehended, they would probably kill or be killed.

On the day of the arrests, the surveillance team followed several gang members from Linda's Beauty Salon to the gang apartment run by Roger Kwok, in the basement of the house on Ithaca Street. New York City police, F.B.I. agents, and SWAT officers armed with M-16s ("dressed in their Ninja suits," one cop recalled) surrounded the house. About a dozen gang members, some of them armed, emerged and headed for two cars. All were arrested without a shot being fired. Sonny Wong attempted to flee through the back door but was stopped by a rifle-wielding officer on the roof.

The next day, police searched Chen I. Chung's apartment in Wood-haven. They found fifteen weapons, including an Uzi machine pistol hidden on top of a ceiling tile, and a bulletproof vest between I. Chung's bed and nightstand. (Police also found a calendar on which I. Chung had marked off each week's extortions.) Guns were recovered from other gang apartments and cars. All in all, the police collected an arsenal of thirty-one weapons—more than enough to fill an evidence cart at the trial, for the awed inspection of the jury.

The police had located the firearms without much difficulty, because someone had tipped them off to where they should look. That person was a suspect who had been persuaded to "flip"—become a government informant—on the first night of his arrest. The informant was Sonny Wong.

It appeared to have been Sonny's destiny. His gang brothers had always suspected him of being weak. At F.B.I. headquarters, Sonny was separated from his colleagues and interrogated by William Murnane and James Hughes, of the N.Y.P.D., and by Peter Blum, of Nassau County. Sonny began to cry. Within a few hours, the officers had extracted a signed confession.

Five months later, Pete Blum bagged another prize. Not long after the murders of Tina Sham and Tommy Mach, one of the killers, Aleck Yim, had quit the gang, because, he later explained, "I wasn't making money." He had gone to Florida for a time, and then returned in April, 1991, to the streets of New York, where Blum and another detective arrested him. Blum was able to persuade Yim that the government could prove he had helped kill Sham and Mach, and that it would be best for him to confess. Yim pleaded guilty to murder and agreed to testify at the forthcoming trial of the Green Dragons.

Meanwhile, Sonny Wong, like his gang brothers, was thrown into the Metropolitan Correctional Center, but segregated on the eleventh floor. (Sonny had agreed to plead guilty to one count apiece of assault, kidnapping, and extortion.) The Green Dragons remained in detention, awaiting trial. Somehow, by the spring of '91 Chen I. Chung had learned that his former right-hand man had copped out.

On June 4, 1991, the F.B.I. monitored a phone call placed by Chen I. Chung from the M.C.C. to Foochow Paul, in China. Though Paul Wong once again promised to "be there" for the young men who had followed him with love and reverence, it was clear that he had callously written them off. I. Chung, however, continued to kowtow to his leader.

"I'm just worried about the one on the eleventh floor," I. Chung said.

"Who?" Paul asked.

"Gu Yu Chai!" (This was Sonny Wong's Cantonese nickname. It meant Playboy.)

"Gu Yu Chai," Paul repeated. "I am still looking for his family members, you understand."

The government took alarmed note of that.

"I'm telling you, you can fight this case," Paul said.

"Mmm-hmm."

"Just in case . . . ten years. When you come out, I'll be still there. . . ."

"I know, Dai Lo. . . ."

"I'll have a plan. . . ."

"Hey, Dai Lo, here we aren't thinking about anything. That is to say, since you have no problem, then all is fine. . . ."

"My head has become swollen with problems!" Paul said. "You know my situation."

"I know."

The trial of the Green Dragons opened on February 18, 1992. It was held on the second floor of the federal courthouse in Brooklyn Heights. Cathy Palmer was joined by two co-prosecutors, Loretta Lynch and Margaret Giordano. On the sixth floor, government lawyers were prosecuting the boss and seven members of Born To Kill. The news media ignored both cases in favor of a trial on the fourth floor, that of the Mafia boss John Gotti.

If the media underestimated the Green Dragons case, so did the nine defendants: Chen I. Chung, Tony (Big Nose) Tran, Brian Chan, Roger Kwok, Alex Wong, Joseph Wang, Steven Ng, Jay Cheng, and Danny Ngo. This was a federal RICO case, and the penalties were severe. Murder in aid of racketeering carries a mandatory sentence of life without parole. In the past, mandatory life had been handed out to the likes of Fat Tony Salerno and other aging mafiosi. The Green Dragon defendants ranged in age from eighteen (Roger Kwok) to twenty-three (Chen I. Chung). Yet the defendants remained very much a gang, arrogant and invincible—laughing and smirking to a degree

almost never seen in federal court. Perhaps they still believed that Foochow Paul would swoop down and rescue them—even though Legal
Aid, and not Foochow Paul, had provided their lawyers.

On February 20th, Loretta Lynch called to the stand Charlie Lo, the
man whose apartment had been robbed and whose wife had been
raped. (Since rape is not considered a racketeering act, the crime was
not charged and was never mentioned in open court.) Within
moments, Cathy Palmer was on her feet, complaining to the judge that
Big Nose was giving Lo the finger. After Lo testified, Palmer fished out
of a wastebasket a graphic drawing of a nude made by Chen I. Chung.
It became a court exhibit. The atmosphere of the trial grew steadily
more tense after that.

On February 25th, Carol Huang identified Alex Wong as the
young man who had shot and killed two people at the Tien Chau
restaurant. Under questioning by Loretta Lynch, Christine Gallivan
described to a stunned courtroom how her husband, Anthony, had
died in her arms.

On February 26th, the government displayed large, graphic photographs of the dead bodies of Tina Sham and Tommy Mach. During
a break, as the defendants marched out, Big Nose stopped at the government table to glance admiringly at a picture of his handiwork. Then
he locked eyes with Tommy's brother Steven, in the courtroom as a
spectator. Cathy Palmer recalled, "He goes 'Hee-hee! Hee-hee! Hee-
hee!' as if to say, 'Yeah, we killed them—and we enjoyed it.' "

On February 27th, the government called Yip Ming Lee, the only
worker at the Crown Palace who consented to testify. Lee was shaking
so hard he had to grip the witness stand. That morning, as he had
walked toward the courthouse, a blue sedan pulled up and a young
Chinese man opened the door. "Hey, kid," he warned Lee in Cantonese. "Be careful of what you say. Be fucking careful."

On March 4th, the government called Sonny Wong. He testified for
more than eight days. In authenticating the wiretaps, Sonny severely
damaged the defense. On March 12th, as the Green Dragons left the

courtroom during a break, Big Nose turned to Sonny and hissed, "Watch yourself!" Under his breath, I. Chung added, "Scum!"

On April 9th, after three and a half days of deliberation, the (anonymous) jury found all the defendants guilty on virtually every count in the indictment. Chen I. Chung got nine concurrent life terms, with no possibility of parole. Six others got life sentences with no parole: Big Nose, Brian Chan, Roger Kwok, Alex Wong, Joseph Wang, and Jay Cheng. The Green Dragons were out of business.

Shortly after the verdicts were handed down, Chen I. Chung agreed to be interviewed. Wearing a brown prison jumpsuit and white Avia sneakers, he was led into the visitors' room on Five North of the M.C.C. He had gained weight in jail. A jade Buddha hung from a gold chain around his neck. He had a hint of a mustache, some hairs on his chin, and a hole in his left earlobe where he had once sported a gold loop. The edges of a tiger tattoo were visible on his left arm. His thumbnails and left little-finger nail were dramatically long and pointed, Fu Manchu style. Unable to get Q-Tips in prison, he said, he had grown his nails to clean out his ears. He was in a bad mood.

After twenty months of prison, I. Chung's English was a bit improved but still subpar. He had learned enough to converse with John Gotti at the M.C.C., and said they had come to an agreement: "The law is dirty, man." I. Chung had nothing but contempt for Cathy Palmer, the federal prosecutor, whom he referred to, inaccurately, as "the D.A." "I don't know why she hate me a lot," he said. "I didn't do wrong." The pornographic sketch he had made in court was meant to be Palmer, he said. "I nothing to do. And they not fair, this court. What I listen for! So I draw, draw, draw, draw, draw that D.A."

He reserved his deepest scorn, however, for Sonny Wong. At the mention of Sonny's name, he nearly spat. To hear I. Chung tell it, it was Sonny who murdered Tina Sham and Tommy Mach. "We went to have tea lunch that day," he began, switching back and forth between Mandarin and English. "After we finished tea lunch, someone noticed

Tina. Sonny Wong leaned over and said, 'Remember this girl? In the jail for nothing, two year. Wo wo wo wo wo.' I say, 'Forget about it.' He say, 'You kill that Tina Sham. Take a gun, shoot her in the chest.' And I say, 'Don't do bad thing, O.K.? Don't do it.' After we saw them leave, all of us went to the parking lot. Then I looked around and said to Sonny, 'What are you doing?' And he said, 'I'm taking them to a place.' "

I. Chung did admit that there were those who believed he was responsible for the murders, including Tina Sham's ex-boyfriend in the gang. "Johnny Walker, he come out of jail. And then he calls up my house, and we got a meeting, you know? Come on and go eat. Korean restaurant. And then Walker, he was sighing, 'Ayyy!' He had become numb. I said, 'You know, this is fate. She was killed; there was nothing we could do to prevent it. Destiny, man.' "

Was he prepared to spend the rest of his life in prison? "I can't do it," he said. "I feel that I might commit suicide. I might hang myself. Nobody could take it. Nobody could say, ha ha ha—happy! Who could happy? Come on. I only born in this world twenty-three year." Wasn't it clear by now that Paul Wong had abandoned him? I. Chung shrugged, and said, "Who am I to him?" Did he have any words for Sonny Wong? He did: "Where is your conscience?"

Throughout the trial, there had been no sign of any defendant's parent or close relative in the courtroom. The shame was too great to bear, particularly in the Asian culture. However, Joseph Young, the uncle and guardian of Brian Chan, sent the judge an ambitious document he had prepared. A computer consultant, Young methodically assembled and captioned a series of photographs of his nephew, tracing his development from infancy. He wanted to show that Brian was a "kind-hearted, outgoing and loving child" who could be "rectified" and "not be a scum of the society," he wrote. But the document only heightens the enigma of Brian Chan. In a snapshot from the summer of 1986, he is happily holding a monkey at Sea World, in Florida. In a government photograph taken after his arrest, only four years later, he is utterly transformed—with two large, menacing eagles tattooed on his chest, and cold, scary eyes.

On being reached by phone, Young said he was still puzzled by how it happened that Brian had turned so bad. Young had lived in the United Kingdom for over twenty years, and spoke with a clipped British accent. He was more eager to talk about Brian's brother, Perry, who was working for a financial company and studying for his M.B.A.

"He's doing B-plus average while working full time," Young said proudly. "Last year, he took thirteen credits, which is a tremendous effort. This year, he took, I think, nine or ten. He never stopped studying all year round. He listens to me, whereas the younger one is not trying to listen. And then got into trouble—sort of the ultimate trouble that one could ever get into. In American society, being so liberal and so free, children will abuse the family rule, and leave the house, even though the regulations stipulate they should not. Because I am not a direct parent, there's a certain limit to what I can do. And, fortunately, one of them I salvaged completely." Young allowed himself a satisfied little laugh. "I'm happy already."

Robert Sham moved to Virginia for a year after his daughter's murder, but he returned to Queens, to play the drums in a band at a Korean nightclub in Flushing. He worked the nine-thirty p.m. to four a.m. shift, and got to take hour-long breaks while soused Koreans sang karaoke. During one of those breaks, Robert consented to an interview. At the entrance of the nightclub was an airport-style metal detector, to prevent gang members from walking in with their guns. The club was enormous, with disco balls and klieg lights; smoke billowed from the dance floor. Robert was the only Chinese in the band, which played pop standards like "Feelings" and the love theme from "The Godfather," along with hit Korean tunes. Now middle-aged, he wore his hair slicked back and tied behind in a ponytail. There was an earring in his left ear. He had on a white tuxedo shirt and black pants—the club uniform.

On the way into the club, Robert's niece Dorothy warned, "He looks depression and skinny and he lost a lot of weight, and his girlfriend told me he was drunk all the time." Robert did seem depressed. A few weeks earlier, he went down to Chinatown to install a picture of Tina at a Buddhist temple on Mott Street, and the previous day he had gone to visit the tomb containing her ashes at a cemetery in New Jersey. His son Trini, recently out of jail, joined him.

"She always next to me, I feel like she always there," Robert said of his daughter. "When I play sad song, especially American song, forget about it. I'm the best. I love sad song, for Tina, my daughter. Sad song remind me. I love her too much. When I see her body, I hit the wall— *pow!* My hand was hurt. Because I know the Buddha punish me, for my drug business—what happen to my daughter, my son. And I pay for it, too. I believe that Tina died because maybe she take all my bad luck away. I believe that. She took all my suffer away. But I feel like no hope. I got a good dream, recording. But what I fight for! I fight for my family, but she gone."

The mood at the Mach residence was equally sombre. Steven continued to live there, with his parents and his wife. Near the dining-room table was a shrine to his brother—a small wooden cabinet upon which stood a framed photograph of Tommy, wearing a tuxedo. In front of the photograph was a brass box containing his ashes. Next to these were fresh flowers and fruit, and electric candles. The shelves held an assortment of Tommy's clothing and other possessions, including a remote-control model Porsche, skin-care products, sunglasses, and the wings Tommy earned when he got his F.A.A. certification. On top of the cabinet was a plate with some food.

"That's dim sum we had this morning, so we put some there," Steven said "A few hours later, we just throw them out. It's a way to express our respect. Every morning, before I go to work I drink a glass of orange juice, so I'll pour him a glass. I'll burn incense for him, I'll tell him I'm going to work. I know this is like useless, it sound kind of crazy, too, but it make me feel better that I don't leave him out, because we always eat dinner together when he was alive. A lot of times, if I go out for dinner, or anything, if I forget to tell him, I feel really guilty."

Steven's mind kept returning to October 2, 1977, the night his family took to the sea to escape Vietnam. "That night the sea was really choppy," Steven said. "Every time our tiny boat go through a wave, it slam down, and the noise it creates is horrifying. Tommy and my little sister were huddled under my mom's arm. And Tommy said, 'Mom, I'm really scared. If this boat is not going to hold and we fall into the ocean, are we all gonna die?' At that time, Tommy was ten years old; I was thirteen. My mom said to him, 'Don't worry, son. If anything happen, we all good swimmers. We'll hold on to you, and we'll all be safe.'

"We went through all that, right? And when we live in Vietnam it was a war-torn country. We survive all that, and we came to America, supposedly a safe haven for us, and this is where Tommy got killed. That's something I can never swallow. People say America is a land of opportunity, a land for the dreamers. I have that dream before, I have that feeling, too. And now I have to say America is not a land of opportunity, it is more a land of opportunists. Because those gangsters, they come here, they just terrorize people, and do anything they want. They have not only terminated a young person's life, and shattered his dreams—Tommy has a bright future and all that—but for the family, we have to suffer, and we have to suffer forever."

The families of Tina Sham and Tommy Mach did not speak to one another. "They mad at us. Maybe we mad at them," Dorothy Chan said. "You can see on their face they don't like us—especially Steven." The last time an attempt was made to communicate was at Tommy's cremation. "I go with Robert, he wants to go, we try to pay some respect," Beatrice said. "But they weren't talking to us, they weren't even look at us. The mother even using her eyes like this. Then we sit for a while, and then we go out. I know the parents is very mad and sad. I don't blame them. Maybe they think the cause is because of Tina. You know Chinese, they always want to blame. But it isn't fair."

Steven: "The thing that kind of bugs me—I don't know whether I should say it—but when we first find out that Tommy was missing, my sister call Tina's cousin. And the first thing they said was: Was Tommy a gangster? My sister said, No, no, he's not anything like that. We didn't even ask the same question for them. Because it's inconceivable for us to think Tommy would date an ex-gang girl. See, I know that Tina is also one of the victims, and I'm not trying to blame anyone, it's not her fault. But I don't think Tommy knows who Tina really is. Because if Tommy knows Tina's background, he would never go out with her. He's not going to do something crazy like that. So the biggest mystery for us is we never know whether Tommy knows why he is killed. Nobody will ever know. Only between them two."

acknowledgments

Thanks to everyone who helped make this Anthology.

At Thunder's Mouth Press and Avalon Publishing Group:
Thanks to Ghadah Alrawi, Tracy Armstead, Will Balliett, Kristen Couse, Linda Kosarin, Shona McCarthy, Dan O'Connor, Blanca Olivieri, Neil Ortenberg, Paul Paddock, Susan Reich, David Riedy, Simon Sullivan, and Mike Walters for their support, dedication and hard work.

Thanks also to Sue Canavan for her design and Maria Fernandez for overseeing production.

At Shawneric.com:
Shawneric Hachey brilliantly handled permissions.

At the Portland Public Library:
The librarians helped me collect books from around the country.

At The Writing Company:aience and creativity. Nate Hardcastle helped find the selections, offered advice, and answered countless questions. Nat May also provided guidance. Mark Klimek, Taylor Smith, and March Truedsson were fun to be around.

Friends and family:
Carol Pickering allowed gang-related books and articles to take over our home for months, and endured many weekends lost to work. My brother Jed was a great sounding board for general ideas and publishing-related questions.

Finally, I am grateful to all the writers whose work appears in this book.

p e r m i s s i o n s

b i b l i o g r a p h y

The selections used in this anthology were taken from the editions and publications listed below. In some cases, other editions may be easier to find. Hard-to-find or out-of-print titles often are available through inter-library loan services or through Internet booksellers.

Adler, William M. *Land of Opportunity: One Family's Quest for the American Dream in the Age of Crack*. New York: Atlantic Monthly Press, 1995.

Asbury, Herbert. *The Gangs of New York: An Informal History of the Underworld*. New York: Thunder's Mouth Press, 2001.

Borges, Jorge Luis. *A Universal History of Infamy*. New York: Dutton, 1971.

Buford, Bill. *Among the Thugs*. New York: Random House, 1991.

Burgess, Anthony. *A Clockwork Orange*. New York: Buccaneer Books, 1996.

Dannen, Fredric. "Bo Ying". First appeared in *The New Yorker* as "Revenge of the Green Dragons," November 16, 1992.

Farrell, James T. *The Life Adventurous, and Other Stories*. New York: Vanguard Press, 1947.

Finnegan, William. *Cold New World: Growing Up in a Harder Country*. New York: Random House, 1998.

Sager, Mike. "Death in Venice". First appeared in *Rolling Stone*, September 22, 1988.

Shakur, Sanyika. *Monster: The Autobiography of an L.A. Gang Member*. New York: Atlantic Monthly Press, 1993.

Solotaroff, Ivan. "Gangsta Life, Gangster Death". First appeared in *Esquire*, December 1996.

Thomas, Piri. *Down These Mean Streets*. New York: Alfred A. Knopf, 1973.

Toobin, Jeffrey. "Capone's Revenge". First appeared in *The New Yorker*, May 23, 1994.

Wallace, Scott. "La Post-Guerra: War Without End in the New El Salvador". First appeared in *Harper's* as "Letter from El Salvador: You Must Go Home Again", August 2000.